Robert Ward

Lee's sharpshooters

The forefront of battle

Robert Ward

Lee's sharpshooters
The forefront of battle

ISBN/EAN: 9783337145552

Printed in Europe, USA, Canada, Australia, Japan

Cover: Foto ©ninafisch / pixelio.de

More available books at **www.hansebooks.com**

"We speak that we do know and testify that we have seen."

..LEE'S..
SHARPSHOOTERS;

OR,

THE FOREFRONT OF BATTLE.

A Story of Southern Valor that never has been told.

MAJOR W. S. DUNLOP.

LITTLE ROCK, ARK.:
TUNNAH & PITTARD, PRINTERS.
1899.

MAJOR W. S. DUNLOP.

TABLE OF CONTENTS.

CHAPTER I.
Battalion of sharpshooters of McGowan's brigade —Organization, equipment and drills...... 17-23

CHAPTER II.
Battle of the Wilderness—General movements of the army — Operations by the sharpshooters, and general results 25-39

CHAPTER III.
Battle of Spottsylvania court house—First four days—Successes of the Northern army—Sharpshooters, etc. 41-55

CHAPTER IV.
Battle of Spottsylvania, continued—Bloody angle —Desperate fighting, and final repulse of the Federals, etc. 57-74

CHAPTER V.
Battle of Hanover Junction or Jericho Ford—Race for position—Race won by the Confederates— Almost a bloodless victory—Valor of the sharpshooters 75-85

CHAPTER VI.
Tilt on Totopotomoy Creek at Atlee's Station, and battle of Cold Harbor—The Unionists outgen-

Table of Contents.

eraled at Atlee's, and fearfully castigated at Cold Harbor..... 87-95

CHAPTER VII.

Battle of Riddle's Shops begun by the cavalry and finished by the sharpshooters 97-102

CHAPTER VIII.

First battles of Petersburg—Desperate valor of Confederates under Beauregard — Transfer of Lee's army to the scene—The city saved—Siege laid, etc. 103-120

CHAPTER IX.

Mahone's fight and splendid success—Sharpshooters engaged, and Wilson and Kautz raid—Gallant defence of Staunton river bridge by the Boy Reserves—Return to north side................ 121-136

CHAPTER X.

Battle of Longbridge or Deep Bottom, by Kershaw, Lane and McGowan—Both sides defeated—Three sharpshooters by a game of bluff chase a thousand 137-146

CHAPTER XI.

Battle of Fussell's Mill, by Field, McGowan and Lane—Brilliant victory—Successful operations by sharpshooters 147-157

CHAPTER XII.

Springing of the mine at Fort Elliott, or Pegram battery—Battle of the Crater—Intrepid valor of

Table of Contents. 5

the Confederates, and bloody castigation of the Unionists 159-187

CHAPTER XIII.

Battle of Ream's Station between Hill and Hancock—Hancock worsted by the loss of nine pieces of artillery and two thousand prisoners—The sharpshooters cover themselves with glory 189-200

CHAPTER XIV.

Incidents and demonstrations — Sharpshooter caught asleep on the vidette post, trial and acquittal—One sharpshooter charges one Federal in the cornfield and captures his hat—Demonstration by sharpshooters while Hampton captures 2500 beef cattle 201-207

CHAPTER XV.

Battle of Jones' farm, by McGowan and Lane—Confederate victory — Sharpshooters' splendid behavior and large captures—Unsuccessful attack on Fort Harrison—Successful at Hatcher's Run 209-220

CHAPTER XVI.

Terrible march to Jarrett's Station through sleet and snow—No fight— Return to Petersburg— Sharpshooters ordered to retire—Dash into the Federals at night and large captures—Christmas dinner 221-229

CHAPTER XVII.

Dash of the sharpshooters into the Union lines at night—Captures, etc.—Sharpshooters go into

Table of Contents.

winter quarters — Description of camp, etc. — Peace negotiations at Hampton Roads and results 231-242

CHAPTER XVIII.

Gordon's attack on Fort Steadman and final failure —Subsequent Federal advance and capture of our picket lines—Storming of McIlwaine's Hill by sharpshooters and results 243-256

CHAPTER XIX.

Last battle of Hatcher's Run—Disasters at Five Forks and Batteries Gregg and Forty-five—Sharpshooters hold their position until the last regiment withdraws, then cover the retreat 257-271

CHAPTER XX.

Battle of Southerland Station, by McGowan's and two other little brigades left as a rear guard— Splendid fight, but overpowered and driven— Sharpshooters behave with distinguished gallantry—Retreat to Appomattox, and the end— "Furl That Banner," and reply.............................. 273-284

CHAPTER XXI.

Roster of sharpshooters—One hundred and forty-two names out of a complete roll of more than two hundred—Rehearsal, etc. 285-304

CHAPTER XXII.

Capture of myself and wife—Experiences in prison —Amnesty and discharge, and return to Dixie....305-331

CHAPTER XXIII.

Promiscuous anecdotes—Poetry: "Fall of Stonewall Jackson," "Carolina-1865," and "Bivouac of the Dead."... 333-358

APPENDIX.

CHAPTER XXIV.

Story of Mississippi sharpshooters, and letter of the correspondent of the London Morning Herald on the battle of the Wilderness 359-418

CHAPTER XXV.

Mississippi sharpshooters, continued; and second letter of London correspondent on the battle of Spottsylvania court house......................................419-475

CHAPTER XXVI.

Short sketch of Lane's North Carolina sharpshooters—Evans' Georgia sharpshooters at Appomatox court house—McRae's North Carolina sharpshooters—Closing remarks by the author....477-488

PREFACE.

The author proposes to add to the great volume of American war history a mere postscript, setting forth in systematic detail the operations of a single battalion of Lee's sharpshooters, whose services on the field of battle entitle it, as a distinctive organization, to some historical consideration. This to be followed by such sketches of its co-ordinates in the same service as may fall within the scope of his own personal knowledge or may be gathered from other legitimate sources.

It is not designed to disturb the record, or detract one iota from the renown achieved by the gallant brigades of which these battalions were proud to compose a part; but only to rescue from oblivion and the shadows of a fading memory, the story of their exploits upon the historic hills of Virginia, is this difficult yet pleasing task undertaken.

The corps of sharpshooters of McGowan's brigade is selected as the "battalion of directions" in this narrative, not for any superiority claimed for it above the sharpshooters of other brigades, either in material or achievement; but only on account of the personal acquaintance of the writer with the history of its campaigns from the date of its organization to its final dissolution at Appomatox court house.

It is used as an example to illustrate the necessity and importance of such a branch of the service at such a period; and to demonstrate the genius and wisdom of our great leader in the selection and organization of such bodies of daring men to guard his lines and lead his brigades into action, when called upon to meet the enemy on the field. They were, as Kingslake puts it, "the spike heads" or case hardened steel points attached to the brigades, whose duty it was to crush the outer lines and admit our columns to the inner lines and strongholds of the enemy. How well they met the purposes of their organization, this volume proposes to tell.

Before entering upon the work in hand, however, it may be well to state for the information of the critical reader, and to remove certain erroneous impressions that now prevail as to the history of this (leading) battalion, that shortly after the battle of Fredericksburg—say January, 1863—a corps of sharpshooters had been organized in McGowan's brigade and placed under command of Capt. Wm. T. Haskell of the first South Carolina regiment, and was ably led by that gallant and accomplished young officer during the succeeding campaigns until he fell at the head of his battalion, July 2, 1863, on the bloody field of Gettysburg. At that time the writer, by direction of the brigade commander, had reinforced Haskell with two companies of the twelfth regiment and assisted him in driving the enemy from a strong and dangerous position directly in front of the brigade. When Haskell fell an order was made directing me to take charge of the sharpshooters, but that order went astray and was not delivered, hence the command was turned over to Major Alston, of the first regiment, who led the battalion until it was dissolved soon after our return to Virginia in the early fall. And, therefore, I had no connection with the first organization other than as above stated; and the impression that I had command of the sharpshooters from the battle of Gettysburg henceforth is erroneous.

And now, to the memory of the heroic dead, and to their widows and orphans, as well as to the survivors of these gallant corps, are the following pages most affectionately inscribed by THE AUTHOR.

INTRODUCTION.

"Lee's Sharpshooters; or, The Forefront of Battle," is the title given to this volume, which tells a story of Southern valor that never has been told; tells it because it never has been told; tells it because it ought to be told; and tells it because the truth of history demands that it should be told.

It treats of the closing period of our great struggle, of that matchless campaign which began in the wilderness of Spottsylvania, May 4, 1864, and ended at Appomatox court house, April 9, 1865. It follows the two great armies of Grant and Lee, and notes with careful pen the salient features of every engagement; gathers up results and engrosses them into a broad black background, through which to trace the crimson thread of its own untold story.

It tells of the great carefulness with which the sharpshooters were selected and organized; of their special drill and extra equipment; and of their high character as men and splendid record as soldiers.

It tells how they hung like a fringe upon the front and flanks of the marching columns to avert a cavalry dash or other contingency, or stood like a hedge between the embattled ranks of Blue and Gray as they swung into line for action; and when the issues were made up and the hours of conflict came, how they combed out the interval between the lines and led the hosts to battle.

It tells of their dauntless courage and headlong charges that crushed the enemy's outer lines and caused their main lines to writhe and squirm, and sometimes to break, under the fiery impact of their splendid *esprit de corps*.

It tells how they massed themselves against the enemy's high entrenchments, stormed out their forces and captured their men. And how, time and again, at the dead hours of midnight they dashed into the Federal outposts and picket lines and swept them out for miles without losing a man.

It tells of many incidents of personal daring and hairbreadth escapes, as well as of numerous independent and successful encounters in full corps, where their opponents were five times their own numbers.

It tells of the disasters at Five Forks and Batteries Gregg and Forty-five; of the evacuation of Petersburg and Richmond, and the last sad scenes at Appomatox court house; how the sharpshooters, with brazen front, stood in the breach when our lines gave way, and with what amazing dexterity they were thrown from front to rear and from flank to flank to ward off the surging columns of Grant and Sheridan as they crowded upon the little army of retreating Confederates. It tells how they made the last charge, captured the last battery and fired the last gun as the tragedy closed and the curtains fell.

Its tells all these and a hundred other things that never have been told; but can not tell why this untold story never has been told.

CHAPTER I.

SHARPSHOOTERS; WHO THEY WERE, AND WHAT THEIR DUTY.

The battalion of sharpshooters of McGowan's brigade was permanently organized on or about the 1st day of March, 1864, and was composed of three companies of about sixty men each, rank and file; with one commissioned and three non-commissioned officers to the company.

A draft was levied upon the regiments of the brigade for three or four men from each company to make up the number requisite for the new organization, to be selected from the best men in the company, with due regard to the peculiar and hazardous service for which they were designed. The regiments promptly responded to the call and detailed the men, with two non-commissioned officers, according to the terms of the requisition, while the brigade commander selected the company commanders, together with the commandant of the corps. The companies of the battalion were designated "first," "second" and "third," and were assigned to their positions in the line according to number, reckoning from the right. Brevet Capt. N. Ingraham Hasell, of the first South Carolina regiment, was selected and assigned to the command of the first company; Brevet Capt. Wm. H. Brunson, of the fourteenth regiment, to the command of the second company; and Brevet Capt. Charles E. Watson, of Orr's rifles (eleventh regiment), to the command of the third company. The honor of commanding the corps was, by the partiality of Gen. McGowan, conferred upon the writer as *chef de battailon*.

Intelligence, sound judgment, accuracy of marksmanship, fidelity to the Southern cause, and unfaltering courage in the trying ordeal of battle were the *conditiones sine qua non*, or necessary qualifications to membership in this command; and by this standard both officers and men were put to the test in due time. First, by the rigid application of the rules of military tactics and the enforcement of army regulations; and afterwards by the hazards and hardships of the active campaign. A few men failed in drill and were promptly replaced by others, while, as will hereafter appear, only one failed in battle. To meet the purposes of the organization, as well as to secure the highest degree of skill and efficiency in movement and action, an unique and concise system of tactics was prepared and compiled from the American skirmish and French zouave drills and introduced by the commander for the government of the battalion on the field, while a "manual of arms" in the form of a brochure upon the subject of rifle training was furnished by Maj. Gen. Wilcox. These, together, became the standard *par excellence* of the sharpshooters, both upon the drill ground and in active operations on the field.

Estimating distance, target practice, movements and dispositions against cavalry, bayonet exercise, etc., were prominent features of the system.

The battalion was first put upon drill in estimating distance. It was drawn up in line in open field; a man or an object the size of a man was stationed in front at an unknown distance, about one hundred yards off, and the roll called; at the call of each name the man stepped forward ten paces, surveyed carefully the object in front, calculated the intervening space, and deliberately announced in exact figures his estimate of the distance between, and a record was made of his judgment; then the next in the same way, and so on through the entire command. The distance was increased from time to time, from one hundred to two, three, five and nine hundred yards, and an accurate account kept of each man's judgment in each drill. The practice in this drill was continued from day to day until every man could tell, almost to a mathematical certainty, the distance to any given point within the compass of his drill. A few, however, were naturally and hopelessly deficient in their powers of estimating distance, and hence were exchanged for others.

The target practice was conducted in the same way. The battalion was formed on the range, a target about the size of a man was placed in front at a distance of one hundred yards, with a bullseye in the center of about five inches in diameter enclosed within an inner circle of about fourteen inches and an outer circle of about twenty-four inches; a tripod was constructed of convenient height, with a sandbag lodged in its fork on which to rest the heavy rifle while the soldier aimed and fired, and the practice began.

The target for 100 yards, pine plank one inch thick, 2x6 feet.

The target for 500 yards, pine plank one inch thick, 4x6 feet.

The target for 900 yards, pine plank one inch thick 6x6 feet.

The bullseye was enlarged, as well as the circles, as the distance was extended.

The roll was called, as in the first drill, and each man in his turn stepped forward to the tripod, aimed and fired; the flag man at the target announced, by signal, the result of the fire, which was recorded; and the practice continued until the entire battalion had taken part in the drill. This practice was continued from day to day, and the distance increased from time to time up to 900 yards, with a complete record kept of each drill, until the results achieved in estimating distance and rifle training were as amazing to the brigade commander as they were gratifying to the officers and men of the battalion.

In the target drill, the Minnie rifle, the Enfield, the Austrian, Belgium, Springfield and Mississippi rifles were put to the test. And while each and all of them proved accurate and effective at short range, the superiority of the Enfield rifle for service at long range, from 600 to 900 yards, was clearly demonstrated, both as to force and accuracy of fire. The ulterior range of the Enfields proved reliable and effective to a surprising degree to a distance of 900 yards, while the other rifles named could only be relied on at a distance of 500 yards.

To meet sudden and unexpected sallies of the enemy, assaults *coup de mein*, and other extraordinary emergencies which might arise while the troops were in bivouac, column of route, or order of battle, as well as to sweep the front and prepare the field for action. The sharpshooters were carefully and thoroughly instructed in all the rules of rapid and extraordinary formation, and were ready to move promptly to the front, flank or rear, as the exigency required.

They were trained to advance in full breast, *en echelon*, by the right, left or center; and could strike at any angle, as well with the left hand as with the right; so that they were equipped for the conflict, whether in field or forest, or in the streets and lanes of a town or city.

During the winter and intervals of rest their position was in front on the outposts and picket lines; and in the active campaigning of the summer they occupied the front in the advance, and the rear on a retreat, as skirmishers.

When the opposing armies met upon the field it became their duty to open and bring on the fight, or to stand like ushers on the vestibule of battle and receive and welcome our friends in blue whenever they choose to visit our lines.

With this training in the higher branches of the science *militaire*, based upon a thorough rudimentary education in the arts of war, the battalion of sharpshooters awaited the opening of the campaign of 1864 in the hope that under the blessings of God it might strike some blow that would tell for the freedom of the South. Nor did it have long to wait.

CHAPTER II.

BATTLE OF THE WILDERNESS.

> All was prepared—the fire, the sword, the men
>   To wield them in their terrible array.
> The army, like a lion from his den,
>   Marched forth with nerves and sinews bent to slay—
> A human hydra, issuing from his fen
>   To breathe destruction on its winding way,
> Whose heads were heroes, which cut off in vain,
>   Immediately in others grew again.
>   —Byron.

Early in March Gen. Grant had been appointed lieutenant general and commander in chief of the armies of the United States. And, while he exercised a general supervision of military operations in all departments of the field, he established his headquarters with the Army of the Potomac, now under command of Major Gen. Meade.

Though conscious of his ability as a commander and of the inexhaustible resources of the Federal government as to men, money and munitions of war, the Federal commander was well aware of the skill and prowess of the great Confederate leader who confronted him with an army of sixty thousand veterans, along the southern banks of the Rapidan. He therefore addressed himself to the task of reorganizing and equipping the forces at his command, preparatory to projecting a campaign, in comparison with which all other campaigns of the Army of the Potomac must pale away into the insignificance of a succession of combats. Troop after troop and division after division were added to the Federal forces along the northern banks of the river, until that army reached the fearful aggregate of one hundred and forty thousand men present for duty in the field. Yielding to the pressure of the Federal government and the clamors of the people of the north, Gen. Grant determined at length to move directly against Richmond by the overland route, regardless of the wall of Confederate bayonets which intervened between his grand army and the Confederate capital. Hence, on the morning of the 4th of May, he struck his tents and put his vast columns in motion toward the lower fords of the Rapidan, with the view of turning the Confederate right by the way of the Wilderness, and thrusting his army between Gen. Lee and the city of Richmond. He had but little more than effected a passage of the river, however, when to his great astonishment he was confronted by his adversary, the ever vigilant Lee, with his gaunt but spirited columns ready to accept or deliver battle. The Wilderness of Spottsylvania was again to be the arena of battle, where Greek should meet Greek, and the two great champions of the divided sections should measure their strength upon the issues of war.

The Confederates had approached the field of action by the two roads leading from Orange court house through the wilderness to Fredericksburg. Hill's corps on the right by the plank road, and Ewell's corps on the left by the old turnpike, while Longstreet's corps with Anderson's division of Hill's corps were to follow on the plank road. Stuart's cavalry, having met and driven back the Federal cavalry, struck Grant's advance columns in the depths of the Wilderness and brought them to bay, while Ewell and Hill urged forward their respective wings toward the position occupied by the Unionists. As the movement progressed, the battalion of sharpshooters was thrown out upon the left of the plank road and deployed, covering the line of march; then, conforming to the movements of the brigade as it proceeded toward the Wilderness, the sharpshooters hung like a fringe on the left of the column, to ward off any disposition on the part of the enemy to thrust himself into the interval between Ewell and Hill and thus disturb our march. We were in the woods for the most part, and maintained our distance of from one to two hundred yards to the left of the brigade for some eight or ten miles before the lines were formed for action, when we were called in.

About 1 o'clock on the afternoon of the 5th, the advance guard of Ewell's corps was met on the turnpike and vigorously assaulted by the leading division of Sedgwick's corps, and for a moment was thrown into confusion. Support, however, was promptly brought up, order restored, and troops designed to meet the attack were thrown into position perpendicularly across the road.

Later in the day Hill's skirmishers discovered the presence of the enemy on the plank road, and the two divisions of Heth and Wilcox formed across the road—Heth on the right and Wilcox on the left. The battalion of sharpshooters was directed to form on the left of McGowan's brigade—which was the left of Wilcox's division—and extend intervals to the left, so as to cover as far as possible the gap between Hill's left and Ewell's right. While this movement was being executed by the sharpshooters, Heth advanced to the attack of Getty's division of the sixth corps, supported by Birney's and Mott's divisions of the second corps. Heth succeeded in driving his opponent back upon his supports, where he maintained his ground with great gallantry against the counter attacks of a vastly superior Federal force until Wilcox came to his support on the left. The fight now became animated and deadly. Meanwhile Ewell attacked the Federal right and drove it back for some distance; then swinging forward his right flank, virtually established connection with Hill's left. The sharpshooters were therefore recalled from their position between the Confederate columns and were ordered in to the support of McGowan's brigade. Finding the gallant brigade abundantly able to take care of itself, the sharpshooters went into action on the left, and there with the troops of the line steadily met and repelled the persistent assaults of the heavy Federal lines which surged against them, taking a deeper and firmer hold upon the field at every repulse of the enemy.

The enemy being thus hard pressed by the two gallant divisions of Heth and Wilcox, ordered to the support of their trembling lines Barlow's division and two brigades of Gibbon's division of the second corps, and Wadsworth's division, and one brigade of Robinson's division of the fifth corps. All the while the Confederates were bearing down upon their adversaries with all their might, driving them back through this *terra incognito* upon their reserves.

The arrival of the enemy's reinforcements in a measure checked the advance of the Confederates, still the battle raged with unabated fury, well sustained by the Confederates, until night put an end to the deadly conflict. Gordon's brigade of Ewell's corps and McGowan's brigade of Hill's corps are specifically mentioned by their respective division commanders in their reports of this engagement, as behaving with conspicuous gallantry throughout the action, which is a distinction worthy of note, especially when all behaved so well. In the language of Gen. Wilcox, "McGowan's brigade swept through the Wilderness like a tornado, driving everything before it—far in advance of the line—and had to be recalled." Caldwell writes, "The pressure became fearful on both flanks, and for a time we had a front of but a single brigade." Again, speaking of the twelfth South Carolina regiment—same brigade —he says: "They continued to advance until they broke the enemy's line, which they followed up, killing large numbers and capturing more. Their charge was too impetuous, if anything. They pushed ahead until they lost connection with the rest of the brigade and found themselves almost entirely surrounded by the enemy. They captured, among others, a brigadier general. * * * Finding themselves thus outflanked by their own exertions, they faced about, put their prisoners before them and drove back for our line, and succeeded in cutting out with small loss."

Owing to the advanced position to which the Confederates had forced their way into the woods, and the superior forces of the enemy drawn across their front and overlapping both flanks, when the curtains of night fell upon the scene the lines of the two divisions lay in the shape of a semi-circle, exhausted and bleeding, with but little order or distinctive organization. Anxious and uneasy, under a felt sense of insecurity, these gallant men spent the live long night in this exposed and disorganized condition, momentarily expecting relief, but no relief came. Longstreet was deliberately approaching, but had not reached the field.

We were without rations and had but little water during the night, and the only water we had was obtained from a branch between the lines, where both the Federals and Confederates got their supplies, and frequently had to fight for that.

At early dawn on the morning of the 6th these two divisions were withdrawn from their advanced positions and had nearly reached the open field in their rear, when they were suddenly attacked by a fresh and overwhelming force, which turned and crushed the right wing and drove it in confusion back upon the left. McGowan's brigade maintained the unequal contest for a while, but it was in turn flanked and rolled up from the right, and retired to the open grounds in rear, where it rallied and reformed on Poague's artillery. The sharpshooters held their ground on the left until the last Confederate regiment retired, when they slowly fell back into the field above referred to. The moment the front was clear of Confederates, the gallant Poague, realizing the importance and peril of the moment, trained his guns accurately upon the wheeling columns of the enemy and poured into their crowded ranks such a storm of grape and canister as for a moment to paralyze their movements. Recovering from the shock in a few moments, the dark lines of Federals, with shouts of victory, again surged forward through the woods into the open field, and the day seemed irretrievably lost. But just at this critical juncture the "Old War Horse" appeared on the scene, and, like Dessaix at Marengo, "just in time to win a victory."

For a moment Longstreet consulted the commanding general and surveyed the field, then poising his intrepid battalions one after another as they came into line, hurled them, as with the right hand of Mars, against the crowded columns of the enemy just as they emerged into the open ground. The throat splitting huzzahs of the exultant Federals were answered back by the ominous cry of the rebel countercharge. One deadly volley and a sweeping charge, and Longstreet's lines were buried in the Wilderness. The veteran corps of Winfield Scott Hancock was beaten and driven back with fearful slaughter to his original position on the Brock road. Suspending his charge for the purpose of rectifying his alignment and observing the situation in front, Gen. Longstreet rode forward with Gen. Jenkins of South Carolina to reconnoitre, when, unfortunately, they were mistaken for the enemy and fired upon by his own men. Gen. Jenkins was killed outright, and Gen. Longstreet severely wounded. This fatal accident necessitated the suspension of pursuit for the time, which gave the Federal commander time to rally and reinforce his broken columns; and but for this unfortunate misadventure Grant's left wing would have been crushed and routed.

Heth and Wilcox, when relieved by Longstreet, were placed in position some distance to the left and somewhat retired. They now confronted Burnside's corps, which lay concealed in a dense pine thicket not exceeding six hundred yards in front. The position taken was on a commanding ridge in an open field, which the men proceeded to strengthen by a slender line of breastworks constructed of fence rails and what earth could be dug up with the bayonets and shoveled with the hands. The sharpshooters were deployed and thrown forward about three hundred yards in front. Here, under a misapprehension of the strength and position of the enemy, the sharpshooters were ordered to go forward and drive the Federals out of the pine thicket. Instantly they sprang to duty and moved down upon the thicket. Silently the beautiful line swept across the field until it reached a point not more than fifty yards from the edge of the woods, when it received a withering volley from a solid line of battle just within the pines. The battalion responded with a will, and volley after volley was received and delivered until an order came to withdraw. A section of artillery was now sent forward to assist the sharpshooters, and again the attempt was made, and twice repeated, to dislodge the enemy, with the same result. The ninth Federal corps could easily repel the assaults of the small force while it lay concealed in the dense thicket awaiting an attack from Heth and Wilcox, which was not made.

About 4 o'clock in the afternoon the troops of Anderson and Longstreet, led by the incomparable Lee on the right and Ewell's forces on the left, simultaneously assaulted the enemy in their now fortified position; and after terrific fighting, partially succeeded in doubling both wings of the Federal army back upon the center, when night closed the contest. The opposing armies occupied substantially the same ground upon which the action was begun, and the battle of the Wilderness was ended. The Confederate loss was heavy, but not to be compared to the damage inflicted upon the Union forces. McGowan's brigade lost in killed, wounded and missing 481 officers and men, including the battalion of sharpshooters, which contributed its full quota of brave men to the list of casualties reported, but the number and names of the unfortunates, I regret to say, can not now be given.

A certain Southern writer thus vividly describes the battle of the Wilderness and the field upon which it was fought: "The land was sombre—a land of thicket, undergrowth, jungle, ooze; where men could not see each other twenty yards off, and assault had to be made by the compass. The fights there were not so easy as night attacks in open country, for at night you can travel by the stars. Death came unseen; regiments stumbled on each other and sent swift destruction into each others' ranks, guided by the crackling of the bushes. It was not war—military manœuvreing; science had as little to do with it as sight. Two wild animals were hunting each other; where they heard each other's steps they sprang and grappled—the conqueror advanced or went elsewhere. * * * Here in blind wrestle, as at midnight, did two hundred thousand men in blue and gray clutch each other—bloodiest and weirdest of encounters. On the low line of the works, dimly seen in the thicket, rested the muzzles spouting flame; from the depths rose cheers; charges were made and repelled, the lines scarcely seeing each other; men fell and writhed and died unseen, their bodies lost in the bushes, their death groans drowned in the steady, continuous, never ceasing crash."

As to results, Brev. Maj. Gen. Webb of the Union army bears this significant testimony in his article in the Century War Series: "The 6th of May was the last day of the battle of the Wilderness. Ewell had most effectually stopped the forward movement of the right wing of Meade's army, and Hill and Longstreet had defeated our left under Hancock. The fact is that the whole of the left was disorganized. From Hancock down through Birney and Gibbon, each general commanded something not strictly in his command. Hancock had the left, Gibbon the left of Hancock; Birney had his own and Mott's divisions, and Wadsworth had Webb's and Stevenson's. The troops of these division commanders were without proper leaders. We had seen the mixed second and ninth corps driven in in detail on our left. We knew that the fifth and sixth corps were blocked, and we felt deeply the mortification consequent upon our being driven back upon the Brock road. From personal contact with the regiments who did the hardest fighting, I declare that the individual men had no longer that confidence in their commanders which had been their best and strongest trait during the past year."

Swinton, in his "Twelve Decisive Battles," says: "The Union troops, wearied and chagrined, sent up no cheer of victory through the Wilderness. Many, indeed, believed we would recross the Rapidan. * * * But there was one man otherwise minded. * * * The battles might have been fought by any other commander; but the difference in results was this: That while any other commander we had thus far seen would have fought the battle of the Wilderness and gone backward, Grant fought the battle of the Wilderness and went forward."

CHAPTER III.

BATTLE OF SPOTTSYLVANIA COURT HOUSE.

*Ez fer war, I call it murder—
There you hev it plain an' flat;
I don't want to go no furder
Than my Testyment fer that.*
—JAMES RUSSELL LOWELL.

The initial battle of the "On to Richmond" having been fought, and the attitude of these two great armies remaining unchanged, the two champions lay all day of the 7th in the midst of their baffled yet defiant troops, like two exhausted giants of the forest, foaming and panting and bleeding; each watching with wild suspicious eye the movements of his antagonist, lest, peradventure, some advantage might be gained unawares and the contest renewed before he was ready. On the afternoon of the 7th, however, the two divisions of Heth and Wilcox, preceded by the sharpshooters, had advanced upon Burnside's position in the pines and discovered that his lines had been withdrawn. Here they were ordered to fortify, but had scarcely begun the work when they were ordered to desist and prepare for the march. Early after nightfall the Federal commander withdrew his forces from Gen. Lee's front and began his second movement by the left flank, in the hope that now at least he could turn the Confederate right and, under cover of night, throw himself unobserved across their line of march somewhere in the neighborhood of Spottsylvania court house. But the very first step taken in the execution of this secret design was discovered and promptly reported to the Confederate commander by that sleepless guardian of the Confederate flanks, J. E. B. Stuart, who planted his cavalry squarely across the pathway of the Union forces and contested every inch of the ground. Meanwhile Longstreet's corps, now under command of Gen. Anderson, was withdrawn from the lines and ordered to hold itself in readiness to move in the direction of Spottsylvania court house. About 8 o'clock the army began to move by the right flank. The leading division of Longstreet's corps took up the line of march promptly at the command, followed after some delay by the second; and each successive division took the road as soon as the way was clear. The rear divisions meanwhile were closing up, and then giving back to the next in front—so that Hill's corps had not moved more than two hundred yards at 10 o'clock. Such delays are always annoying even to the veteran soldier, although he knows it to be an inevitable necessity in the movements of every large army, it matters not what may be the exigencies of the case; yet a good soldier will submit to any necessity and make the best of it. In this case our patience was beginning to weaken just a little, when away to the right, from the depths of the forest, in the stillness and darkness of night, a sound is heard—the sound of a charge or good cheer, which we could not tell. In the hush of expectancy we listened to catch the significance of the strange outburst; when lo! here came the swelling tide of ten thousand voices sweeping down the lines of Longstreet to Hill's right. We lifted our voices as our turn came, and sent the grand chorus echoing along the lines of Ewell to the distant left.

Thrice repeated, this overflow of enthusiasm *viva voce*, issuing from Anderson's column, swept down through the Confederate lines from right to left, when the last vestige of impatience and complaint seemed to have been removed, and every man stood ready to do and to dare for the honor of his country. It was the grandest vocal demonstration ever witnessed on this continent; under the inspiration of which Gen. Anderson urged forward his troops toward Spottsylvania, while the other corps went into bivouac for the night.

To remove all doubt as to the designs and movements of the enemy, early on the morning of the 8th the battalion of sharpshooters was ordered to make a reconnoisance of the Federal lines in front. We deployed and moved forward through the woods in the direction of Sedgwick's position on the Federal right, until we struck the line of breastworks. Here we discovered the evidence of a hasty withdrawal of the enemy from our front, in the shape of abandoned fly tents, knapsacks, oilcloths, and the like. Continuing our advance, we ascended a commanding ridge which overlooked the country for some distance beyond.

Here we encountered the richest field of spoils we had ever seen. The whole face of the earth was literally covered with valuable plunder and the signs of demoralization. Tempted by the vast amount and endless variety of army stores scattered around in every direction, and the entire absence of the enemy, and considering the urgent needs of the command for the very articles that lay scattered around us, the assembly was sounded and the battalion ordered to stack arms, break ranks and help themselves. Instantly the command, from a compact body of daring men, was converted into a wild and reckless mob, rushing hither and thither in search of plunder. The danger of the situation became manifest at once, and an effort made to reform. For a period of half an hour every effort to rally and reform proved ineffectual and vain—during which an organized body of twenty men, if present, could have captured the entire command. Fortunately there was no enemy present. After awhile, when the raid was completed, the officers recovered control of the men, reformed the battalion, and we proceeded on our drive. Wheeling to the right, we swept down the enemy's deserted lines to the Orange plank road, where changing again to the right, we drove out and rejoined the brigade. All questions as to the movements of the Federal commander had thus been settled, and now the brigade took up the line of march with other troops for Spottsylvania.

While Gen. Grant was pushing his immense columns along the Brock and Chancellorsville roads against the strenuous efforts of the untiring Stuart, to delay him as much as possible, Anderson was urging forward the Confederate van with all possible dispatch toward the point of convergence and the objective point of both commanders. The race for position was an exciting one, but Anderson won. Reaching the field before daylight, he placed his leading division in position on the range of hills covering Spottsylvania court house, and upon it formed the rear divisions as they successively arrived on the field. So that when the 8th of May dawned, and Gen. Grant essayed to sweep from his front the cavalry force which had hung upon his advancing columns and seize the range of hills north of town, what should he behold but the "stars and bars" defiantly

The Forefront of Battle. 47

floating in the morning breeze over a solid line of Confederate infantry firmly established upon the coveted hills, quietly awaiting his arrival.

Warren's corps was the first to confront Anderson, and while other troops on both sides were rapidly approaching the field, two divisions of Warren's corps advanced against the Confederate position. This attack was easily met and repelled, and resulted in considerable loss to the attacking column, including its leader, Gen. John C. Robinson, who was severely wounded by the first volley and carried off the field. Sedgwick's corps joined Warren about noon, and late in the afternoon was thrown heavily against Anderson's right, which, assisted by the timely arrival of a part of Ewell's corps, repulsed the attack with great slaughter. Thus ended the first day of the battle.

Hill's corps reached the field early on the morning of the 9th, and was placed in position east of the court house, on the Confederate right. This day was principally spent by both armies in active preparations for the impending conflict, with now and then a sharp fusilade between the opposing skirmish lines, as when one or the other of the great captains pressed his lines here and there too far to the front and trespassed upon the territory claimed by the other. In the settlement of these preliminary difficulties the sharpshooters took a lively interest; and whenever or wherever their services were needed for the adjustment of any misunderstanding as to the rights of parties, they were freely contributed.

As soon as McGowan's brigade was assigned its place on Hill's line the sharpshooters were ordered out, with instructions to cross the small stream in front and sweep through the thicket beyond, until the position and strength of the enemy were discovered.

The order was promptly obeyed, and we drove forward across the stream and through the woods until we reached the backbone of the ridge, near the edge of a field which lay out beyond. Here we could plainly see Sedgwick's corps in line of battle on the crest of another hill, busily engaged in rectifying their lines and constructing breastworks, with their skirmishers well advanced. Upon these we opened a scattering fire with some effect. We discovered an angle protruding from their main line towards the right of the battalion, which brought a four gun battery with its infantry supports placed there for the defense of the salient, barely within reach of our long range rifles. And to these Ben Powell with his "Whitworth" and a few files on the right paid their respects. Presently an officer of rank with his staff approached the salient, and adjusting his field glasses began to take observations of the front. A few shots only had been fired at the group, when the ringing peal of Powell's "Whitworth" was heard some distance to the right; the officer was seen to stagger and fall; and the brilliant career of that gallant and distinguished soldier, Maj. Gen. Sedgwick, commandant of the fifth Federal army corps, was closed and closed forever. Powell reported at once that he had killed a Federal general, but we knew not his name or rank until it came out a few days later in the Northern papers, announcing that Gen. Sedgwick had been killed by a Confederate sharpshooter; which fact, so published at the time, has gone into history, but the name of "the man behind the gun" has never before been mentioned. Upon the death of Gen. Sedgwick, Maj. Gen. Wright took his place, and the Federal sharpshooters opened on us with increased animation, while a column of infantry on our left and a column of cavalry on our right were discovered swinging forward upon our flanks, with the evident intention of cutting us off from the main line and bagging the entire command. To avoid such a disaster we threw back our wings and retired to the little stream before mentioned, where Watson's company engaged, at long range, the column on our left until it was withdrawn. We maintained our position here without further trouble until some time after nightfall, when we were relieved.

Baffled by the genius and audacity of the Confederate commander, and chafing under defeat and disaster, Gen. Grant determined to mass his forces before the Confederate position and by sheer weight of numbers to overwhelm and crush his opponent, regardless of costs, and at once addressed himself to the disposition of his troops to that end. With Hill's corps on the right, Ewell in the center, and Anderson with Longstreet's corps on the left, in a strong position carefully selected and well fortified, Gen. Lee awaited the movements of his adversary. These positions were substantially maintained during the struggle, though brigades and sometimes divisions were detached from their proper commands and sent to other parts of the field to meet pressing emergencies.

Early in the morning of the 10th the movement of Hancock's corps against the Confederate left and rear was gallantly met and defeated by Heth and Mahone under Early, on the banks of the Po. Meanwhile Grant was not idle on other parts of the field. Pursuing his determination to crush Lee, by 10 o'clock the Federal commander had organized a column of assault in front of Anderson's right, consisting of Warren's and Burnside's corps. This column moved promptly and with great intrepidity against the position occupied by Field's division, which received the attack with a galling fire, followed by volley after volley with such deadly effect that the front lines recoiled upon the second, when both retired.

About 3 o'clock in the afternoon the attack was renewed with still more disastrous results. A lull of something more than two hours succeeded the last attack, but proved to be only a breathing spell preparatory to the culminating effort of the day. These repeated and unsuccessful assaults against the Confederate lines seemed only to exasperate the Federal commander and to goad him to a more desperate determination to carry the works at this point. Hence, about 5 o'clock, increasing the dimensions and weight of his assaulting columns, by the addition of Wright and Hancock, with all the energy of his indomitable will, Gen. Grant hurled the flower of the Federal army against the Confederate left center. One after another the dark lines came rushing forward, at first in quick time, then at a full charge, as if nothing could stay their impetuous onslaught. The front lines dissolved before the pitiless storm that beat against them, but the succeeding lines, rushing forward over the prostrate forms of their fallen comrades, succeeded in penetrating our lines at two points; the one where stood the gallant Texas brigade of Anderson's corps, the other where stood Dole's brigade on Ewell's left. These gallant brigades stubbornly yielded to the weight of overwhelming numbers, but promptly rallying upon the supports at hand, succeeded in forcing the enemy back through the breach with terrible slaughter.

Again repulsed on every part of the line, the assailants fell back in disorder to their works, leaving the ground thickly strewn with their killed and wounded.*

The 11th was a wet and disagreeable day, with little or no serious fighting. During these two days, however, the battalion of sharpshooters occupied a position in front, some distance to the left of its former position, and where the opposing lines were drawn much more closely together. The Federal sharpshooters were in our immediate front, and displayed an animus of vindictive spite, which the boys in gray were not slow to reciprocate. The perpetual cry of their deadly rifles—as from every tree and bush and boulder they spurted fire and smoke and death, which to be understood needed the aid of no expert or scientific interpreter—aroused in the Confederate sharpshooters a glow of patriotic ardor which could be restrained only by the most peremptory or-

---

* Throughout the day the divisions of Heth, Field, Kershaw and Wilcox * * * maintained a firmness and displayed a valor that well became the veterans of a hundred battles. The Army of the Potomac never fought with more desperate courage, nor had its ranks ever been visited with such frightful havoc.—*Long.*

ders; and, although the activity of the litter bearers on the other side testified to the skill of these trained riflemen, to stand and fire was not to their mind like the sweeping charge. The ground between the lines at this point was for the most part in the woods, covered with underbrush and seamed with sharp ravines and gullies, which meandered abruptly hither and thither across the interval. These furnished an inviting field and fair protection to the adventurous on both sides to crawl upon the rifle pits of the other side and get in some good shots before their movements and whereabout could be discovered, and were utilized with fatal effect by each upon the lines of the other. In one instance two men in Young's North Carolina battalion were killed by a Federal sharpshooter with a single ball fired from one of these ditches; and many a gallant soldier of the gray, as well as the blue, paid the forfeit of his life for the part he took in this unremitting fusilade. The sharpshooters occupied this line for something over two days, being relieved at night after dark, and going on duty again before daylight in the morning.

Our rations were scant and sometimes unsavory, but our appetites bold and aggressive. I devoured the hindquarter of a muskrat with vindictive relish, and looked with longing eyes upon our adjutant general's fat young pointer. One day, during these fights at Spottsylvania, when the Federals were making an assault on our lines and the onset was persistent and furious, while passing along the lines to encourage the men, I discovered in a little branch a turtle of the loggerhead variety. I stopped, threw him out of the water with my sword, turned him on his back, and when he poked out his head to recover his all fours I popped my sabre through his neck and pinned him to the ground, and went on. When the fight was over and the hour of relief came, I went and got him, and such a stew as I had that night! It does me good to think of it to this day.

CHAPTER IV.

BATTLE OF SPOTTSYLVANIA.
[Continued.]

In the thick of the fight,
When the incessant roar
Of the volleying guns
Grew clearer, louder;
And the deadly storm
Of shot and shell
Swept back before it
The sharply smitten
Confederate legions,
Sudden is heard
Through the clang and the roar
Of sabres and guns,
The peal of a bugle
That sounds the charge,
And the cry of one
(Who laughs the while),
"Forward the flag of the battalion!"

Like a stream of light,
Of red, red light,
The red, red flag
Leaps forth to the front,
By the hands upborne
Of a boy in years
But a veteran old

In the ways of war,
Whose face has never
By the edge of a blade
As yet been shorn,
Save as a scar
On his cheek betrays
The stroke of a horseman's sabre.
(That horseman sleeps
In his grass grown grave
By the edge of a wood
On the Rapidan.)

Like a stream of light,
Of red, red light,
The red, red flag
Leaps forth to the front,
A shining mark
To the foe advancing.
Forth, but no faster,
Then speeds the battalion,
With voices uplifted
In cheer on cheer,
As they follow the course
Of the meteor bright,
That pauses never
Until it has launched
Them, reckless of death,
Full on the enemy's breast.

Then the lines of battle,
The blue and the gray,
Are mixed together;
And the air is filled
With shouts and groans,
And with curses wild
And mocking laughter,
And the clash of steel:
And the roar of guns
Grows deeper, louder.

The Forefront of Battle.

In the heat of the fray
The flag goes down—
The flag of the battalion—
And is trampled
Under the feet of men.
But a hand uplifts it,
It is held aloft,
All dripping wet
With the blood of the slain.
Lo, now it is one
Whose wrinkled cheeks
A gray beard hides,
Whose hand upbears
The flag of the battalion.

And the fight grows fiercer
And deeper and louder;
And with shouts unceasing,
Mid cursing and laughter,
And the clash of sabres,
And the roar of guns,
The conflict rages,
Till the foe relaxing
Their strong endeavor,
Yields at length
To the impetuous tide
That beats against them.
Forth to the front
As the foe gives way
The flag is pushed
By the hand that bears it;
Forth in pursuit
Like a leash-hound slipt,
It follows them fleeing,
Answering ever
The cry and the laugh
That are heard through the din,
"Forward the flag of the battalion!"

As the sound dies away
Of the shifting battle,
There is one draws near
To the boy that lies
On the wet, red field,
Who bathes his wound
With water and tears,
The wound in his breast
By a bayonet made.
Too late to save,
But still he may bear
Some message of love
To father or mother,
Or sister or brother,
Or other, yet dearer,
In his far away home.
He kneels to listen,
The plainer to hear
The mutterings low
That echo the visions
Of life that are flitting
Through the wandering sense
Of the dying boy.

But his dreams they are never
Of home or of love,
Of father or mother,
Or sister or brother,
Or other, yet dearer;
But still he is fighting
The fight of today,—
Still he is bearing
The flag that he bore,—
And the words that come forth
From his lips in a murmur,
As fearless he passes
The portals of death, are
"Forward the flag of the battalion!"

—BERRY BENSON.

Late in the afternoon of the 11th an impression prevailed that Grant was about to take another step to the left, and the constant stir and shifting of troops on the Federal lines somewhat justified the impression. Our trains were therefore placed under marching orders; the artillery posted in the salient occupied by Johnson's division was withdrawn, and every arrangement made for a move during the night, if necessary. The Federal commander readily discovered the mistake of his opponent and determined to make an attack at this point early the next morning, and to that end massed a heavy column during the night in front of Johnson, consisting of the second and sixth, with two divisions of the fifth corps. Gen. Johnson became aware of the enemy's designs against him, and realizing the peril of his position without artillery in the event of an attack in its absence, dispatched a courier with orders for the return of his batteries to the front by daylight in the morning. The orders were promptly delivered, and the dangers fully appreciated by the artillerists; but the numerous difficulties of the way, added to the darkness of the night, greatly delayed their execution of the orders. In the meantime the brave men stood to arms in the angle, in deep anxiety awaiting the approach of day and the return of their guns—which was their only safety.

The morning dawned—the morning of the eventful 12th—and just as the rays of light began to penetrate the blinding mist which had settled down upon the field, an immense column, well saturated with Dutch courage, led by Gen. Hancock, emerged from the pines in front and rushed forward to the attack. The little division defended its position with commendable gallantry, but could not stay the onward rush of the Federal column, which stormed over the works, capturing Gen. Johnson himself and nearly the whole of his division, with about twenty pieces of artillery, which reached the field just in time to be gobbled up by the exultant Unionists. Amazed at the completeness of his own success, the Federal commander stood for a moment bewildered at the mad rush of his confused columns as they crowded into the breach. But recovering his self possession, as well as the formation of his divisions, Hancock urged forward his men to the attack of the interior lines, driving further and further apart the severed wings of the Confederate army as he advanced. Lane's brigade of Hill's corps, which occupied a position to the right of the salient, and Ransom's brigade of Ewell's corps, which occupied a position to the left of the angle, each throwing back their exposed wings, poured into the Federal column such a storm of withering fire that they began to stagger and recoil. At the same time the heroic Gordon, planting his division (Early's) across the base of the salient, effectually checked the rolling tide of battle and held it back within the triangular area, while Perrin's Alabama, Harris's Mississippi and McGowan's South Carolina brigades were hurried forward to the rescue.

Gen. Lee determined to drive the Federals out, if possible, and recover his lines; but directed the construction of a new line of works some distance in the rear, upon which to rally and reform his troops in the event of failure. He therefore ordered up all the artillery that could be spared from other parts of the field to assist in the restoration of his broken center.

Everything ready, about 9 o'clock the artillery opened from the adjacent hills, right and left, and poured into the compressed masses of the enemy a perfect storm of shot and shell. As many guns answered back from the other side. The roar of artillery fairly rent the air and shook the earth as the infantry lines began to move. The attack was by brigades *en echelon* against the two sides of the salient at the same time. Lane on the right, and Ramseaur on the left, first sprang forward with a rousing cheer, and swept the trenches the full length of their brigades. Then rushed the fiery Gordon into the breach with his Georgians and Virginians, and cleaned out the right face of the angle to the left of Lane. At the same time the dashing Perrin launched his brave Alabamians, closely followed by Harris's Mississippians, each carving his way across the seething chasm, and landed successively in full breast on the outer line to the right of Ramseaur. Then came our own intrepid McGowan with his gallant Carolinians—sharpshooters and all—like a blazing meteor rushing through the blinding storm, and planted his brigade on the outer line to the right of Harris and in the very heart of battle. Gen. Perrin fell dead just as he leaped his horse over the first line of works, and Ramseaur and McGowan were both seriously wounded in the charge.

When the troops were ready to move to the recovery of the lost salient, Gen. Lee rode to front of Gordon's division—as he had of Gregg's Texans at the Wilderness—and proposed to lead the charge. He uttered not a word—he was not the man for display—but as he quietly removed his hat and sat his war horse, the very personification of the genius of battle, the great purpose of his great soul was evident. Just then Gen. Gordon spurred to his side, seized the reins of his horse and exclaimed: "Gen. Lee, this is no place for you! Go to the rear! These are Georgians and Virginians, sir!—men that have never failed, and will not fail now; will you, boys?" Loud cries of "No! No! Gen. Lee to the rear! Gen. Lee to the rear!" burst forth from the ranks. While two soldiers led Gen. Lee's horse to the rear, Gordon placed himself in front of his division, and his clarion voice rang out above the roar of battle, "Forward! charge!!" and "remember your promise to Gen. Lee." Not Napoleon's words to his old guard, "The eyes of your emperor are upon you," produced a happier effect. The right face of the angle was swept clean, and Gordon and Lane reoccupied our lines nearly to the center of the breach.

> "Never hand waved sword from stain so free,
> Nor purer sword led a braver band,
> Nor braver bled for fairer land,
> Nor fairer land had a cause so grand,
> Nor cause a chief like Lee."

The interior of the salient was now effectually rid of the obnoxious Federals, but rallying upon their supports they firmly held on to the vertex or tip of the angle, the possession of which now became the single issue of the desperate struggle. The gaping incision made in the Confederate lines at early dawn had been partially closed—as the physician would say—by first intention, but the center of the wound could not be healed. Gen. Lee, however, continued to press his wings toward the broken center, in the hope that by persistent effort he might be able to expel his adversary and restore his lines completely. But the Federal commander, by massing his forces around the protruding angle and concentrating the fire of his immense columns upon that point, successfully resisted every attempt to close the breach, and ever and anon himself thrust forward his right or left, in the vain hope of retaking that part of the lines which the Confederates had recovered from him. Neither side could gain any advantage or make any impression upon the other, and therefore both settled down to their work of death and destruction. Hour after hour the livelong day and far into the succeeding night "the incessant roll of the volleying guns" proclaimed the desperate nature of the bloody conflict going on in the "bloody angle."

Fortunately the works at this point were strongly traversed and mounted by heavy head logs, beneath which the contestants aimed and fired, otherwise no living thing could have survived for a moment the terrific cross current of musket balls, which literally combed the parapets from every point of the compass. Around this storm center the battle surged and swayed, and men fell by scores and hundreds, like leaves before an autumn gale. Indeed, so close was the fight that the rival standards were frequently planted on opposite sides of the breastworks, and men were seized and dragged across the lines as prisoners of war, while the call to surrender was repeated again and again by the determined Confederates, each time receiving a defiant answer with the same demand. During the day diversions were made by both sides, with the hope of relieving the pressure in the center. Wright attacked Anderson on the left and was repulsed with heavy loss, while Early, who with Hill's corps was moving to strike the Federal flank on the other side, met and defeated Burnsides, who was advancing at the same time to attack the Confederate right. Still the storm raged with unabated fury around the famous salient until a short while before daylight on the morning of the 13th, when the Confederates sullenly retired, by order of the commanding general, to the new line of works erected some half a mile in the rear and across the base of the salient.

An incident which illustrates the fierceness of this battle, and which by various writers has received historical notice, may properly be mentioned in this connection. A large oak tree, eighteen inches in diameter (besides a number of smaller trees of different varieties and dimensions), standing some twenty feet or more in rear of the Confederate works, was literally shot down by the incessant converging fire of the Federal musketry—to the truth of which the writer, as an eye witness of the fact, here bears testimony. The trunk of the tree is now preserved in Washington as a memento of the desperate struggle.

Gen. McAllister, of the Union army, writes: "It was in our immediate front that the large tree was cut down by rifle balls, the stump of which was exhibited at the Centennial exposition at Philadelphia." James L. Bowen, historian of the thirty-seventh Massachusetts regiment, says: "This regiment was in action continually for more than twenty hours, during which time it fired over four hundred rounds per man. * * * It was in front of the right wing of this regiment, and almost in the rear of the apex, that the oak tree, twenty-one inches in diameter, was cut down by bullets and fell within the Confederate lines. * * * The tree fell after midnight, and after the firing had ceased everywhere except at this vital point." Several men of the twelfth South Carolina regiment, which occupied the right of the line on the left face and near the tip of the angle, were crushed down and severely stunned by the lap of the falling tree, but not permanently injured.

Swinton writes: "Of all the struggles of the war, this was perhaps the fiercest and most deadly. * * * The enemy's most savage sallies were directed to retake the famous salient, which was now become an angle of death, and presented a spectacle ghastly and terrible."

The ground was literally covered with the dead and dying, and the water that rippled along the trenches from incessant rain, ran red with the blood of the slain. In the absence of specific orders, the sharpshooters had thrown themselves into the line of the brigade at their proper intervals and fought like tigers throughout the struggle, sharing the perils and dividing the honors with their sturdy comrades of the brigade; and contributing withal their full pro rata of heroic men to the roll of 451 fallen braves, which constituted the aggregate number of casualties reported in McGowan's brigade. Indeed, so large was the list of casualties in the sharpshooters to this juncture that Gen. Wilcox, our division commander, ordered that thereafter the sharpshooters should not be required to fight in the line of battle, as theretofore, except in cases of extreme necessity, but should confine themselves to their legitimate duties as skirmishers.

Upon retiring from their position in the "bloody angle," these grimy, blear eyed veterans, finding Longstreet's corps occupying the new line of works, went into bivouac some distance in their rear, where we were permitted to rest and recuperate. On the afternoon of the 14th we were moved to the little church east of town, but on the next afternoon were ordered back and went into position west of the court house. Here we remained several days awaiting the movements of the enemy. The sharpshooters again took the front and resumed their practice upon the enemy's skirmish lines.

Never was respite more welcome than the comparative rest that followed the terrible battle of the 12th, and which continued up to the 18th, for we had been marching and fighting without intermission since the 4th of May; and our comfort was materially enhanced by the supply of sugar and coffee and other delicacies obtained from Federal haversacks during the campaign. These luxuries contributed as much as any other material agency to recover and sustain the spirits and physical energies of the men in a campaign that had taxed both to their utmost limit.

Longstreet's corps had been moved to the right, and now lay beyond the Fredericksburg road, while Ewell occupied the lines in rear of the salient. On the morning of the 18th a last effort was made to force the lines at the only point where previous efforts had partially succeeded, and this was destined to a more signal failure than any of the other attacks. Under the fire of thirty guns, which swept every approach to Ewell's lines, the attacking force was broken and driven back in confusion before it came within range of our musketry of the line. On the next morning it was discovered that Gen. Grant had begun his third movement by the left flank, and in the afternoon Ewell's corps was thrown round the Federal right to ascertain the extent of the movement. After a severe engagement, which lasted until night, Ewell withdrew with some loss. This attack delayed Grant's movement for twenty-four hours. On the afternoon of the 19th, however, while Ewell was engaged in his movement against the Federal right, the sharpshooters were thrown forward to cover the interval between his right and Hill's left. This brought the sharpshooters across the line of works in the famous salient, at the very point where we had fought on the memorable 12th, and where the timber had been cut down by Federal musketry, as heretofore mentioned; and while here I took it upon myself to measure the stump of the "large oak tree," and found it to be exactly fifty-five inches in circumference, or a little more than eighteen inches in diameter. Every tree and bush and shrub were literally riddled with bullets. The ground was covered with the debris of battle. Small arms of every variety, bent and broken, with every conceivable article of accoutrement and clothing, were scattered in every direction. Horses lay as they fell; and the bodies of the thousands slain, expanding under the process of putrefaction, and bursting the thin covering of earth which had been thrown upon them in their hasty burial, emitted a stench that was almost stifling. The whole scene was a perfect picture of gloom, destruction and death—a very Golgotha of horrors. For the next two days the sharpshooters, like the "Fierce Demoniac," lived among the tombs and deserted Federal breastworks, driving their rear guard from one position after another until late in the afternoon of the 21st, when they made an obstinate stand, covering the house which had been occupied by Gen. Warren as his headquarters. Their position was a strong one and well fortified, but we thought it could be carried. So adjusting our lines to the work in hand, we gathered up our full strength and sounded the charge. Instantly the whole battalion sprang forward, stormed over the breastworks, and swept the field of the last trace of the Union army in our front. The troops of the line, in the meantime, had been shifted from left to right, and now the race began for a position on the banks of the North Anna.

CHAPTER V.

BATTLE OF HANOVER JUNCTION, OR JERICHO FORD.

> And when the fight becomes a chase,
> Those win the day that win the race,
> And that which would not pass in fights
> Has done the feat with easy flights.
> —BUTLER.

The consciousness of personal courage, which alone had animated the members of the battalion at the opening of the campaign, and which soon extended to the *comrades de bataille*, or groups of four, now embraced the entire command, and, as Bancroft said of Morgan's Scotch-Irish riflemen, the sharpshooters were "fashioned into one life, one energy and one action." When ordered into the fight they moved as a unit. No skirmish line, or force of equal numbers, could withstand the momentum of one of their headlong charges; and even a line of battle was often made to squirm, and sometimes to break, under the fiery impact of their splendid *esprit de corps*. To hold them in control in presence of the enemy, and to restrain them from pursuing a broken column beyond the limits of safety, constituted the principal difficulties experienced by their officers in the management of this gallant corps. And their reckless impetuosity on the field caused the needless sacrifice of many a brave man, whose services were afterwards needed, but sadly missed, in the prosecution of the pending vigorous and unremitting campaign. One member alone failed to stand the test of of battle, and his place was promptly supplied with another man.

Sergeants Madison F. Hawthorn and Berry Benson, two regularly commissioned scouts of the battalion, had rendered valuable service to the army in gathering information for the commanding general as to the position and movements of the enemy, both in the Wilderness and around Spottsylvania court house. Their discoveries were always promptly reported to Gen. Lee, and had their influence upon the movements of the army. They were sometimes too reckless in their adventures, and subjected themselves to dangers not contemplated in their commissions and beyond the necessities of the service. They operated not only closely upon the front and flanks of the Union army, observing critically their position and movements, but frequently entered their lines and conversed intimately with the Federals themselves with regard to the progress and prospects of the campaign. On one such occasion (I believe it was the night of the 10th of May) they went into the Federal lines, and after gathering all the information they could get, Benson mounted a general's horse, a magnificent animal, and right before their eyes deliberately rode him off into the Confederate lines, while Hawthorn retired from a different part of their lines afoot. Both landed safely within our lines and reported. A few nights later they attempted the same thing, when Benson was caught, and for six long months was held in restless confinement in a Northern prison, from which he made his escape by tunneling some time in the fall or early part of the succeeding winter, and rejoined his command in the trenches before Petersburg. Hawthorn was not so unfortunate, but succeeded in eluding detection and returned to our lines in due time—ever afterwards a wiser and more cautious scout. Benson's place was filled by his brother, B. K. Benson, and the campaign progressed.

Gen. Grant having received heavy reinforcements, again disappeared from our front and began his third movement by the left flank. But Gen. Lee, with his usual alertness, had his depleted columns in motion the instant Grant began to move. Gen. Ewell led the van, followed by Anderson, with Hill's corps bringing up the rear. McGowan's brigade, now under command of Col. Brown, of the fourteenth South Carolina regiment, took up the line of march soon after dark on the night of the 21st, and continued the march until after midnight, when it went into bivouac. I had been seized with a violent form of dysentery and had to retire from the front, and hence the command of the sharpshooters devolved upon Capt. Brunson. Resuming the march at daylight the next morning, the brigade crossed the North Anna in the afternoon on a bridge near Noel's Station, and went into bivouac about a mile beyond the river. "Lee had the inside track this time, as the Telegraph road on which he moved was the direct route, while Grant had to swing round on the arc of a circle of which this was the chord." So that when Grant approached the north bank of the river on the morning of the 23rd, he found that his third movement against the line of Lee's communications had been completely circumvented. There stood his opponent with forty-five thousand muskets, occupying a strong position on high ground south of the river, covering Hanover Junction. The hammering process was again his only alternative, so Grant got his mallets ready. McGowan's brigade continued the march toward the Junction on the morning of the 23rd, but had not reached the position on the line it was designed to occupy, when it was suddenly halted. Gen. Warren, who commanded the Federal right, had succeeded in driving off the small cavalry force which guarded the crossing at Jericho Ford, and had crossed his whole corps to the south side of the river, and was taking position on the Confederate left. Gen. W. H. F. Lee, who commanded the cavalry on that flank, under a misapprehension of the strength of this movement, reported a small Federal force south of the river, and McGowan's brigade was ordered to report to Lee. When the brigade reached the position occupied by the cavalry, the rifle regiment was ordered forward to make a reconnoissance. Capt. Cothran, who commanded the regiment, promptly advanced, but had gone but a short distance when he encountered a heavy force of Federal infantry, and his regiment was driven back in confusion. Calling the sharpshooters, Col. Brown ordered Brunson to advance and feel the enemy. Nothing daunted by the failure of Cothran's experiment, Brunson moved to the front and deployed, and the feeling process now began. Cautiously advancing until the Federals were fully discovered, then delivering a volley and sounding the charge, the sharpshooters went crashing through their lines like an Alpine avalanche, dispersing the force and capturing a number of prisoners. Again resuming their carefulness, the sharpshooters continued the advance until a second and much stronger line was discovered, posted in an old roadbed on a commanding ridge in an old field, thinly clad in scrubby pines and broomsedge, and halted. The light division was now brought up and formed, with Lane's brigade on the right, McGowan in the center, and Thomas on the left. Scales's brigade was held in reserve. It was now about 5 o'clock in the afternoon, and the sharpshooters were again ordered to drive in the Federal advance line and prepare the field for action. Accordingly Brunson led his men across the ravine in front, and ordered them to dispose of the Federal sharpshooters on short notice, which they did, sending them flying through the pines and broomsedge up the hill to their front line in the old roadbed. Without hesitation Brunson attacked and carried this line, and engaged their second line, which was covered by a strong line of earthworks at the edge of the woods, and behind which the first line rallied and formed. The division now advanced to the attack. The assault was gallantly made and vigorously maintained by the Confederates, and as gallantly met and repelled by the Federals until long after nightfall, when the firing ceased and the division was withdrawn. The sharpshooters were left in position to cover the withdrawal, and continued their lonely vigils the livelong night, while the division retired to a well favored position near Anderson's Station, where the commanding general had planted his left, and where he designed to make the fight.

About daylight on the morning of the 24th Brunson swung back his left flank and retired at the run, back to cover of the woods behind him, pursued by a heavy line of infantry. The instant they reached the woods the sharpshooters turned and opened on their pursuers. The Federals continued their advance, but with abundant caution, while the sharpshooters stubbornly contested every inch of the ground back to the station. For four mortal hours this gallant corps detained the Federal line of battle in a belt of timber not exceeding three miles wide. The incessant cry of their deadly rifles, rising from the depths of the forest and falling upon the ears of their comrades of the line—at first faintly, and by slow degrees more and more plainly, as they slowly fell back—proclaimed the obstinacy of their resistance to the Federal advance. At length, reaching a point some four hundred yards in front of the line of battle, the sharpshooters made a stand in a strong position and effectually held up the advancing line.

Meanwhile Hancock had succeeded in overpowering a small detachment of Kershaw's division, and crossed the river below, and now confronted Anderson and Ewell on the Confederate right, while Wright had crossed above and with Warren confronted Hill's corps on the left. The two wings of the Union army were on the south side of the river, but there was no connection between them. Lee had purposely thrown back his flanks and let them cross on either side, while he held the river between. Burnside, who confronted Lee's center, threw forward a strong division against the sharp angle, in the hope that he might gain a foothold on the south bank of the river and establish connection between the severed wings of the Union army, but was driven back by Mahone with heavy loss. "The game of war seldom presents a more effectual checkmate than was here given by Lee. For after Grant had made the brilliantly successful passage of the North Anna, the Confederate commander, thrusting his center between the two wings of the Army of the Potomac, put his antagonist at an enormous disadvantage, and compelled him, for the reinforcement of one or the other wing, to make a double passage of the river." Whereas, Lee could readily transfer his troops from one wing to the other across the narrow space between them whenever necessary; and but for the necessity of economy in men—and expecting the Federals to attack—Gen. Lee could have ruined the Union army right here. Gen. Grant saw the point, and after a formidable demonstration withdrew his army during the night of the 26th to the north bank of the river, and moved again by the left flank down the river—defeated without a battle.

Brunson says: "During the night of the 25th the enemy made several attempts to capture our lines, with his usual success; and finally, when drowned out of their pits during a thunder storm and giving us a view of their heads, we drove them back upon their main line."

The brigade lost in this engagement, including the casualties in the battalion, 211 officers and men—killed, wounded and missing; and among the missing Col. J. N. Brown, the brigade commander, who was captured in the fight of the 23d. Lieut. Col. J. F. Hunt, being the senior officer present, took command of the brigade.

On the morning of the 27th it was discovered that the Army of the Potomac had disappeared from Lee's front, and was already on its march for the Pamonkey river at Hanovertown, where the leading division had crossed early in the day.

CHAPTER VI.

TILT ON THE TOTOPOTOMOY AT ATLEE'S, AND BATTLE OF COLD HARBOR.

> Cease to consult, the time for action calls;
> War, horrid war, approaches to your walls.
> —POPE.

The Confederates began to move at once to head off their opponents. Crossing Little river and South Anna, Lee hurried forward his army toward Atlee's Station, on the Central railroad, where he arrived early on the morning of the 28th, and formed his lines in a strong position fronting the Totopotomoy creek. Gen. Wade Hampton had succeeded the lamented Stuart (who, it will be remembered, had been mortally wounded in a cavalry engagement at Yellow Tavern on the 11th, and had subsequently died), and now commanded Lee's cavalry corps. Hampton planted a strong division of cavalry, under Fitzhugh Lee, across the main line of approach to the army at Atlee's, at Haw's shop, between the Totopotomoy and Pamonkey, and here fought successfully one of the severest cavalry engagements of the war. Sheridan was defeated, but the Federal infantry coming up, Hampton retired, and the two armies again confronted each other on the banks of the Totopotomoy.

The sharpshooters again took the front and resumed their rifle practice upon the Federal lines. Grant had evidently grown sick of his hammering process, and here concealed his mallets and resorted to a game of small strategy. For two days there was constant shifting of troops in the Confederate front, with now and then, and here and there, a demonstration. But Gen. Lee was master of the situation and readily confronted his adversary at every point. Again thwarted in his attempt to thrust his army between Lee and the Confederate capital, Gen. Grant moved off by the left flank, with the battlefield of Cold Harbor as his objective point.

Gen. Long writes with regard to the movements of the Union army: " Proceeding on his march from the Pamonkey, Grant found his advance upon Richmond again arrested by Lee, who awaited him on the Totopotomoy, in the neighborhood of Mechanicsville and Atlee's Station. Grant did not attempt at this point to force his opponent from his path, but moved slowly by his left flank toward the Chickahominy, while Lee, by a similar movement by his right, kept pace with him and constantly confronted him at every stage, until the flank of each army rested on the Chickahominy on the first day of June. The old battlefield of Cold Harbor was again occupied by the contending forces, though in an inverse order; and was about to become the theater of a second conflict more desperate than the first."

When Gen. Lee moved from Atlee's Station, however, Sergt. B. K. Benson writes: "The sharpshooters were left in position facing the enemy, with instructions to hold the position at all hazards until night. The line occupied was on a commanding ridge, covered with heavy timber, which broke off abruptly in front into a short valley below, then gradually rose again to another hill of equal height beyond. The Federal sharpshooters occupied this hill in strong force, well protected by rifle pits. Several times during the day they made ineffectual attempts to dislodge us, and as many times were repelled and forced back to their rifle pits. Late in the afternoon orders were received to withdraw quietly and follow the army. To save himself from the annoyance of pursuit, Capt. Brunson determined to drive the Federal pickets from their position by a dash and then retire. So the order was given, and about dark the sharpshooters descended the hill into the valley, and after rectifying their alignment sounded the charge, and at a full run mounted the hill in front, cheering and firing as they advanced, stormed the Federals out of their works and drove them in confusion into the darkness beyond, capturing a number of prisoners and considerable spoil. Among others was a noble specimen of Yankee soldier, who fearlessly asserted his honest convictions as to the final results of the war, and supported his views with such potency of argument that the officers, fearing the effect of his reasoning upon some of the men, hurried him off with other prisoners to the rear under guard. The battalion was withdrawn without molestation, and rejoined the brigade."

Brunson himself, writing of the same period, condenses his report into a single paragraph, and modestly says: "We were at our usual trade, marching, watching, fighting, somewhere on the face of the earth in the State of Virginia, between Hanover Junction and the old battlefield of Cold Harbor."

SECOND BATTLE OF COLD HARBOR.

The two great armies of the civil war again confronted each other on the historic field of Cold Harbor. The army of Northern Virginia, with the reinforcements of Breckinridge's, Hoke's and Pickett's divisions, numbered about 50,000 men, while the Army of the Potomac, reinforced by the eighteenth army corps from Butler's army and other troops, notwithstanding its enormous losses, still numbered 140,000 men. Lee occupied the lines from which McClellan was driven two years before, with his back upon Richmond, while Grant confronted him, with his face turned longingly towards the Confederate capital. Hancock held the Federal left, Wright and Smith the center, and Warren and Burnside the right. Hill's corps, with Breckinridge's division, confronted Hancock and Wright on the Confederate right; Longstreet in the center confronting Smith, and Ewell on the left confronting Warren and Burnside. McGowan's brigade occupied the right of Hill's corps and the extreme right of the Confederate lines, holding the last shoulder of the ridge which rises from the Chickahominy swamp on McClellan's military road. Both armies spent the first and second days of June in erecting fortifications and making general preparations for the impending conflict, with now and then a slight collision barren of results. The Confederate lines ran in general directions north and south, but the works were angular throughout; so that no line could approach the front without subjecting itself either to a converging fire, or to both a direct and enfilading fire at the same time. No doubt preparations on the other side were just as formidable and complete; but Gen. Lee would not make but awaited the assault.

Accordingly, on the morning of the 3d, with the seeming intention of blotting out the memory of the defeat of the Federal arms on the former occasion, Gen. Grant massed the flower of his army for battle, and on they came. "The battle that succeeded was one of the most desperately contested and murderous engagements of the war. Along the whole Federal line a simultaneous assault was made on the Confederate works, and at every point with the same disastrous results. Rank after rank was swept away until the columns of assault were almost annihilated. Attack after attack was made, and men fell in myriads before the murderous fire of the Confederates. While Hill Breckinridge, Anderson and Pickett repulsed Grant's desperate assaults on the right, Early, with Rodes, Gordon and Ramseaur on the left, successfully opposed Burnside and Warren. In the brief space of one hour the bloody battle of the 3d of June, 1864, was over, and 13,000 dead and wounded lay in front of the lines, behind which little more than 1000 of the Confederate forces had fallen." Grant ordered a renewal of the attack shortly afterwards, but the men, silently protesting against the useless slaughter to which they had been subjected, refused to move. Thus the second great battle of Cold Harbor was ended, and the curtain dropped upon the fifth and last act of Grant's bloody drama, "On to Richmond," by the overland route. That part of the line occupied by McGowan's brigade was not attacked, and hence the sharpshooters had nothing to do but guard the front and gather up fragments of Hancock's broken columns as they scattered out and came within their grasp.

"But the June of 1864," says a certain Northern writer, "found Grant almost in sight of the city, upon the very ground which McClellan had held on the banks of the Chickahominy two years before. Four times he had changed the line of operations, chosen in obedience to Lincoln's strong desire, on which he had declared his intention to fight it out on this line if it takes all summer. Four times he had recoiled from the attempt to force his way direct to the rebel capital, for his indomitable and watchful adversary ever barred the way. Once more, on the morning of June 3d, he flung his masses fiercely against the line held by Lee, which ran across the very field of battle where that general had won his first triumph over McClellan. The result was so fearful and useless a slaughter that, according to the chief Union historian, when later in the day orders were issued to renew the assault, the whole

army, correctly appreciating what the inevitable result would be, silently disobeyed."
* * * "Not even the vast resources on which he had power to draw could spare long 20,000 men a week for the continuance of the experiment. He had lost in the first three weeks of battle with Lee 60,000 men; and as Lee had commenced the campaign with only 63,000, Grant could not but reflect that had their armies been equal Lee would not have left him a vestige of his army with which to retreat."

CHAPTER VII.

BATTLE OF RIDDLE'S SHOPS.

> Be stirring as the time; be fire with fire;
> Threaten the threat'ner, and outface the brow
> Of bragging horror: So shall inferior eyes,
> That borrow their behaviors from the great,
> Grow great by your example, and put on
> The dauntless spirit of resolution.
> —SHAKESPEARE.

Grant now determined to lay siege to the Confederate capital and accomplish its downfall by the slow process of investment, which he had most signally failed to do in a determined campaign of more than thirty days in the open field, and so began the movement of his troops to that end. On the 7th of June, Sheridan with two divisions of cavalry was dispatched to cut the Virginia Central railroad, join Hunter at Charlottsville, and after cutting off and destroying the sources of Confederate supply in that direction, to rejoin the

Army of the Potomac wherever it might then be.

On the 10th, Gilmore, with a strong force of infantry, and Kautz's division of cavalry were dispatched from Butler's army to capture Petersburg and to destroy the railroads there, together with the bridges across the Appomattox, thus to sever the lines of communication and sources of supply in that direction. Both these expeditions failed. Gen. Smith, with the eighteenth army corps, was next ordered to Petersburg by water, via the White House, in the hope that he might reach there before the Confederates were aware, and capture the city in advance of the army. This expedition also failed.

On the 12th, Warren's corps and Wilson's cavalry crossed the Chickahominy at Long Bridge and moved to White Oak Swamp to cover the passage of the other corps to the James. The advance corps of the Federal column crossed the James river for Petersburg at Charles City court house and Wilcox's Landing on the 13th, followed by a large part of Grant's army.

Gen. Lee, of course, was advised of these movements the instant they began, and promptly reinforced Beauregard who was in command at Petersburg. At the same time he began to crowd and harass Grant's rear. The Confederate cavalry and the several battalions of sharpshooters hung like a festering incubus upon the retiring Unionists, persistently annoying their columns, and ever and anon precipitating a sharp engagement—driving in their covering detachments and capturing their men.

About this time Gen. James Connor, of Charleston, S. C., was temporarily assigned to the command of the brigade (Gen. McGowan being still disabled by wounds received at Spottsylvania court house), and on the morning of the 13th, at the request of Capt. Brunson, relieved the sharpshooters from duty for one day, to wash their shirts, which had not been off their backs for more than five weeks. They had about gotten their washing under good headway when they were ordered to assemble and prepare to move at once. The battalion was promptly formed and moved off, followed by the brigade, and after a march of some twelve miles through the woods and along obscure bypaths, the sharpshooters reached the Charles City road at or near Riddle's Shops. Here they met Gen. Gary's brigade of cavalry in full retreat before a heavy line of Federal infantry.

Gen. Connor ordered the sharpshooters to advance and feel the enemy, but be very cautious and not go beyond supporting distance from the brigade, which would follow in line of battle. The battalion advanced at once, supported by one company of the line from the fourteenth regiment in rear of the right flank. It met the Federal skirmishers as they slowly pursued the retiring horsemen, and drove them back upon their main line, which was posted behind an improvised line of breastworks built of earth and fence rails. The company in reserve was now ordered up; but before it could be brought into line, the sharpshooters, led by Hasell, whose company extended beyond the Federal left, swung forward his right, and striking the enemy in flank drove him from cover.

The whole line now moved forward, and despite their obstinacy, drove the Federals through the woods mile after mile to their original position, recovering all the ground that Gary had lost. About sunset Gen. Connor ordered the battalion to halt and dig rifle pits. The position on which the sharpshooters were ordered to halt was not at all satisfactory to Capt. Brunson, who discovered some distance in front a much more eligible position for a permanant line—a wooded hill which was still in the hands of the enemy; and therefore dispatched a courier to Gen. Connor for permission to charge the hill. Before the courier had time to obtain the order and return, the position was carried and the enemy driven back upon a second and more formidable line supported by a section of artillery. Here they rallied and made a stand. The two battalions of Scales and Thomas now came into line on Brunson's left; and, together, the three battalions advanced to the attack. The Federals received the sharpshooters with a galling fire from the full length of their line, and turned loose their artillery with grape and canister at short range.

Onward moved the beautiful line through the leaden storm that swept the face of the hill, until it was almost lost to view in the smoke of the enemy's guns. So close was the fight that, viewed from a distance, the contending lines seemed to merge, and for a moment the issues seemed doubtful; but the Confederates were determined. At this critical moment Hasell again swung forward his right across the road and struck the enemy squarely in flank, crushing their line and closing upon their artillery, which was almost within his grasp, when they broke and fled the field in every direction. The artillery made its escape by the opposite end of the road, which, but for the failure of the left battalion to seize the road as Hasell had done, would have fallen into our hands and completed the already brilliant affair.

Night intervened and the sharpshooters were withdrawn.

Gen. A. P. Hill had witnessed the operations of the day and complimented the battalion very highly for the splendid successes achieved.

The losses of the brigade in the battles of Cold Harbor and Riddle's Shops, which fell almost exclusively upon the sharpshooters, were only twenty-five men.

CHAPTER VIII.

FIRST BATTLES OF PETERSBURG; BEAUREGARD IN COMMAND.

"Soldiers of the South! Defenders of our soil!
Who from destruction save us; who from spoil
Protect the sons of peace, who traffic or who toil;
Would I could duly praise you, that each deed
Your foes might honor, and your friends might read."

By this time the entire army had been withdrawn from the lines of Cold Harbor, and now extended from the south bank of the Chickahominy on the left to the neighborhood of Malvern Hill on the right. On the 15th of June McGowan's brigade was advanced a few hundred yards and fortified—the sharpshooters in front, but not disturbed. Here the troops enjoyed for a few days a restful respite from the arduous duties of the campaign. But the constant exposure to sun and rain, scant rations, lack of clothing, miserable water, miasma of the swamps, and constant anxiety for the continued success of our arms, had begun to tell upon the health of the men. Numbers of them were attacked with malarial fever, dysentery and other forms of disease, and had to retire from the front; some never more to return.

On the afternoon of the 17th the light division, in obedience to orders, marched off in the direction of the James river, went into bivouac about dark, resumed the march at daylight the next morning, crossed the river on the pontoons at Drury's Bluff, and hurried on, as for the life of the Southern Confederacy, toward Petersburg. The small force under Beauregard had been confronted by the eighteenth army corps under Smith and other Federal troops from Butler's army on the 15th. Hancock and Wright had joined Smith on the day following, and the entire Union army seemed to be concentrating upon the lines of Petersburg. Already a part of Beauregard's outer line had yielded to the weight of Grant's superior columns, and the second and interior line attacked. It therefore behooved the Southern commander to hurry forward his troops with all possible dispatch to the rescue.

The boom of distant cannon saluted the ears of the light division the moment it emerged from the valley of the James, and continued at intervals throughout the day, as the division pressed forward toward the scene of action. The spirit of lofty patriotism alone sustained the men as they struggled on through clouds of dust, under a burning sun, in great distress, to the point of conflict, and the exceeding scarcity of water along the route added no little to the suffering endured on this hurried march. The head of the column met a train of box cars about five miles out, and as many as were up mounted the train and were soon landed in the city. Others came in during the night, and others still, of less physical energy, did not report until some time the next day. The division reached Petersburg late in the afternoon of the 18th, marched through the city to the front, and went into position on the right of our line. The right of McGowan's brigade rested on or near the Weldon railroad. The sharpshooters were ordered to the front and took position some four hundred yards in advance of the brigade, enjoyed a good night's rest, and were ready for business the next morning.

Kershaw's division had arrived early in the morning of the 18th, about 5000 strong, and two hours later Field's division, of about the same strength, had marched into Petersburg.

The arrival of these reinforcements surprised the enemy and saved the city. Other troops followed the light division, and very soon our lines of defense were complete.

The past several days constituted an exceedingly critical period for the Confederates in their great struggle for independence; and, but for the masterful genius of Gen. Lee and the sturdy valor of his veteran battalions, the Southern cause must have suffered.

The city of Richmond was universally recognized as the grand objective of the Federal commander, notwithstanding the energy with which he pressed his heavy columns against the lines of Petersburg. These demonstrations were regarded at first by the Confederate commander as so many movements in strategy to divert him from his purpose to defend the Confederate capital, and to scatter his forces, that the gates might fall ajar and the downfall of our citadel be accomplished before he was aware. And there is but little doubt that these surmises were correct as to the incipiency of this movement. But his sad experiences at Cold Harbor and the failure of Butler's movement from Bermuda Hundred, led Gen. Grant to convert his *ruse de guerre* into a genuine purpose to reduce Petersburg.

Gen. Beauregard was in command of the Confederate forces confronting Butler between the rivers and covering Petersburg. He had only about 2000 men south of the Appomattox when the eighteenth army corps under Smith confronted him east of the city on the 15th of June; and these were largely transient troops and local militia, drawn out to a thread and covering a line of some four or five miles in length. Smith advanced to the attack about 8 o'clock in the morning, but was met by these untrained Confederates with the resolute fortitude of veterans, and repulsed. Smith reinforced his columns of assault and repeated his attacks again and again; and as many times was driven back with heavy loss. The enemy, continuing to mass his columns toward the center of the Confederate lines, pressed it more and more, concentrating his heaviest assaults upon batteries five, six and seven. Thinned out and exhausted as they were, the heroic Confederates resisted still, with such unflinching stubbornness as to equal the veterans of the Army of Northern Virginia. Shortly after 7 o'clock p. m. the enemy entered a ravine between batteries six and seven, flanked battery five and made a breach in our lines. The fall of Petersburg seemed inevitable.

Meanwhile the seriousness of the situation had induced Gen. Beauregard to call for reinforcements again and again, which were not furnished; and the alternative was upon him, either to withdraw troops from Butler's front, between the rivers, or give up Petersburg. He elected to hold Petersburg, and therefore ordered Hoke to report at once with his splendid division, which he did, and soon marched into the city. These reinforcements were shown their position, on a new line, a short distance in rear of the captured works, and were kept busy, with the other troops, all night in throwing up breastworks.

Strange to say, Gen. Smith contented himself with breaking the outer Confederate lines, and attempted nothing further that night. Stranger still was his inaction since Gen. Hancock with his strong and well equipped second army corps had reached the city soon after dark. A little later in the night Gen. Beauregard ascertained that Gen. Burnside with the ninth Federal corps was approaching the lines of Petersburg. He further ordered Gen. Bushrod Johnson to withdraw from Butler's front and march his division as rapidly as possible to the assistance of Petersburg. Johnson reported with his division early on the morning of the 16th. Beauregard now had an effective force of about 10,000 men, which were confronted, after the arrival of Burnside, by three full Federal army corps, which mustered some 65,000 veterans.

Fortunately this heavy force was held inactive during the day and did not attack until 5 o'clock in the afternoon. The Federals then attacked with considerable vigor. The Confederates met them with great fortitude and repulsed them again and again for three mortal hours. Finally Birney's division of Hancock's corps broke into a part of our lines and effected a lodgement. The contest was continued with varying results long after nightfall, with advantage to the Confederates on the left and some serious loss on the right. It then slackened and gradually came to an end.

In the meantime Butler had advanced from Bermuda Hundred, seized and occupied the Confederate works between the rivers, and Warren's corps had been added to the forces in front of Petersburg. The enemy now confronted the 10,000 Confederates with an army of some 80,000 men. Hostilities were resumed early on the morning of the 17th.

Here quoting from Gen. Beauregard: "Three times were the Federals driven back, but they as often resumed the offensive and held their ground. About dusk a portion of the Confederate lines was broken and the troops in that quarter were about to be thrown into a panic, which might have ended in irreparable disaster, when happily * * * Gracie's brigade of Johnson's division, consisting of about twelve hundred men * * * came up from Chaffin's Bluff, whence, at last, the war department had ordered it to move. It was promptly and opportunely thrown into the gap on the lines and drove back the Federals, capturing about two thousand prisoners. The conflict raged with great fury until after 11 o'clock at night."

When the Federals had become quiet in his front, Gen. Beauregard, realizing his inability further to resist the immense Federal columns concentrated in his front, and the peril of his position, with his inadequate force on his extended lines, determined to withdraw during the night to an inner, shorter, stronger and permanent line of works, which had been laid off some distance in rear of his present position. Accordingly, a while after midnight, he ordered his picket lines advanced as far as possible without provoking a conflict, his camp fires to be lighted all along his lines, and the greatest possible display to be made of his strength and determination to continue the struggle at this point, then withdrew to his interior lines as aforesaid, and spent the remainder of the night in strengthening his new position and making preparations for a renewal of the conflict in the morning.

Meanwhile Gen. Lee had become convinced of the seriousness of Grant's designs against Petersburg and had sent forward to the support of Beauregard the three splendid divisions of Kershaw, Field and Wilcox, two of which reached Petersburg early on the morning, the third late in the afternoon of the 18th. Before these reinforcements were assigned their several positions on the line, Gen. Lee himself appeared and took command.

The Federals, however, advanced to the attack early in the morning, but when they came upon our deserted outer lines they were surprised and disconcerted, and hence called a halt to take new bearings. About 12 o'clock m., or perhaps a little later, the grand attack was made. The immense columns moved forward in a half hearted, disconnected and desultory manner, and were repulsed all along the lines.

At 4 o'clock in the afternoon another grand attack was made with Hancock's, Burnside's and Warren's full corps, and, as Gen. Meade himself says, "Without success." And he adds, "Later in the day attacks were made by the fifth and ninth corps, with no better results."

The truth is, that despite the overwhelming odds against us, every Federal assault on the 18th was met with most signal defeat, "attended," as Swinton says, "with a mournful loss of life." This was, in fact, very heavy, and exceeded the Confederate loss in the proportion of nine to one. Gen. Humphries, of the Union army, in his Virginia campaign of 1864 and 1865 places the Union losses at 10,000 men killed, wounded and missing in the several engagements from the 15th to the 18th.

Gen. Grant seemed to be satisfied that further efforts, at present, against the lines of Petersburg would prove as disastrous to his army as previous attacks, and hence addressed himself to rectifying, entrenching and protecting his own lines. Therefore, everything became quiet in front of Petersburg. When the body of the Army of Northern Virginia had concentrated in front of the five army corps of Smith, Hancock, Burnside, Warren and Wright, Gen. Beauregard conceived the plan of massing the Confederate forces on the banks of the Appomattox, east of Petersburg, attack and break the Federal right, take their lines in reverse and sweep them out before they could fortify. This plan was suggested to the commanding general, but declined on the ground of the great fatigue of the troops, and the further objection that the defensive policy theretofore pursued had been so successful and satisfactory, he thought it unwise to change to-the aggressive at this stage of the game. Heaven forbid that the humble author should presume to criticise the movements of any of our great leaders in the "lost cause," much less to tarnish the lustre of a single star that blazes in the crown of glory, which, by universal verdict, has been placed upon the brow of our immortal chieftain; yet, I am constrained to believe that this was one of the few errors committed by the incomparable Lee. This conception of Gen. Beauregard and the distinguished ability with which he conducted the defense of Petersburg, if he had done nothing more, is sufficient to stamp his name in high relief in the annals of our great struggle among the names of our greatest Southern heroes.

To go back a little: On or about the 15th of June Gen. Lee had despatched Early and Breckinridge with a column of about 10,000 men to meet Gen. Hunter, who with a large Federal force was marching up the Shenandoah valley toward Lynchburg, laying waste the country as he advanced. Early met Hunter in front of Lynchburg on the 18th, and sent him scurrying down the valley to the Potomac.

When Grant set out for the James, Lee threw a corps of observation between him and Richmond. Grant moved his troops rapidly in order to capture Petersburg by a *coup de main*, as heretofore recorded. On the night of the 15th Lee tented on the south side of the James, near Drury's Bluff. On the 16th and 17th, his troops coming up, he superintended *personally* the recapture of Beauregard's Bermuda Hundred line, which had been seized by Butler's forces as soon as Hoke and Bushrod Johnson had been withdrawn. After taking the left of the line evacuated by Beauregard, there remained a portion, the approach to which was more formidable. The order had been issued to Gen. Anderson, commanding the corps, to retake this portion of the lines by joint assault of Field's and Pickett's divisions. Soon afterwards the engineers, upon a careful reconnoissance, decided that a good line could be occupied without the loss of life which might result from the recapture. The order to attack was therefore withdrawn. This rescinding order reached Field but failed to reach Pickett. Pickett's division, therefore, began the assault under the first order. The men of Field's division, hearing the firing and seeing Pickett's men engaged, leaped from their trenches—first the men, then the officers and flag bearers—rushed forward and were soon in the formidable trenches, which were held by only a small force. Our lines, therefore, were complete and fully occupied not only in front of Petersburg, but also between the rivers and north of the James covering Richmond.

Both armies were engaged for several days in building and strengthening their respective lines of protection and defense, with no fighting save between the sharpshooters and opposing picket lines; so that we had time to cast about, take our bearings and note the attitude of the armies and progress of the struggle.

We found that Butler had been re-bottled at Bermuda Hundred, and the bottle re-corked; Hampton had met and defeated Sheridan at Fravillians; Early and Breckinridge had wiped the earth with Hunter, liberated the valley, and were preparing to invade Maryland; while Lee, with Beauregard, Hill and Anderson, for the sixth time had effectually circumvented Grant's movements, and now stood between the Union army and the city of Petersburg ready for battle.

The pertinacity with which the Federal commander had pursued his purpose to overwhelm and crush Lee, even in the face of failure and defeat, had inspired the Federal administration with a hope that, with the vast resources of the government now pledged to his support, Grant would finally destroy the Army of Northern Virginia and seize the Confederate capital. And so the siege was laid, the burrowing begun, and "why should we war without the walls of Troy."

The anti-war element had been silenced or coerced, and the great North, now practically an unit, stood pledged to the overthrow of the Southern Confederacy. The earth and the fullness thereof had entered into a quasi-alliance with the Federal government, and even the forces of nature were laid under contribution to compass the destruction of the South and her institutions.

With will and muscle the spade, pick and ax were plied with such vigor that within a very few days there sprang up before the Confederates a vast cordon of redoubts of powerful profile, connected by heavy infantry parapets, stretching from the south bank of the Appomattox to the Jerusalem plank road, where rested the Federal left. A military railroad was constructed for the supply of the army and the rapid transit of troops, beginning at City Point and sweeping around the rear of Grant's lines their full length. Telegraphic communication was established between the commanding general and every division and corps commander, for the prompt transmission of orders and instructions.

A tower, like unto that which was built some years ago in the land of Shinar, suddenly rose up from the depths of the forest in rear of Grant's lines, and stood some 300 feet above the tops of the tallest trees, to be occupied by some faithful sentinel, and from which to observe and report the position and movements of the different divisions of the Southern army. The interval between the lines, and every approach to the more vital points of their works, especially, were covered with *abatis*, *cheveaux de frise* and other entanglements, to stay the Confederates and protect their own troops in the event of an attack. And, besides all this, the sappers and miners of Burnside's corps were busily engaged in the construction of a mine, to be charged with 8000 pounds of giant powder, for the purpose of blowing up Fort Elliott—sometimes called Battery Pegram—which occupied a strong salient on the Confederate left center, and supposed to be the key to the whole position.

"Their wits larded with malice, and malice forced with wit," day and night the work went on. Notwithstanding these vast preparations for the final struggle, and the concentration of forces in his front, on the one hand, and the depleted ranks of his own army, on the other hand—to say nothing of the fatal paralysis which had seized upon the extremities of his own beloved South land—the great Lee, in the full consciousness of the gravity of the situation, moved along the thin lines of his gaunt and ragged but spirited battalions with the mien of a master in the arts of war—that he was—without the least apparent anxiety, as if only waiting another opportunity to encounter and defeat his adversary; which he did time and again, as his lines were assaulted here and there, and day after day, for months to come.

The calm and dignified bearing of their beloved chieftain inspired the men with the same invincible determination to stand to their colors and fight it out to the bitter end. The *clan* of the Army of Northern Virginia was never better.

CHAPTER IX.

MAHONE'S FIGHT; SHARPSHOOTERS ENGAGED; WILSON AND KAUTZ RAID.

> "A thousand glorious actions, that might claim
> Triumphant laurels, and immortal fame,
> Confused in crowds of glorious actions lie,
> And troops of heroes undistinguished die."

Gen. Grant, having completed his fortifications to the Jerusalem plank road, as before stated, was free to begin that series of attempts against Lee's communications which, despite his numerous and disastrous failures, he continued with slight intermissions to the end. And hence, on Tuesday, the 21st day of June, he ordered the second and sixth corps to move to the left, and, maintaining connection with Warren's left, to swing forward west of the Jerusalem plank road, and if possible to strike and hold the Weldon railroad, while Wilson with 6000 sabres should gallop round the Confederate right, cut the Weldon railroad farther to the south; thence, sweeping westward, strike and sever Lee's communications by the South Side and Danville railroads. The second corps under Birney, after some sharp skirmishing with the Confederate cavalry, succeeded in taking position on Warren's left, and the sixth corps, moving out behind the second, took position to the left, but some distance in rear, with its right slightly covering the left of the second corps. But the next morning Grant discovered such an array of Confederate cavalry confronting the sixth corps, that he suspended his movement against the railroad and ordered Birney to swing forward his left so as to envelope the Confederate right. Discovering this change of plan, and the opportunity the new movement would likely afford him to strike his opponent a telling blow, Lee ordered Mahone to take his own and two other brigades of Anderson's division, pass along a certain ravine that ran out from the Confederate right and which would screen him from view, form his line in the neighborhood of the Johnson house and await Birney's swinging movement. A section of artillery was to assist Mahone on the left. By the time Mahome had gotten into position Birney had so far progressed with his movement—which was made without reference to the sixth corps, and left an ever widening gap between the two lines—that the naked flank of the wheeling column stood almost directly in front of Mahone's line, inviting attack. The gallant Virginian was not the man to decline a good thing; so, with the suddenness and swiftness that startles and paralyzes, Mahone's men burst, "like a clap of thunder on a clear day," upon Birney's flank. A rousing cheer and a pealing volley awoke the echoes of the forest, and with a stream of wasting fire the brawny veterans swept forward, shrivelling up brigade after brigade and division after division as lightning shrivels the autumn leaves. Cleaving their fiery pathway diagonally across Birney's front, and spreading dismay and destruction without check, they rolled up the second corps and swept it from the field. Four pieces of artillery, eight standards and over 1700 prisoners, besides other trophies, fell into the hands of Mahone's men in this brilliant affair. Mahone returned to the lines soon after dark.

Gen. Wilcox was sent out at the same time with the light division to relieve our cavalry and attend to Gen. Wright and the sixth corps, but for some reason, unknown to the writer, failed to attack. When the division had marched down the Weldon railroad some two miles, however, it changed direction to the east and approached the position occupied by the sixth corps. The sharpshooters were thrown forward and deployed across the narrow country road, along which the division moved in column of route, and were ordered to advance until they reached a small farm house, which Gen. Wilcox discovered some distance in front.

The battalion moved forward at once, and with difficulty made its way through the tangled brushwood. Watson's company soon became engaged; but with his usual promptness and gallantry, that accomplished young officer drove the enemy's sharpshooters before him, slightly breaking his connection with the battalion; which meeting no opposition on the right of the road, outmarched him. When Watson recovered his position on the line, however, he had somewhat lost his temper and began to upbraid his commander and comrades on the right for deserting him in the hour of need; but when they assured him of their confidence in his ability to take care of himself; and furthermore, that in this instance his action was so prompt and successful, "they supposed that he had only encountered a flock of wild turkeys, which they saw flying from his front," he withdrew his complaint, and with a smile on his countenance resumed his place in line. Continuing the advance, the battalion soon found larger game, well covered by a line of breastworks near the farmhouse on which it was ordered to advance, and with a right good will went at it with a yell and a charge.

The line of battle from behind the breastworks received the charge with a galling fire, which surprised the sharpshooters and caused them to stagger and recoil. The assault was renewed again and again, and maintained with great gallantry by the sharpshooters for more than an hour, but was finally repulsed with considerable loss, Capt. Brunson himself receiving a painful wound in the foot, which caused him to retire, and from which he was disabled for service for some two months. The command of the battalion, therefore, devolved upon Capt. Hasell, who dropped back to a safe position, from which he continued the fire and contented himself with holding the Federal sharpshooters close under their guns. The division was withdrawn after dark without a fight, and returned to its position on the lines, leaving the sharpshooters to cover the movement. The failure of the light division to attack may have been a part of the program: to hold the attention of Wright while Mahone skinned Birney.

The enemy soon discovered the absence of the division; and, knowing the insufficiency of the slender line in front, advanced upon the sharpshooters and drove them back; but not being satisfied with this, concluded to cut them off from the road in their rear —which was their only way of escape—and capture the whole command. The darkness was intense and the underbrush thick and tangled, yet, when the purpose of the enemy was discovered, the sharpshooters delivered a stinging volley and made a dash for the road, with the Federals upon each flank and close upon their heels. A furious race ensued, in which a number of vicious curs from the Federal lines participated, but the light weighted, clean heeled Confederates won by half a neck, and made good their escape to the main lines.

The brigade lost in this expedition, while lying under fire, and in the part played by the sharpshooters, some thirty-five or forty men, more than half of whom were sharpshooters.

On the same day Wilson struck the Weldon railroad at Ream's Station and destroyed the track for several miles; then pushed on to the South Side railroad. Having sent Kautz to Burkville, he (Wilson) was assailed by the Confederate cavalry under W. H. F. Lee and the road wrested from destruction. He then made a dash for Meherrin, on the Richmond and Danville railroad, where, uniting with Kautz, the two struck out for the Staunton river bridge. Here the local militia defended the bridge with great gallantry and held Wilson in check until Lee again interposed his fiery squadrons, when Wilson was again defeated. Lee pursued his retreating columns as they fled before him, now in the direction of Petersburg. Hampton, from the north side of the James, joined Lee in the pursuit at Sappony church, where Wilson was inclined to make a stand; but discovering the increased number of his pursuers, spurred onward toward Ream's Station. The chase now became wild and exciting. Mahone, with two brigades of infantry and two batteries of artillery, had been hurried forward to Ream's Station for the purpose of intercepting the raiders, and now stood squarely across their line of retreat. But Wilson, discovering the trap set for him, abandoned his artillery, set fire to his trains, and ridding himself of all unnecessary impedimenta, eluded the grasp of the Confederates and made good his escape to Grant's lines, with the additional loss of a few hundred prisoners.

Maj. J. T. Brame, of Helena, Ark., one of the boys who participated in the gallant defense of Staunton river bridge, thus describes that encounter:

HELENA, ARK., March 25, 1899.
COL. W. S. DUNLOP, Little Rock, Ark.

Dear Sir and Comrade: At your request I send you a few notes drawn altogether from memory, and bearing on events leading up to and including the battle of Staunton river bridge, which was fought on the 17th of June, 1864. I do not remember that I have ever seen, since the war, any mention of this battle in print, though for inequality of numbers, and a further fact that an overwhelming force of veterans were pitted against a handful of inexperienced boys, and the further fact that the superior force was not only held at bay, but defeated with heavy loss, and that they (the enemy) utterly failed in every assault made to break our line, I think that under the circumstances this fight should rank under the most desperate minor engagements of the war. The first regiment of Virginia reserves, commanded by Col. B. F. Farenholt, and numbering about six hundred, composed mostly of boys under eighteen years of age, was encamped on the south side of Staunton river, about seventy miles from Richmond. On the south side of the river the hills rose almost abruptly from the water's edge. On said hills we had planted a few pieces of obsolete artillery, which proved in the coming battle to be a disadvantage to us for want of experienced gunners, as several times in firing, while using grape and schrapnell, they fired too low, thus endangering our own men. On the north side of the river there was a level bottom perhaps three-quarters of a mile wide, with hills beyond. Through this level stretch of bottom land had been cut four or five ditches which ran parallel with the river. Said ditches were perhaps two miles long and four or five feet deep. So much for the lay of the field.

About two days prior to the battle our commander received information that a large force of Federal cavalry and field artillery had gotten in the rear of Gen. Lee's army, and were rapidly approaching with the intention of burning the bridge and destroying the Richmond and Danville railroad. Our force was at once thrown across the river, where we soon threw up a slight line of earth works on each side of and at right angles to the railroad bridge. About 2 p. m. the Federals got six or eight pieces of artillery planted on the hills, about one mile in front of us, and commenced shelling. In the meantime their cavalry had dismounted and made their way unseen by us to the head of the aforementioned ditches, got in them and marched down opposite our line. They then charged, coming three columns deep at once. We succeeded in beating them back as often as they came. It was charge after charge from 3 o'clock till dark. We often fought across the breastworks, but never did they succeed in breaking our line. The artillery in the meantime kept up a continuous fire, and many times it looked as if it were folly for us to longer resist. The Federals were armed with the latest make of improved Henry repeating rifles, the first we had ever seen, and quite a number of which we captured. Late in the evening of the second day we noticed a cloud of dust in a northwesterly direction; whether friend or foe we knew not. Friends they proved to be, and we soon saw our enemy in full retreat. After burning the railroad depot at Roanoke they continued a running fight with the cavalry command of Gen. W. H. F. Lee, who had given us such timely succor. The Federals were under command of Gen. Wilson, and we learned that they numbered about five thousand. The loss on the Federal side was very heavy both in killed and wounded. I there saw wounded men who could not speak the English language—mercenaries, of course. Was it any wonder that we were finally overpowered? I do not remember our exact loss, but the army records should show exact numbers engaged and losses on both sides. Had Gen. Wilson succeeded in burning the bridge the war would have been at an end so far as the Army of Virginia was concerned, as Gen. Lee could have gotten neither supplies or ammunition. The Richmond and Danville was the only railroad open from Richmond south, the Petersburg and Weldon railroad having been captured by the Federals. A few days after the fight I heard Gen. Walker say to a field officer of our regiment that had our command been composed of veterans we would not have held out an hour; that the Federals had us whipped often during the engagement, but did not know it; and that owing to our inexperience we did not know when we were whipped, but held on with bulldog tenacity till the last. He did not give us credit for any unusual amount of bravery, but thought it more a lack of sense of danger, or rather the foolhardiness of youth.

At any rate the bridge was saved and communication with Lee's army maintained. If you can make the above or any part of it of use to you, you are welcome to use it as you may see fit.

With kindest regards, I am very truly yours,

J. T. BRAME.

On the 23d McGowan's brigade was moved about a mile to the left, and took position on the right of Bushrod Johnson's division, where the hostile lines approached much more closely together. The change was made in daylight, in full view of the enemy on our left, who opened on the brigade an enfilading fire from one of his batteries, as it approached the works. A rapid plunge into the works behind the traverses saved the brigade from any casualties. The sharpshooters were ordered to the front, and, deploying in the trenches, dashed forward and threw themselves into the rifle pits without loss. Here the two skirmish lines were uncomfortably near to each other, and opened at once, and maintained a sharp fire, day and night, for about a week; which resulted in considerable loss to both sides.

On the afternoon of the 30th McGowan's and Lane's brigades received orders to prepare for a move to the north side of the James. Accordingly, as the shadows of night began to settle upon the beleaguered city, the two brigades withdrew from the lines, marched through Petersburg, crossed the Appomattox, and moved off from Richmond. All night long in great suffering this blear eyed, struggling column pressed forward along the dusty roads toward their destination. Bearing eastward from the Richmond and Petersburg railroad, we crossed the James at Drury's Bluff early the following morning, and reached the lines at Chaffin's farm about 10 o'clock, completely broken down. McGowan's brigade took position on the line with its right resting on Fort Harrison, with Lane's brigade on the left—relieving Heth's division, which moved off for Petersburg. The sharpshooters were thrown forward some three or four hundred yards in front; and, there being no enemy present, disposed themselves for a season of quiet and repose, and for several weeks were not disturbed.

Having recovered from a protracted spell of sickness, I returned to the front about the 1st of July and resumed command of the battalion.

Beside the small force of cavalry on our left, and the garrisons of Forts Harrison, Gillmore,

Chaffin's Bluff and the supporting batteries along the river, there were no troops on the north side other than the two brigades of McGowan and Lane, except the Richmond city battalion and perhaps a few regiments of reserves. Notwithstanding our small force, we felt ourselves strong enough (in the absence of the enemy) to hold the position at all hazards, and for the first time in two months we unbuckled our armor, relaxed our high nervous tension and laid ourselves down to rest. The days were hot but the nights were delightful; hence we had no occasion to invoke the aid of Morpheus or other somnolent deity to steal away our senses and soothe us to sleep; for nature was exhausted, and we had not a care.

Caldwell, in his history of McGowan's brigade, in describing the condition of the troops at this period, says:

"The contentment of the troops here was a sad commentary on their previous existence. We had no tents except scraps of Yankee flies; we were fed on wretched bacon, wormy peas and cornmeal, with a small sprinkling of coffee; we lacked shoes and clothing; we were exposed to great heat and kept constantly on some sort of duty; yet we constructed arbors of branches, picked blackberries, smoked pipes (when we had tobacco), and felt very comfortable indeed. We did not envy the city battalion their fine clothes; we did not envy the heavy artillery their vegetable gardens or their pig pens; we did not even envy the boat hands on the river, who fattened on government bacon; we were perfectly satisfied to be left in the shade for a while. * * * But in spite of the one-third pound of crawling bacon, the pint of cornmeal, and the peas alive with worms, we improved wonderfully both in mind and body. Our numbers also increased by the return of recovered sick and wounded, so that the brigade now numbered about a thousand men, all told."

The sharpshooters, however, were not seriously affected by the scarcity or poor quality of grub furnished the army; for, be it known, they were just as faithful foragers as they were furious fighters. A chicken, turkey, goose or pig, prowling about their camp or picket lines, night or day, or trespassing upon the territory over which they exercised jurisdiction, was in just as much danger as the full panoplied bluecoat who was so unfortunate as to fall within their clutches.

During this lull in active hostilities they traversed the country for miles around in quest of food to supplement their rations; and if perchance they should stumble on a Yankee, they took him in, all the same. Lying along the James river in front of our lines was a large field of wheat just ready for the harvest, but it lay immediately under the guns of Butler's men of war patrolling the river and protecting his operations in Dutch Gap canal, and the Federals laid claim to the entire crop by virtue of the rights of conquest. The sharpshooters, however, were not disposed to respect their rights, and ever and anon would slip into the field and gather sufficient wheat to cover, in exchange at the mills, a peck or half a bushel of flour.

On one occasion, during our stay here, John Parrott, Isaac Daley, James Wood, Crockett Henderson and —— Bundricks slipped out to get a turn of wheat. When they reached the edge of the field they discovered one of Butler's best equipped boats lying in the river alongside of the field and covering with its heavy guns every acre of wheat; they also had three men stationed as sentinels on the yard arms near the top of the main mast, to watch, and report to the gunners below, any trespasser who might enter the field.

They (the sharpshooters) also discovered a large ditch 6x6 feet in width and depth, running diagonally across the field from the road where they stood to the bank of the river, a little above where the boat lay.

Henderson and Bundricks were, by agreement, set off to cut wheat, while Parrott, Daley and Wood should slip down the ditch and attend to the sentinels on the boat. They reached a point not exceeding 400 yards from the boat, when, by lot, it was determined that Parrott should pick off the top man and Daly and Wood the other two. At a given signal they all fired, and the three men dropped from the rigging as if struck by lightning. The guns of the boat were opened on the ditch and the field, but the boys got their wheat and made good their escape to our lines.

CHAPTER X.

BATTLE OF LONG BRIDGE, OR DEEP BOTTOM.

"The death-shot hissing from afar—
The shock—the shout—the groan of war—
Reverberate along the vale,
More suited to the shepherd's tale:
Though few the numbers—their's the strife,
That neither spares, nor speaks for life."

On the 23d of July Kershaw's division arrived from Petersburg and joined us on the right, but moved to our left the next day to meet a demonstration of the enemy, who had also returned in considerable force to the north side of the James. There was some manœuvreing of troops on our lines for several days, which finally resulted in a collision on the 28th. Early in the morning McGowan's brigade withdrew from the lines and moved rapidly to the left, passing in rear of Kershaw's division, which now occupied the trenches from the Williamsburg road to Fussell's Mill. The

Federal batteries were playing on Kershaw's lines, and occasionally dropped a shell into the road along which we moved, but without damage. Lane's brigade was in front, and a short distance beyond the mill formed to the right into line. McGowan's brigade, following by the same movement, formed on Lane's left. It now transpired that the enemy's designs were against the Confederate left; Kershaw therefore moved and formed to the left of McGowan. Skirmishers were thrown forward, and a short distance in front became engaged. The line of battle now advanced through the swamp and tangled underbrush. The numerous difficulties and exceeding roughness of the ground over which the lines moved soon resulted in the separation of brigades one from the other, and even the different regiments lost connection with their neighbors, right and left. All moved forward, however, and each went at whatever appeared in front. The enemy gave way before the determined Confederates as they tore and plunged through the tangled woods. McGowan's brigade soon cleared the woods and entered a cornfield, where the vigor of their assault was increased. The Federals gave way before the furious onset of the gallant Carolinians, leaving one piece of artillery in our hands, the honor of capturing which both the twelfth and thirteenth regiments claimed. Reaching a skirt of timber beyond the cornfield, the retiring Federals rallied and reformed. The brigade halted in the valley to retake its bearings, water, and adjust its alignment.

Meanwhile Lane's brigade came struggling forward through the swamps on the right, endeavoring to recover its connection with McGowan's line. It came up just in time to strike the enemy a vigorous blow and save McGowan's right. Smarting under the stinging fire which the Federals had poured into its naked flank, just as Lane struck and drove them back, and before the North Carolinians had made the connection sought, McGowan's brigade again moved to the attack, followed by Lane. The enemy received the charge with a galling fire which caused the brigade to stagger. Seeing the effect of their fire upon McGowan's line, and discovering the interval between the two brigades, the enemy inserted between the two an active, compact body of riflemen, which struck first one and then the other brigade in the flank, driving them farther and farther apart, while a heavy column moved directly against each brigade, and drove them one after the other from the field, and recovered their original position. Kershaw was more successful on the left, and drove his opponents from one position after another until ordered to desist.

Gen. Connor, who was in command of McGowan's brigade, was greatly mortified at the failure of his last attack, but attributed his defeat to the difficulties of the field and the failure of his regimental commanders to observe the movements of the battalion of direction, to which they should have conformed, but failed to do. The lines were reformed with considerable difficulty on the original position. About this time the battalion of sharpshooters, which had been left on picket, reached the field and was ordered to the front. We deployed and advanced, and struck the advance line of the enemy some three hundred yards in front of the brigade, and opened. The familiar cry of our deadly rifles, reverberating through the forests, fell upon the ears of our comrades of the main line like vesper music at the close of day, and contributed materially to the restoration of order. In a little while the formation of the regiments was complete and the brigade stood ready to meet the enemy in the event of an attack, which seemed imminent.

The Federal advance line responded to our fire with spirit, but the deliberate and accurate aim of these trained riflemen soon began to puncture their resolution as well as their ranks, when they began to yield. The sharpshooters steadily pressed them back until night intervened, when they were recalled, and both sides retired to their respective original positions on the general line. The loss of the brigade, including the few casualties in the sharpshooters, was 239 officers and men—in killed, wounded and missing.

The Confederates had failed to recover possession of the Long Bridge road across Deep Bottom, which was their objective, and the Federals had failed to gain ground on our left towards Richmond, which was their purpose; hence both sides were defeated.

Nothing of importance was done on the 29th. There was some shifting of positions on the 30th and 31st, but all finally settled in their same positions on the line—the sharpshooters in front. Here we remained again without disturbance for ten days or two weeks, with nothing to do beyond the quiet routine of company drills, dress parade and picket duty.

About this time an expedition was planned against Butler's forces, now busily engaged in the construction of the Dutch Gap canal. Our artillery, supported by a strong detachment of infantry, was to move out under cover of darkness to a strong position selected by scouts, surprise and attack the gunboats supporting the working force, drive them off or sink them, and thus put a stop to the work.

Accordingly, late in the afternoon of the 11th of August, the two brigades of McGowan and Lane were sent some distance in advance of the fortifications, with instructions to entrench during the night, and on the next morning to support and assist the artillery in dispersing the Federal squadron. We took our position and made every preparation for the work assigned us, but for some reason, unknown to the writer, the expedition was abandoned; and after receiving a good shelling from the Federal gunboats, the brigades returned to the lines, with the loss of several men. Upon our return to the works we found that Field's division had arrived from Petersburg, and now occupied the position of Kershaw's division, next on our left, Kershaw returning to Petersburg.

Late in the afternoon of the 13th the enemy appeared in large force in front of Field's division, and early the next morning advanced and drove in his skirmishers and occupied their line. McGowan's skirmishers, being left without support on that flank, also retired upon the brigade. The sharpshooters, who were off duty at the time, were ordered out with instructions to re-occupy the line abandoned, which they did.

This line was upwards of half a mile in advance of the breastworks and covered by thick woods. But, when we took position, it was discovered that our left flank rested mid air, near the edge of an open field, in which there stood a large two story frame tenement house, just beyond which in the field and on the same line, the enemy had planted a four gun battery; which, with their skirmishers in front, had opened fire on Field's line. Their line of battle was in the woods a short distance in the rear, where they were making preparations to fortify. To guard against a movement against our flank or rear, now so invitingly exposed to attack, Sergts. Hawthorn and Benson (B. K.) with one other—whose name I cannot recall—were ordered to take position in the house, and observe closely every movement of the enemy and to report promptly any disposition shown to disturb our flank. When they reached the house and surveyed the field, it was discovered that the Federal battery was not more than four or five hundred yards off and could be easily reached with their long range rifles; and they began at once to tease and fret the artillerists by picking off their men and horses.

The effect of their unerring aim was so pungent and disastrous that the artillerists turned their guns upon the house, to dislodge them. But the ready witted sharpshooters evaded the effect of their shells by dropping into the basement while the artillerists fired; then, mounting the second story while they loaded, they let them have it again. This movement was repeated again and again, and the sharpshooting continued so persistently and with such fatal effect that the artillerists could stand it no longer, and hence began to limber their guns for a change of position. Instantly, upon the discovery of this movement, the trio sounded the charge, raised the Confederate battle cry, and at a full run—yelling and firing as they ran—made for the battery; the battery, at a sweeping gallop, made for the rear; and charging through under whip and spur, broke and stampeded the line of battle; when the whole force—artillery, infantry and engineering corps fled the field, in wildest panic, pursued by the three Confederate dare devils, leaving the ground literally covered with cartridge boxes, knapsacks, haversacks, oil cloths, fly tents, cooking utensils and ditching tools. Each man returned with a prisoner or two and loaded down with valuable plunder. A detail was made from the battalion and sent out, which soon returned with a complete outfit for the entire command.

The sharpshooters were not otherwise engaged, and Field's division was relieved of further annoyance.

Of course, the ferocious bellowing of these audacious sharpshooters impressed the Federals with the conviction that Field's whole division in front, with McGowan and Lane on their flank, were after them; otherwise the three sharpshooters would have been gobbled up.

The 15th was a day of perfect quiet along our lines; the sharpshooters were relieved about 9 o'clock in the morning and dropped back in the rear to rest.

> "It is a sultry day; the sun has drunk
> The dew that lay upon the morning grass;
> There is no rustling in the lofty pines
> That canopies our bivouac, and their shade
> Scarce cools us. All is silent, save the faint
> And uninterrupted murmur of the bee,
> Settling on the sick flowers, and then again
> Instantly on the wing, is gone."

CHAPTER XI.

BATTLES OF FUSSELL'S MILL.

On the morning of the 16th a courier reported the enemy, in strong force, again moving against our left. We moved at once, and rapidly, to the left; passing in rear of Field's division, the two brigades of McGowan and Lane went into line of battle on his left—Lane first, and McGowan on the left of Lane. McGowan's brigade was deployed into one rank, to cover the Federal front and to intercept any movement that might be made against our flank.

The sharpshooters were deployed and advanced, and soon became engaged. The main attack, however, was made on the right against Field and Lane. The enemy massed a heavy column in front of Field, charged and drove the Confederates from their works. McGowan's brigade was withdrawn from the left and hurried to the rescue.

The brigade, forming into two ranks as it marched, moved rapidly to the right, in rear of the lines, a distance of about half a mile—halting about opposite the captured works.

Here it was fronted and ordered to advance. The works, now in the hands of the enemy, ran obliquely across McGowan's front, approaching his line more closely on the left than on the right. The brigade advanced in splendid order, but with great caution, for the strength and position of the Federals were not definitely known.

The enemy opened on the advancing line at long range, and were answered by a slow and deliberate fire.

The twelfth regiment, which was on the left, first struck the works, and by a desperate plunge, succeeded in driving the enemy out. But the other regiments failing to carry their part of the works, the Federals turned a withering fire into the naked flank of the regiment and drove it out. This was repeated the second time with the same results. The gallant regiment, again rallying on the brigade, pushed forward with unabated ardor in a third assault; when the whole brigade was repulsed, leaving their killed and wounded between the lines. Rallying again a short distance back, and hearing their wounded comrades calling to them to charge, a wild impulse of desperate determination seized the entire brigade, when it rushed forward against the fortifications, stormed out the dense lines crowded there, and slew them by scores and hundreds as they fled in irretrievable panic. There had been two lines of Federals crowded into the works—one of whites and one of blacks—numbers of whom fell into our hands, with an immense amount of plunder.

After a few faint attempts to retake the works, the enemy sued for a truce to bury their dead, which was granted. And so the battle of Fussell's Mill was ended.

The sharpshooters held the Confederate left against every assault, and justly claimed a fair pro rata of the honors won by the gallant brigade and other troops engaged.

Gen. Lee was present in person during the action, and pronounced the results a brilliant victory to Southern arms. The brigade lost in killed, wounded and missing, including the casualties in the sharpshooters, 119 officers and men.

On the next day the brigade moved some distance to the left, and Gen. Hampton, with a strong division of cavalry, moved round on the Federal right and made an attack—for what purpose and with what results, I am not informed. This I know, however, that at the very hour when Hampton's guns were thundering away to the left, the sharpshooters were ordered to advance. We drove forward, struck and routed the Federal sharpshooters, and sent them scurrying through the woods to cover of their main line. Here we found their main line of battle fully intrenched behind a solid line of earth works, protected by acres of abatis and defended by a solid line of infantry, with here and there a field piece placed in battery along the line of works. We halted at the edge of the abatis and engaged the line of battle; which, from the confusion produced by our fire, I am satisfied we could have carried but for the entanglements in front, and the orders of the brigade commander, restraining further effort.

Our line of battle was not advanced, and the sharpshooters were at length withdrawn. We lost seven men in this encounter.

Late in the afternoon of the same day, Lane's brigade joined McGowan on the right; and Major Wooten with his sharpshooters united with us in front, when both battalions were ordered to advance. We moved forward again, with somewhat of caution, upon their breastworks, but found the enemy gone. There were evidences of a hasty withdrawal all along the works, and we quickened our pace and pursued. We overtook their rear guard some distance back and opened fire. The Federals responded with spirit but continued to retreat. We pressed forward and drove them mile after mile through the forests of Deep Bottom, until the shadows of evening began to settle down upon the dark valley, when the lines were ordered to halt. A consultation was held between the two battalion commanders as to what should be done for the protection of our lines in their advanced and isolated position, in the absence of orders; and it was determined to post a strong chain of videttes and bivouac in line—rifles in hand—until morning, or until orders should reach us. Wooten's scouts, who had been sent forward to reconnoitre, returned and reported the enemy gone. To make assurance doubly sure, I concluded to take a view of the front in person, and so advanced some hundred yards or more along a narrow path leading to the front, when the cry of two wicked Federal rifles a short distance in front, and the whistling of bullets, reminded me of danger, and I beat a hasty retreat to the lines. Orders were now received, and the sharpshooters withdrew to their proper position in front of the brigades.

The next day M. F. Hawthorn and J. G. Love, with one other—whose name I cannot recall—were sent to the front on a scout, with in-instructions to ascertain, if possible, the attitude and temper of our Union friends, whose courtesies for the last several days we had received and so highly appreciated; especially, to discover the position of their right flank. They approached the Federal lines in front, then turning to the left had gone some distance, when voices were heard in the woods to their right. Then cautiously approaching a road which ran perpendicularly across the interval between the lines, they discovered a Federal vidette post of five men some distance down the road. They also saw a woman coming from that direction with a number of canteens, which she was to fill with milk and return to the videttes. Concealing themselves in the bushes until she came up, they sprang out and captured the woman and canteens. To get rid of their fair captive, after examination, as well as to avoid the possibility of her giving notice of their presence, she was informed that they were going to fire on the videttes, and of course they would return the fire.

Being released, and already frightened, the woman beat a hasty retreat for home. By this time the vidette post was definitely located, and instead of firing, they set about to capture the entire squad. By making a detour of some distance, they gained the rear, then cautiously approaching, they got nearly to the post before they were discovered, when by a brisk charge they captured the five men without firing a gun, and marched them into the Confederate lines.

In pursuance of orders, the two brigades of McGowan and Lane returned to Petersburg on the 20th. McGowan's brigade was placed on the lines near the "Crater"—an immense mine, sprung early on the morning of July the 30th,

170 feet long by 65 feet wide and 30 feet deep, which was conceived in malice and consecrated in blood, and which remains today an abiding monument to Grant's folly and failure, as well as to the unswerving valor of the Southern soldier.

The hostile lines at this point were not exceeding one hundred and fifty yards apart, with a strong line of rifle pits in front scarcely beyond the width of a good lane, into which the sharpshooters were thrown and at once began their work. For two or three days the shrill music of their rifles, punctuated by the deep tones of opposing mortars, ceased not day nor night. Much damage resulted to both sides from the unerring aim of these trained riflemen, both Federal and Confederate, in this sharp and unremitting fusilade. In one instance two of my most skillful and daring sharpshooters—William Kennedy and C. W. Parrish—were instantly killed by a single shot, fired by a Federal rifleman just as they were passing each other in their pit.

Fortunately we were moved to the right on the 22d, and were placed in position near the

Weldon railroad—the brigade on the line, the sharpshooters in front.

A period had now been reached in the progress of the great struggle where the extraordinary conditions which prevailed all along the lines seemed to demand some modification in the rules of official responsibility, which would justify the commanding general in distributing to his lieutenants, and through them to the different divisions and brigade commanders, such power and discretion in their respective commands as would authorize them to strike whenever in their judgment an effective blow could be delivered, without formal authority from their superiors in rank. And now that the enemy were constantly in our immediate presence, the importance of an active, vigilant and spirited picket line, largely free from control of the officers of the line, became more and more vital and indispensable to the safety of our lines. These exigencies of the service were fully appreciated by Gen. Lee, and the liberty suggested, with proper limitations, henceforth became the rule in the Army of Northern Virginia. The movements of the different brigades from this time, therefore, as well as the operations of the battalions of sharpshooters, became much more distinctive and independent.

About this time Gen. McGowan returned to the front and resumed command of the brigade, and Gen. Connor was temporarily assigned to the command of Lane's brigade.

On the afternoon of the 22d, and immediately after the sharpshooters had taken position on the Weldon railroad, Sergt. B. K. Benson was sent forward through the woods in front to reconnoitre, and when the enemy was discovered to return and report their position and strength, if the same could be ascertained. About two hours later Benson returned and reported that a heavy line of Federal skirmishers was posted at the opposite side of the woods, some half a mile off, well covered with rifle pits, with a strong vidette occupying the Davis house, about 100 yards in advance of their line. This isolated vidette post was a tempting bait to the sharpshooters, and soon after dark Watson's company was ordered to hold themselves ready for service at 4 o'clock next morning. Accordingly, awhile before daybreak on the morning of the 23d, the company moved out and stealthily passing around the Davis house, between the pickets and videttes, completely surrounded and quietly captured the entire force consisting of fourteen men, without firing a gun, and returned to our line before daylight in the morning.*

There existed an active spirit of rivalry between the different battalions of sharpshooters, as to which should perform the greatest number and the most daring feats in the line of legitimate duty, to the annoyance and damage of their opponents operating in their respective neighborhoods; and each kept a sharp lookout for opportunities to make a dash into the enemy's lines, stampede their pickets, or capture their men.

---

* Sergt. Benson insists that Watson made the capture as above stated, but my impression is that Maj. Wooten, of Lane's sharpshooters, anticipated Watson's movement and captured the post just before Watson got there.

CHAPTER XII.

BATTLE OF THE CRATER.

The morning's still; th' artillery strangely quiet
On Pegram Hill, where Elliott's men stood by it;
Where nothing stirred, not e'en a bird;
Nor sound is heard, to mar the hellish fiat.

The hilltop quakes, and suddenly bursts asunder
The silence breaks in tones of deepest thunder;
When earth and men in tons ascend,
To meet the end, of Grant's gigantic blunder.

Fort Elliott, or Battery Pegram, as it was sometimes called, occupied a prominent elevation on the Confederate left center, somewhat south of east from the city of Petersburg, which projected, point foremost, toward the Federal lines, and constituted a conspicuous salient in the wide circular sweep of the Confederate lines. The four gun battery of Capt. Pegram of Virginia, Coit's battalion of artillery, occupied and defended the fort, while Elliott's South Carolina brigade supported the battery and manned the trenches to the right and left of the fort. The city cemetery was also on high ground, about five hundred yards in rear of Fort Elliott, and between the two ran a deep depression, in which reserves could be held in comparative security from the enemy's guns, or along which reinforcements could be brought up without the knowledge of the enemy operating in front of the salient. Ransom's brigade of North Carolinians and Wise's Georgia brigade occupied the trenches to the left and right of Elliott, respectively. Wright's four gun battery assisted Ransom on the left, while a single gun of Maj. Gibbs' battalion aided Wise on Elliott's right.

The Federal works in front of Fort Elliott were occupied by the ninth army corps, under Gen. Burnside, at a distance of not exceeding one hundred and thirty yards, and on much lower ground, with abundant artillery placed in battery here and there along his lines.

During our absence on the north side of the James but little had transpired to emphasize the progress of the siege in front of Petersburg. The roar of hostile guns and the perpetual cry of the sharpshooters' rifles, which ordinarily stiffens the sinews and summons up the nerves, had become commonplace and monotonous, and evoked but slight consideration either in military or civil circles in this section.

On the 25th day of June, however, Gen. Burnside, at the suggestion of Col. Pleasants, of the forty-eighth Pennsylvania volunteers, who was a mining engineer of considerable experience and reputation, began the work of constructing a tunnel underneath Fort Elliott, with the view of blowing up this Confederate stronghold and making a breach in our lines at this point. Gen. Grant having failed to make any considerable or permanent breach in the Confederate lines by the ordinary methods of warfare above ground, readily approved Burnside's plan of tackling the Confederates by the underground route. The work was therefore begun and vigorously prosecuted for more than a month; day and night the work went on. About the last of July the mine was completed. The main tunnel was 510 feet in length. The lateral galleries were built perpendicularly across the farther end of the main gallery in the shape of a T, and extended on either side a distance of some 38 or 40 feet. The magazines, eight in number, were placed in the lateral galleries, two at each end, a few feet apart, in branches at nearly right angles to the side galleries, and two more in each of the side galleries, similarly placed in pairs, were situated equi-distant from each other and the end of the galleries. These magazines were charged severally with one hundred pounds of giant powder and strung to the main fuse, which ran from the entrance the full length of the main gallery, by so many tributaries or short branches, which reached out into the lateral galleries, and entered into the several magazines in direct connection with the powder, and ready for the match.

Gen. Ferrero's division of colored troops was selected by Gen. Burnside to lead the charge, and were thoroughly drilled and instructed in all the details of the intended movement. At the last moment, however, Gen. Grant interposed serious objections to the selection; when the order was countermanded and Gen. Ledlie's white division was designated to lead the attack. Four divisions of Burnside's corps, towit: Ledlie's, O. B. Wilcox's, Potter's and Ferrero's, were set off as the column of assault; and were to succeed each other, in open column, in the order in which they are named. Supported by the fifth and eighteenth corps, this column was to move forward through the breach made by the explosion, seize Cemetery Hill; and, as soon as a sufficient force could be brought up, to strike the Confederate lines in flank and reverse and sweep them out, right and left. Meanwhile, the whole Federal army was to stand to arms and be ready to strike the final blow, which now seemed just at hand.

The Confederates were not altogether ignorant of this fiendish plot, and had sunk several shafts in a vain effort to strike the mine and neutralize the work. But they failed utterly to locate the mine, and hence the work went on to completion. For sometime after the tunneling had been discovered, the Confederates were considerably exorcised as to where the blow would fall and what would be the result; but as the days passed by and nothing occurred, they ceased to prepare for the uncertain emergency and relaxed into their wonted carelessness.

The hour fixed for the explosion was 3:30 o'clock on the morning of the 30th. The columns of assault were organized and in their places by 3 o'clock. The brazen mouthed cannons, which from a hundred hostile batteries had roared in perpetual thunder for more than a month, grew suddenly strangely quiet at this fateful hour; and the sensitive sharpshooters, whose nervous vigilance had not relaxed, nor the ceaseless clatter of their faithful rifles for a moment abated since the siege was laid, in ominous silence hushed their practice, to speculate upon the significance of the strange stillness.

The hour arrived and no explosion. The assaulting column stood to arms in painful suspense awaiting the signal for action. The Confederates slept. Everything ready! At 4:30 o'clock the match is applied to the fuse. The fire speeds along the main gallery and out into the wings and touches the magazines. The earth quakes, the hilltop writhes and bellows. And Fort Elliott shoots up into the air a hundred feet—earth, guns, tents and men;—trembles in awful poise; parts asunder and descends in broad sheets, covering everything, dead or alive, in tons of earth for acres around the gaping chasm. Dust and smoke fill the air. Sulphurous gas stifles the men, and dismay and terror seizes the minds of all, both Federals and Confederates. Everybody stood in motionless consternation for several minutes, in contemplation of the awful catastrophe. At length the opposing forces began to recover their senses as well as their attitude and bearings, and began to shape themselves for the impending conflict.

Col. McMaster, who commanded Elliott's brigade after Gen. Elliott fell, thus describes the scene:

"The mine was exploded one-quarter of 5 a. m., 30th of July, 1864, with 8000 pounds of powder. It overwhelmed the battery, the whole of the eighteenth, three companies of the twenty-third, and part of Company A, seventeenth regiment. For some minutes there was the utmost consternation among our men. Some scampered out of the lines; some, paralyzed with fear, vaguely scratched at the counter scarp as if trying to escape. Smoke and dust filled the air.

"A few minutes afterwards Gen. Ledlie's division began to charge. This aroused our officers; they began to cheer; and our men bounded on the banquette and commenced firing on the ranks of men who were rushing in without firing a gun.

"By this time some of the men of the gallant eighteenth, who had extricated themselves from the bank which covered them, came rushing down the trenches, and as many as could picked up guns and began firing. For a considerable time the firing was done entirely by the infantry. In a few minutes after the explosion Maj. Coit, who commanded the most effective artillery on our side, came up to see if any of his guns were uninjured. As soon as he could reach Wright's battery of four guns in the ravine to the rear Ransom's brigade, which was at least half an hour after the explosion, he began to fire, and shot six hundred balls into the divisions of Potter, Wilcox and Ferrero, which succeeded Ledlie's division. These guns were the only ones on our lines which, besides enfilading the enemy at close range, could also fire on the Crater and part of our lines. Maj. Gibbs, who had only one gun on the right of the Confederate line capable of enfilading the enemy, began with this gun about one hour after the explosion and killed many of the enemy. One or two hours later

Maj. Gibbs and Maj. Haskell moved their mortar batteries and dropped a number of balls in the Crater and lines.

"In fifteen or twenty minutes after the explosion Gen. Elliott came up through the crowded ditch, followed by Col. Smith of the twenty-sixth regiment, with a few of his men, and ordered the twenty-sixth and seventeenth to form a line on the crest of the hill and charge the Crater. He and a few men gallantly jumped upon the crest of the hill, about fifty yards of the Crater; he pointed out the line, and was in less than five minutes shot down and brought back. The command then devolved on your colonel (McMaster), who countermanded the order to form on the crest of the hill, which was utterly impracticable, and formed some of the men in the ditches which went to the rear and commanded some yards in rear of the Crater. Courier after courier was sent to the division commander, and one courier to the regiments on the right of the Crater. I ordered Col. Smith to take his regiment, with three companies of the seventeenth under Capt. Crawford (which then were larger than the twenty-sixth regiment), to form in the ravine in the rear of the Crater and cover up the gap, there to lie down, and rise up and fire when necessary, so as to prevent the enemy from rushing down the hill and getting in the rear of our lines. This order was promptly executed and gave the remainder of the seventeenth in the main trench more room to use their guns."

As to the damage, let the enemy tell. Gen. Meade says: "The assault came principally from the right (our left) of the Crater. The enemy brought guns from all points and threw shells into the Crater. Gen. Potter began his movement towards the crest, and was met by another force of the enemy and was compelled to fall back."

Gen. Potter says: "The next fire I saw came from the right; there was a battery behind some timber which it was very difficult for our batteries to reach. I ordered my own batteries to turn their whole attention to that one, but they apparently produced no effect."

Many officers testify that repeated assaults were made to secure the crest. Some say they saw them make two distinct charges early in the morning, but were repelled by men who rose up in the ravine. One fixes the number of these men at 200, some as high as 500. These men who repelled these charges were the seventeenth and part of the twenty-sixth.

The negroes, numbering 4300 muskets, under Gen. Ferrero, rushed to the mine at 8 o'clock, and one distinct charge, as alleged, occurred soon after. Some of the officers allege their men got 200 yards toward the crest, which was 500 yards in the rear, but this is a clear mistake. None ever advanced fifty yards beyond, for I watched their efforts with great anxiety up to about 9 o'clock, as I believed the fate of Petersburg depended on it. The officers frequently attempted to urge their men forward, and some would rush across a few yards and then run back. Col. Smith informed me after the battle that the enemy made a charge, and upon his men rising and pouring a volley, they did not make the attempt again.

Capt. Crawford, who commanded the detachment of the seventeenth, says:

"The Federal officers succeeded in getting about 200 men, three different times, outside of the Crater, and they never advanced more than thirty yards before they were driven back."

We saw at one time fourteen beautiful banners waving in the Crater, and gallant officers, trying to urge their men on in the direction of the Cemetery Hill. But all efforts to reach this point, from the rear of the Crater, failed by 9 o'clock. And they then attempted to effect their purpose by taking the lines north of the Crater, which would secure them a chance to reach the point of their destination, by the ravine which passed through Ransom's lines. This, together with the conformation of the ground, necessarily forced the burden of the battle on the Confederate line north of the Crater and in close proximity to it; and especially on Elliott's brigade, the right of Ransom's brigade and the artillery under the command of Maj. Coit.

The enemy, having thus changed their tactics, would occasionally rush on our right flank. We made barricades to oppose them. Then they would run down the front of the line and jump over, and were met with the bayonet and clubbed with the musket. Generally they were repelled; occasionally they succeeded and captured some men. Private Hoke, of Company A, was thus cut off, and refused to surrender, and struck down several of the enemy before he was bayoneted. Few battles could show more bayonet wounds than this. After a severe hand to hand fight, disputing every inch, and losing the gallant Lieuts. Lowry, Pratt, McCorwell and Capt. Dunovant, whose arm was shot off, and many brave men, we were driven down the hill to Ransom's brigade, which at this time was pouring in an enfilading fire.

The four divisions in front of the lines of Elliott's brigade must have numbered 16,000. Besides this, Gen. Turner with 4000 men charged Ransom's brigade on our left, and was driven back. * * *

Some time after, Mahone came up; when the seventeenth South Carolina regiment was turned over to him, by order of Gen. Johnson. Mahone's men were formed in the line already there. It took probably two hours before all of Mahone's men came into line, and then a splendid charge was made. The final charge which captured the works was made about 1 o'clock p. m. * * * Elliott's brigade lost 677 men—more than half its strength, and fully half of the Confederate loss; whereas, the enemy's loss, according to Gen. Grant's estimate, was above 5000 men, including twenty-three regimental commanders and two commanders of brigades.

Major J. C. Coit, in his account of the part taken by his artillery in this desperate conflict, thus describes the conduct of Elliott's brigade:

"The dread upheaval had rent in twain Elliott's brigade, and the men to the right and left of the huge abyss recoiled for a moment, in terror and dismay. But when I reached the Crater, which could not have exceeded ten minutes after the explosion, I found Elliott's men standing firm and undaunted, almost up to the very borders of the Crater. From my position in Wright's battery, the whole of the line from the ravine to the Crater was exposed to my view, and I witnessed the hand to hand engagement in each successive charge made by the enemy, and I venture to say that more men were killed with the bayonet and clubbed guns than in any other engagement during the war. The only thing separating our men and the enemy in the same ditch were hastily thrown up traverses, over the tops of which the opposing forces crossed their bayonets and delivered their fire. So stubbornly did Elliott's men contest every inch of the ground that the enemy, failing to press down the line from the direction of the Crater, resorted to the expedient of rushing from the Crater down the front of our works and jumping pellmell upon Elliott's men in the trenches. I witnessed this manœuvre executed several times; sometimes with success, but oftener they were repulsed or bayoneted as they leaped the works. In this manner did they gain the little ground they held of our lines to the left of the Crater. * * * The only mistaken movement I noticed was when one of our regiments—the twenty-sixth South Carolina volunteers; I think Smith's—attempted to leave the line and occupy the open ground between the Crater and Elliott's headquarters. It was an effort gallantly made to interpose and prevent the advance of the enemy in the direction of Cemetery Hill and the plank road.

"The whole of this ground was swept by the enemy's artillery and musketry from their main line, not to speak of the fire from those within our works. No troops could stand a moment exposed to such a fire, and such as did not fall were immediately withdrawn. I think it was at this time Elliott was wounded. The saddest sight I saw was the wounded left in this exposed position appealing for help until they sank down in death. Any attempt to remove them would have been vain under that fire.

"It was thus the battle raged from daylight until the arrival of Mahone's division, which, I think, was near 11 o'clock. The troops under Mahone were formed in the ravine in rear of Elliott's headquarters, extending from the covered way in a direction between the Crater and the plank road. New hope was inspired by the arrival of reinforcements, and not without good cause, for no sooner did Mahone's men emerge from the ravine at a double quick than did the immense mass in rear of the Crater break, and without standing upon the order of their going, sought shelter in the cover of their main line. The fire of the artillery was increased, and as Mahone's men neared the Crater Wright's guns were turned upon the flying masses in front of the salient. The slaughter was terrific, and probably more men were killed in the retreat than in the advance. The victory was virtually won, but those of the enemy within the Crater continued for some time the desperate contest. In my opinion they remained in the Crater more from fear of running the guantlet to their own lines than from any hope of holding their position. At 1 o'clock p. m. the white flag was raised and the final surrender of the Crater made.

"From the time of the explosion until the charge of Mahone's division the men of Elliott's brigade bore the brunt of the battle and, with a portion of Ransom's, were the only infantry troops that I saw opposing the advance of the enemy to Cemetery Hill and the plank road, at least to the left of the Crater. To the bravery and skillful handling of the brigade is due, more than to all other infantry troops, the credit of saving Petersburg on that day."

Wise's brigade on the right doubtless did its duty as faithfully and well as Ransom's brigade on the left; and with the assistance of the artillery on their respective lines, together with the enfilading fire of our heavy batteries north of the Appomattox, confined the charging columns of the enemy to a narrow field directly in front of and covering the exploded salient; so that when Mahone arrived his division covered the full Federal front, and thus the superior weight of the enemy's crowded columns was neutralized. Hence, the crowded and demoralized condition of the enemy gave the heroic Confederates the advantage, and they knew it. Therefore, on the arrival of the reinforcements, both the infantry and artillery on either side of the Crater opened with increased zeal upon the seething mass, while Mahone charged up in front, and with a perfect cataract of consuming fire swept out the entire Federal force and re-established our lines completely.

Maj. Wm. H. Powell, of the Union army, an active participant, describes this battle substantially as follows, to-wit:

"It was a magnificent spectacle, and as the mass of earth went up into the air, carrying with it men, guns, carriages and timbers, and spread out like an immense cloud as it reached its altitude, so close were the Union lines that the mass appeared as if it would descend immediately upon the troops waiting to make the charge. This caused them to break and scatter to the rear, and about ten minutes were consumed in reforming for the attack. Not much was lost by this delay, however, as it took nearly that time for the cloud of dust to pass off. The order was then given for the advance. As no part of the Union line of breastworks had been removed (which would have been an arduous as well as hazardous undertaking), the troops clambered over them as best they could. This in itself broke the ranks, and they did not stop to reform, but rushed ahead toward the Crater, about 130 yards distant, the debris from the explosion having covered up the *abatis* and *chevaux de frise* in front of the enemy's works.

"Little did these men anticipate what they would see upon arriving there: An enormous hole in the ground about 30 feet deep, 60 feet wide and 170 feet long, filled with dust; great blocks of clay, guns, broken carriages, projecting timbers, and men buried in various ways— some up to the necks, others to the waists, and some with only their feet and legs protruding from the earth. One of these near me was pulled out, and proved to be a second lieutenant of the battery which had been blown up. The fresh air revived him, and he was soon able to walk and talk. He was very grateful and said that he was asleep when the explosion took place, and only awoke to find himself wriggling up in the air; then a few seconds afterwards, he felt himself descending and soon lost consciousness.

"The whole scene of the explosion struck every one dumb with astonishment as we arrived at the crest of the debris. It was impossible for the troops of the second brigade to move forward in line, as they had advanced; and, owing to the broken state they were in—every man crowding up to look into the hole—and being pressed by the first brigade, which was immediately in rear, it was equally impossible to move by the flank, by any command, around the Crater. Before the brigade commanders could realize the situation the two brigades became inextricably mixed, in the desire to look into the hole.

"However, Col. Marshall yelled to the second brigade to move forward, and the men did so, jumping, sliding and tumbling into the hole, over the debris of material, and dead and dying men, and huge blocks of solid clay. They were followed by Gen. Bartlett's brigade. Up on the other side of the Crater they climbed, and while a detachment stopped to place two of the dismantled guns of the battery in position on the enemy's side of the crest of the Crater, a portion of the leading brigade passed over the crest and attempted to reform. In doing so members of these regiments were killed by musket balls from the rear, fired by the Confederates who were still occupying the traverses and intrenchments to the right and left of the Crater. These men had been awakened by the noise and shock of the explosion, and during the interval before the attack had recovered their equanimity, and when the Union troops attempted to reform on the enemy side of the Crater, they had faced about and delivered a fire into the backs of our men. This coming so unexpectedly caused the forming line to fall back into the Crater. * * * After falling back into the Crater a partial formation was made by Gen. Bartlett and Col. Marshall with some of their troops, but owing to the precipitous walls the men could find no footing except by facing inward, digging their heels into the earth, and throwing their backs against the side of the Crater, or squatting in a half sitting posture, and some of the men were shot even there by the fire from the enemy in the traverses. It was at this juncture that Col.

Marshall requested me to go to Gen. Ledlie and explain the condition of affairs, * * * which was done.

"While the above was taking place the enemy had not been idle. He had brought a battery from his left to bear upon the position, and as I started on my errand the crest of the Crater was being swept with canister. Special attention was given to this battery by our artillery, but for some reason or other the enemy's guns could not be silenced. * * * But the firing on the Crater was incessant, and it was as heavy a fire of canister as was ever poured continuously upon a single objective point. It was as utterly impracticable to reform a brigade in the Crater as it would be to marshal bees into line after upsetting the hive; and equally as impracticable to reform outside of the Crater, under the severe fire in front and rear, as it would be to hold a dress parade in front of a charging enemy. * * * Gen. Griffin's line, however, overlapped the Crater on the left, where two or three of his regiments sought shelter in the Crater. Those on the right passed over the trenches, but owing to the peculiar character of the enemy's works, which were not single, but complex and involuted, and filled with pits, traverses, and bombproofs, forming a labyrinth as difficult of passage as the Crater itself, the brigade was broken up, and meeting the severe fire of canister, also fell back into the Crater, which was then full to suffocation. Every organization melted away as soon as it entered this hole in the ground, into a mass of human beings clinging by toes and heels to the almost perpendicular sides. If a man was shot on the crest he fell and rolled to the bottom of the pit.

"From the actions of the enemy, even at this time, as could be seen by his moving columns in front, he was not exactly certain as to the intentions of the Union commander; he appeared to think that possibly the mine explosion was but a feint and that the main attack would come from some other quarter. However, he massed some of his troops in a hollow in front of the Crater, and held them in that position. * * *

"Orders were, however, being given constantly to the division commanders of the white troops to push the men forward as fast as could be done, and this was, in substance, about all the orders that were received by them during the day, up to the time of the order for the withdrawal. When Gen. Wilcox came with the third division to the support of the first, he found the latter and three regiments of his own, together with the regiment of Potter's second division, which had gone in on the right, so completely filling up the Crater that no more troops could be got in there, and he therefore ordered an attack with the remainder of his division on the works of the enemy to the left of the Crater. This attack was successful so far as to carry the intrenchments for about 150 yards; but they were held only for a short time.

"Previous to this last movement, I had gone to Gen. Ledlie, and urged him to try to have something done on the right to left of the Crater, saying that every man who got into the trenches to the right or left of it used them as a means of escape to the Crater, and the enemy was re-occupying them as our men left. All the satisfaction I received was an order to go back and tell the brigade commanders to get their men out and press forward to Cemetery Hill. This talk and these orders, coming from a commander sitting in a bomb-proof inside the Union lines, were disgusting. I returned again to the Crater and delivered the orders, which I knew beforehand could not possibly be obeyed; and I told Gen. Ledlie so before I left him. Upon my return to the Crater I devoted my attention to the movements of the enemy, who was evidently making dispositions for an assault.

"About two hours after * * * Gen. Ferrero, commanding the colored division of the ninth corps, received an order to advance his division, pass the white troops which had halted, and move on to carry the crest of Cemetery Hill at all hazards. Gen. Ferrero did not think it advisable to move his division in, as there were three divisions of white troops already huddled together, and he so reported to Col. Charles G. Loring of Gen. Burnside's staff. Loring requested Ferrero to wait until he could report to Gen. Burnside. Gen. Ferrero declined to wait, and then Col. Loring gave him an order, in Gen. Burnside's name, to halt without passing over the Union works, which order he obeyed. Col. Loring went off to report to Gen. Burnside, came back, and reported that the order was peremptory for the colored division to advance at all hazards. The division then started in, moved by the left flank, under a most galling fire, passed around the Crater on the crest of the debris, and all but one regiment passed beyond the Crater. The fire upon them was incessant and severe, and many acts of personal heroism were done by officers and men. Their drill for this object had been unquestionably of great benefit to them, and had they led the attack, fifteen or twenty minutes from the time the debris of the explosion had settled would have found them at Cemetery Hill before the enemy could have brought a gun to bear on them. But the leading brigade struck the enemy's force, which I had previously reported as massed in front of the Crater, and in a sharp little action the colored troops captured some two hundred prisoners and a stand of colors, and recaptured a stand of colors belonging to a white regiment. * * * In this almost hand to hand conflict the colored troops became somewhat disorganized, and some twenty minutes were consumed in reforming; then they made the attempt to move forward again. But, unsupported, subjected to a galling fire from batteries on the flanks.

and front infantry fire in front and partly on the flank, they broke up in disorder and fell back to the Crater, the majority passing on to the Union line of defenses, carrying with them a number of the white troops who were in the Crater and in the enemy's intrenchments. * * * When they fell back and broke up in disorder it was the closing scene of the tragedy. * * *

"The enemy's guns suddenly ceased their long continued and uninterrupted fire on the Crater, and the advancing column charged in the face of feeble resistance offered by the Union troops. * * * Over the crest and into the Crater they poured, and a hand to hand conflict ensued. It was of short duration, however; crowded as our troops were, and without organization, resistance was vain. Many were bayoneted at the time—some probably that would not have been, except for the excitement of battle. About 87 officers and 1652 men of the ninth corps were captured, the remainder retiring to our own lines."

The above, added to the casualties in killed and wounded, runs the Union loss up to about 5000; whereas the Confederate losses did not exceed 1200, killed, wounded and missing.

More than twenty centuries have elapsed since the Spartan king and his little band of heroes were crushed to death by the Persian hosts in the bloody defiles of Thermopylæ; still the fame of their exploits goes echoing along the corridors of time to the distant future.

A little more than half a century has passed since that immortal trio, Travis, Crockett and Bowie, with the little garrison of Texas patriots stood to death within the walls of the historic Alamo, their mutilated bodies consumed in one funeral pile, and from whose ashes the fires of liberty sprang up to light the infant republic to glory and independence; and who has not heard the blood curdling story of their sacrificial death?

Later still, we read of Lord Cardigan and the immortal Six Hundred, who dashed to death on the fatal field of Balaklava.

A halo of glory imperishable radiates from all these honored names, which now grace and shall forever adorn the pages of history while time shall last. And I fain would say that the sturdy heroism and unswerving valor of Pegram's artilerists and Elliott's Carolinians, who—after they were blown up, then buried—rallied and stood in the breach against the combined and persistent assaults of more than 16,000 veterans for six mortal hours—and until relief came, the enemy expelled, and Petersburg saved—entitle them and each of them to a name and a place alongside of Leonidas, Cardigan and the Texas trio, and among the world's greatest heroes.

CHAPTER XIII.

BATTLE OF REAM'S STATION.

"Shall we go throw away our coats of steel,
And wrap our bodies in black mourning gowns,
Numbering our Ave Marias with our beads?
Or shall we on the helmets of our foes
Tell our devotion with avengeful arms?"

The Weldon railroad had been seized by the enemy during our absence on the north side, and was now held by Warren's corps in the neighborhood of the Globe Tavern. Hancock had also been ordered back from Deep Bottom and was operating on Warren's left, destroying the Weldon railroad in the vicinity of Ream's Station. We had met and defeated Hancock at Deep Bottom on the Long Bridge road and at Fussell's Mill on the north side, and on the afternoon of the 24th of August were ordered to tackle him again at Ream's Station. Accordingly, at 2 o'clock the light division—minus Thomas's brigade—accompanied by Heth's division and Pegram battalion of artillery, all under command of our dashing corps commander, A. P. Hill, moved out of the works, and by a circuitous line of march, west of the Weldon railroad, proceeded to discharge the duty assigned us.

About dark we went into bivouac some three miles west of Ream's Station, cooked rations and spent the night. About 8 o'clock the next morning we moved up to within half a mile of the station and formed into line of battle, Wilcox on the right and Heth on the left. Scales's brigade had led the light division, and before McGowan's brigade could be placed in position Scales's sharpshooters, under Maj. John D. Young, had advanced and engaged the Federal sharpshooters. McGowan's sharpshooters were called for the moment the brigade came into line, and I was directed to move to the front, and cover and support Young while he disposed of the Federal cavalry in his front.

Gen. Wilcox further directed that if on advancing it should transpire that the enemy was too strong for Young, or overlapped him on one or the other flank, I should uncover and move up on the exposed flank, and assist him in dispersing the insolent raiders. The battalion was promptly deployed and moved forward through the woods to a point some seventy-five or one hundred yards in rear of Young's line, when it was discovered that the enemy was present in large force, and extended indefinitely on both flanks of the battalion in front. We therefore uncovered Young and moved up on his right. After consultation with Young, and a survey of the situation in front, it was determined to make a drive at whatever might oppose us, and orders were so given. We advanced slowly through the woods, struck a strong line of Federal sharpshooters at the edge of a field beyond, well covered with rifle pits, and went at them with a yell and a charge. The Federals responded to every shot, and defiantly clung to their position until we were about to overwhelm them, when they broke and fled across the field to cover of their main line on the railroad at the opposite side of the field. Here the roadbed was graded up to the height of from three to four feet, and behind which, instead of a small force of cavalry, lay Hancock's entire corps of infantry, with nine pieces of artillery placed in battery along the line of the road. They received us with a blizzard as we cleared the field of their skirmishers. We engaged them at short range for a few minutes furiously, and until we developed their full strength—which was too great for us—when we dropped back to the crest of the ridge, a distance of about 400 yards, as our rifles measured it, where we settled ourselves for business. Our line lay just back of the crest, from which we delivered our fire, and which offered us fair protection from their guns. The line of battle lay some 600 yards behind us in the wood. Here, deliberately, but without malice, planning the destruction of their enemies, the sharpshooters carefully estimated the distance between the lines, the depression of the ground where the enemy lay, the course the ball would take in its trajectory flight, and the exact point where it would cut the line of fire; then adjusting their sights accordingly, they entered upon the work in hand.

At the command the entire battalion stepped forward to the crest and delivered a volley, then dropped back to load. The enemy responded from the length of their line with musket and gun in full chorus, fairly raking the crest of the ridge with shot and shell and the deadly minnie. The sharpshooters, continuing the fire at will, but rapidly, for five mortal hours swept the Federal breastworks with a perfect sheet of lead. A relay of active couriers played between the front and main line, and replenished our cartridge boxes from the brigade from time to time as the battle progressed. The battalion fired one hundred and sixty rounds per man during the five hours of conflict. At noon the roar and crash of the Federal guns was terrific, but as the day declined the vigor of their defense relaxed and finally subsided. The sharpshooters mounted the crest and with unerring aim proceeded to split the scalp of every mother's son that dared to lift his head above the breastworks. The tenacity with which the gentlemen in blue hugged the trenches, at first amusing, at length began to touch the sympathies (just a little bit) of these trained riflemen, who now turned their attention to the artillery horses hitched a short distance in the rear; and at almost every shot some gay steed would rear and squeal and writhe and die, so that a great many of their best horses were killed or disabled before the final assault was made.

At the beginning of the action J. G. Love and Oscar Bookman had been sent some distance to the right of our line, which was without connection in that direction and therefore exposed, with instructions to take position in an old road which crossed the ridge we occupied and ran diagonally across our front into the enemy's lines, about opposite to the right of the battalion, there to watch the enemy and guard our flank. The road was hedged on both sides by a heavy growth of bushes and afforded ample cover to the videttes; who, discovering the advantages of their position, slipped down the road some distance in advance of the line and put in some good shots before they were discovered. The artillerists at one of the Federal guns spotted the videttes in the road, then training the gun and cutting the fuse at proper length, awaited their opportunity. About this time B. K. Benson and another man, whose name I cannot recall, who had been sent to relieve Love and Bookman, reached the post and were receiving instructions. The four were standing close together when Love and Benson, seeing a puff of smoke shoot out from the muzzle of the gun, sprang as far as they could, fell flat to the ground and escaped unhurt, while Bookman and the other man, standing with their backs toward the enemy, saw not the smoke, and were literally riddled by a shrapnel shell thrown plump to the spot. A braver man than Oscar Bookman never laid down his life for the Southern cause, and I fain would name the other, as the peer of Bookman or any other Southern soldier, but cannot. This was about the last Federal gun fired before the final assault.

At 4 o'clock in the afternoon Maj. Pegram brought up his artillery and placed it at proper intervals along the crest of the ridge occupied by our left, and not a Federal dared to raise his head above the works. The line of battle also advanced, and Pegram opened, dropping shot and shell just over the breastworks. The enemy responded feebly. The sharpshooters had nobly done their duty, and as the line of battle passed were ordered to cease firing and rest upon their arms, while the brigade should complete the work which they had so skillfully conducted to this point.

But when the Confederate battle cry was raised and the lines went sweeping across the field amid the roar of artillery and the clash of arms, the sharpshooters could not be held; so they were turned loose, and the whole force—sharpshooters and all—like a "rushing mighty wind" stormed down upon the Federal lines and over the breastworks, completely routing the whole force, which fled through the woods in the wildest confusion, leaving in our hands the nine pieces of artillery, with such horses as had not been killed, and more than two thousand prisoners. As well might King Canute have said to Old Ocean's swelling tide, "Thus far and no further!" as to try to stay that determined onset.

Some of the captured guns were turned upon the fleeing Federals; and among others, Capt. Hasell took charge of a captured gun on our right, but finding no lanyard, jerked off one of his suspenders to supply the deficiency, and sent the shells screaming and crashing through the tops of the trees, more than fifty feet above the heads of the tallest Yankees.

The Forefront of Battle. 197

Heth's division had been repulsed in its first assaults on the Federal right, but gallantly carried its part of the works in the final assault. Our success was complete and our losses slight. The sharpshooters, besides a large number of prisoners, brought out some thirty or forty excellent horses, first choice of which Gen. McGowan awarded to the battalion commander in acknowledgment of the valuable services rendered by that gallant corps in the brilliant affair. The brigade only lost 22 men in killed and wounded, including the casualties of the sharpshooters.

Gen. O. B. Wilcox, of the Union army, writing of the results of this engagement, says: "At 5 o'clock Hill had opened with his artillery, both shot and shell, some of which took the works in reverse, but did little actual damage other than demoralizing the men; of whom there were many, even of the old regiments, who never had come to fight, but to run on the first chance, or get into the hospital—and ho! for a pension afterwards. 'Some of their officers could not speak a word of English,' says Hancock in his report, 'and were therefore without that mutual intelligence and support which battle demands, and with nothing in common with their men but panic.' The first assault came on Miles, opposite his fourth brigade, and at a point of the line held by the consolidation of material of different regiments. For a time the severity of Miles's fire, the slashing and other obstacles on the ground, staggered the assaulting column, and they must have baffled it completely if the fire had continued only a few minutes longer. As it was, the assailants were thrown into considerable confusion, when suddenly our recruits gave way and a break occurred of two regiments on the right, and though Miles ordered up what little reserve he had, these men would neither move forward nor fire. Still Lieut. Geo. K. Dauchy, of McKnight's twelfth New York battery, turned his guns on the breach with effect, until the enemy crept along the silent rifle pits, captured the battery, and turned a gun inside our lines. Murphy's brigade of the second division being likewise driven off, the enemy captured the tenth Massachusetts battery and Battery B, first Rhode Island artillery, on his front, though it was served with 'marked gallantry' to the last." * * *

"The Union loss was 140 killed, 529 wounded and 2073 captured or missing—2742. The loss of the Confederates reached a total of 720, mostly in killed and wounded."—*Editors Century War Series, vol. iv., page 573.*

Gen. Grant says: "On the 25th the second corps and Gregg's division of cavalry, while at Ream's Station destroying the railroad, were attacked, and after desperate fighting a part of our line gave way, and five pieces of artillery fell into the hands of the enemy."—*Ibid, page 577.*

Mr. Grant had overlooked the four other pieces of artillery, and the two thousand prisoners, horses, etc., which at the same time fell into our hands.

I am not informed as to the part taken in this action by Lane's sharpshooters, or the different corps of Heth's division, but am sure their part of the work was well and faithfully done. The two battalions of McGowan and Scales, I personally know, bore a conspicuous part in the contest on the Confederate right, and literally covered themselves with glory, to which the short engagement and insignificant loss of the brigades clearly testify.

Both Gens. Wilcox and McGowan complimented the conduct of the sharpshooters in the most gratifying terms, and attributed the magnificent results of the affair largely to their skill and daring in demoralizing the enemy and tying them down behind their works before the final assault was made. And Gen. McGowan ever afterwards spoke of the battle of Ream's Station as "the sharpshooters' fight."

> "Sound, sound the clarion, fill the fife!
> To all the sensual world proclaim,
> One crowded hour of glorious life
> Is worth an age without a name."

We remained at Ream's Station until next morning, when we returned to our position on the Weldon railroad in front of Petersburg. The sharpshooters resumed their place in front and enjoyed a short season of comparative rest, which proved a panacea for all the physical discomforts which they had been required to endure in the unremitting activities of the campaign for more than four months.

CHAPTER XIV.

INCIDENTS AND DEMONSTRATIONS.

> And light is mingled with the gloom,
>   And joy with grief;
> Divinest compensations come,
> Through thorns of judgment mercies bloom
>   In sweet relief.
> —WHITTIER.

The postion taken by the sharpshooters was some 600 yards in front of the brigade, and well covered with rifle pits. The right on the edge of a cornfield, the left in a dense forest. The Federal pickets confronted us on the opposite side of the cornfield, with their right in the woods at a uniform distance of some 400 yards.

During the night we maintained a chain of videttes about 100 yards in advance of the rifle pits, and for several days gave ourselves up to relaxation and rest. The stillness of the forests, the softness of the atmosphere and the moaning of the pines—scarce rising above a whisper—stole away our senses and invited us to sleep. We yielded, and for three days and nights—save the videttes—everybody slept.

The videttes were relieved every two hours, and their lines visited regularly by the officers, once at least, between reliefs. I took my turn with the other officers. A vidette is never allowed to sleep on his post, and the penalty attached to this rule is death. Notwithstanding the sanctity of the trust and the terrible penalty of the law, men would sometimes give down under sheer exhaustion, and not only risk their own lives, but hazard the lives of their comrades and the safety of the cause they are placed there to guard and defend. On one of my rounds about midnight I approached a post and found the poor fellow lying prone upon the ground, with his rifle underneath him, clasped in both hands, fast asleep. I walked around him several times to arouse him, then seized the gun and wrenched it from his grasp; and still he slept. My heart sank within me and my eyes filled with tears, as I stood there in the stillness of that dark night, contemplating that manly form, whose proud spirit had led the charge on many a gory field, prostrate upon the ground, nature exhausted, sound asleep in the very presence of the enemy, and in full consciousness of the penalty prescribed for such an offense. I was almost overcome with grief. But my duty was plain. Returning to the lines I delivered the gun to a sergeant and ordered the man arrested, which was done before he awoke. Charges were preferred the next day, the court martial called and the day set for trial. Time elapsed, the day of trial came, and the stern judge advocate took his seat with his associates around him and the offender before him. The charges were read and not denied; and there remained nothing to be done on the part of the court but pronounce sentence. At this point a *brief*, in mitigation of the offense, was submitted by the prosecutor on behalf of the offender, which after reciting the circumstances of the offense, the story of his exploits on the field, and the unsullied character of the offender as a man and soldier, closed with a prayer for clemency and the suspension of judgment. This paper, after due consideration by the court, was declared to be not only ample as a ground of clemency, but a complete vindication of the offender's honor as a soldier. And so he was discharged with a sound admonition by the court, and returned to duty without punishment—to the joy of his comrades of the line. It is needless to say that we never had another such offense.

The corn in the field between the lines was in a full state of roasting ear, and being on neutral ground, both sides claimed the right to forage from it, at least to the center of the field. This foraging was continued, without objection, until the field was stripped to a narrow belt running across the center, when the sharpshooters were ordered to stop. Despite the order, however, a few shifty, hungry, daring fellows, leaving their arms and accoutrements on the rifle pits to deceive their officers, would now and then slip off and get a mess of corn. This was continued on both sides until there remained only a scattering ear here and there along the center. Finally, John Kilgore, a thin ribbed, self sustaining, nimble jointed sharpshooter, slipped out to get a few ears of corn, when he met one of his blue coated, well fed neighbors on the same errand. He discovered that the gentleman in blue supported a brand new hat, the like of which he had not seen for years, and determined to capture him, hat and all—at all events the hat. Accordingly, sounding the charge, he made for the fellow at full speed; and now they had it up and down, and round and round through the dense mass of growing corn, until the Federal dropped the hat and made a bee line for home. Kilgore suspended the charge, picked up the hat, gathered his corn and quietly returned to his post satisfied, and reported the results of the expedition.

Like the prophet of the Lord at Dothan, Lee and his little army at Petersburg were compassed about with horses and chariots and a great host, awaiting the opportunity to overwhelm and destroy them. But there was a ring of fire intervening, which so far could not be evaded or overcome. Strategy and dash and blundering audacity were alternately resorted to by the investors, but to this juncture of no avail. Meanwhile our numbers and means of support were diminishing, with no prospect of assistance or relief.

On the 16th day of September Gen. Wilcox ordered the two battalions of McGowan and

Lane to drive in the Federal sharpshooters and discover the attitude and temper of their main line in front of the light division. We accordingly formed and deployed; Wooten on the right and Dunlap on the left of the Weldon railroad, the general himself being present in person and directing the movement.

We advanced through the cornfield, at common time, until the enemy discovered our approach and opened on us. We returned the fire, and with a yell and charge went crashing through their picket lines like a cyclone. We pursued them to cover of their fortifications and engaged their main line. After teasing and worrying their line of battle for some time we were recalled, and returned to our position with a number of prisoners. Gen. Wilcox complimented the sharpshooters upon the promptness and skill with which his orders had been executed. But we could not quite understand the purpose of the demonstration. It afterwards transpired, however, which explained it all, that Hampton, with a select body of daring horsemen, had galloped round the Federal left, gained their rear, and at the very moment we were entertaining Mr. Grant in front, Hampton was engaged some miles in the rear, dispersing his guards and capturing his beef cattle. The expedition was completely successful, resulting in the capture of a herd of 2500 fine fat beeves and a number of prisoners, which were safely landed within the Confederate lines.

So passed the time, until near the close of September, during which time we were resting, eating fat beef and gathering strength for the next tilt.

***

A gallant Union soldier thus describes his intense nervous excitement on going into battle: "My knees knocked together and my teeth clattered like a thundergust of woodpeckers in a forest of dead chestnuts." A good description.

CHAPTER XV.

BATTLE OF JONES'S FARM.

"Half a hundred cannon threw up their emetic,
   And thirty thousand muskets flung their pills
Like hail, to make a bloody diuretic;
   Mortality! Thou hast thy monthly bills!
Thy plagues, thy famines, thy physicians; yet tick,
   Like the death watch, within our ears the ills
Past, present, and to come; but all may yield
   To the true portrait of one battlefield."

On the 29th the tenth and eighteenth Federal corps under Ord and Birney, from Butler's army, assaulted the five brigades under Anderson at Fort Harrison, north of the James, and succeeded in capturing and holding a part of our works. On the next morning early, McGowan's brigade was ordered to reinforce Anderson on the north side. About 9 o'clock the brigade was put in motion, marched through the outskirts of Petersburg, crossed the Appomattox above town, and took the road for Richmond. We had only gone a few miles when we were halted and ordered to return to our position in front of Petersburg. Grant, taking advantage of the absence of troops sent to reinforce Anderson, had assailed our right and carried our works in the neighborhood of Poplar Spring, and with a heavy column was advancing on the South Side railroad. McGowan's brigade was halted on its return near Battery No. 45, and lay there until about 3 o'clock in the afternoon, when it was moved out on the Boydton plank road, to a point where the Church road crosses, along which the Federal column was advancing. Here we found Lane's brigade already in position, and formed on his left. Our line ran perpendicularly across the Church road, fronting the Jones house, which sat on a ridge or elevated plateau some six hundred yards in front. The enemy had already occupied the ridge and basement of the Jones house with a heavy line of sharpshooters, who began to pepper us with a scattering fire the instant our lines were formed.

The sharpshooters were deployed and advanced under a stinging fire into a basin shaped depression in the face of the hill this side of the Jones house, where we were protected from the enemy's fire by the rising ground in front. Here our line was adjusted to the work in hand, and orders extended to prepare for action. When everything was ready, with arms at a trail and bodies well stooped, the beautiful line slipped across and up the sloping side of the inclining basin, until our movements could no longer be concealed, when at the command, "Up, guards, and at 'em! fire and charge!" the entire line rose and fired; then with a rousing cheer stormed up the hill, broke and routed their entire line, and sent them flying across the field to cover of the woods beyond, save and except those occupying the Jones house, who fought savagely for their position for a little while. The sharpshooters closed upon the house and poured into the doors and windows of the brick basement a murderous cross fire, which soon moderated their zeal and caused them to cry out for quarter. We captured in the house some thirty-five or forty prisoners, including the major commanding and several other officers, which were marched to the rear under guard. Both lines of battle now advanced, the sharpshooters dropping to the rear.

The artillerists sprang to their places and let loose the dogs of war. Twenty-four guns from the hills behind, trained upon the advancing lines of blue, opened; as many guns from the opposing hills answered back like a deafening echo from the caverns of hades. Thunder and fire and smoke issued from the opposing hill-tops in roaring volumes that rent the air and shook the earth, while shot and shell swept across the field hissing and screaming and crashing into the ranks of the opposing columns as they rushed together. The two lines met just beyond the Jones house, and the shock was terrific. But the Unionists could not withstand the fury of the determined onset, and broke at the first or second volley and fled the field in confusion, leaving the ground thickly strewn with their killed and wounded. The two brigades pursuing, encountered a second line at the edge of the woods which fought with more obstinacy, but it also gave way before McGowan's and Lane's intrepid Carolinians. A third line was engaged near the Pegram house, more than a mile back from where the action began. But night intervening, the conflict ended with the Confederates masters of the field. About 9 o'clock the brigades dropped back into the woods and bivouacked for the night. The enemy remained on Pegram Ridge and fortified.

During the night a movement was planned to strike the enemy in flank while we were to make a demonstration in front. What became of the flanking expedition I am not informed. In pursuance of the plan, however, about 8 o'clock the next morning, the two battalions of Lane and McGowan were advanced, while the brigades stood to arms in line of battle. We drove forward through the woods, square to the front, struck the Federal skirmishers in strong rifle pits at the edge of the field about 250 yards in advance of their line of works, which ran along the Pegram House ridge. We charged and routed the skirmishers without firing a gun, and pursued them up the sloping ridge, yelling and firing at every jump; stormed over their fortifications, crushed their line of battle into fragments, and sent them swarming through the woods in complete route. We captured at least two men to every *one* engaged.

Such was the headlong fury of the charge, and such the amazing results achieved, that our batteries in the rear, supposing that we had been gobbled by the Federals, who came pouring over their breastworks as we entered, turned their fire upon us, and continued to pelt us with shot and shell until a courier was dispatched to Maj. Pegram with notice of our success, who ceased firing. The prisoners were turned over to the brigade, and the sharpshooters moved forward and engaged another, and the Federal main line. After a short while the sharpshooters were recalled and the two brigades returned to their position on the main line. We heard nothing more of our flanking column.

The brigade lost 162 killed and wounded, including the casualties in the sharpshooters, in the two days' operations.

Among the killed, the lamented E. F. Bookter, the gallant colonel of the twelfth South Carolina regiment, and M. F. Hawthorn of the sharpshooters, than whom a better soldier never wore the gray, may be mentioned.

On the 2d day of October the brigade was moved out on the Boydton plank road and placed in position a little westward of the Jones house, and the men put to building breastworks. The work was carried on from day to day by heavy details from the different regiments under the supervision of certain officers detailed by the regimental commanders for that purpose—each regiment building in its own front; and each day being the exact reflection of its antecedent. The sharpshooters took their proper position on the picket line about half a mile in front, and for their protection constructed a strong line of rifle pits, which they occupied each alternate day during our stay on this part of the lines. These works became a part of a permanent line extending from Battery Forty-five to Hatcher's Run. The enemy, being engaged at the same or similar work, were disposed to behave themselves, so there was no disturbance for several weeks. Meanwhile drills were resumed and the ordinary routine of camp life observed.

The two opposing armies, however, were not so quiet and peaceable on other parts of the field. After the fall of Fort Harrison, Gen. Grant, of necessity, had to maintain a heavy force on the north side, to hold the ground taken from Anderson; and Gen. Lee, of course, must confront him with a sufficient force to meet any aggressive movement Grant might make. For several days both sides quietly awaited some demonstration on the part of the other. At length Gen. Lee determined to make effort to recover possession of Fort Harrison and the adjacent works now in the hands of the Federals; and hence, on the 6th, ordered Anderson to make the assault with the two divisions of Hoke and Fields. These divisions were to attack in two columns simultaneously, Fields on the right and Hoke on the left face of the fort. Both were ready a little before the hour appointed, and Fields ordered his leading brigade to move up a little closer to the enemy and await orders. The men, however, mistook the order and made a dash for the fort. This necessitated the advance of Fields's other brigades, which attacked with great impetuousity and with some prospect of success. But Hoke, awaiting the hour agreed upon, failed to attack, and hence Fields's column was repulsed. Hoke then attacked and was also repulsed; and so the movement was a failure. Kautz's division of cavalry, however, was defeated on the Federal left by Bratton and Gary, and ten guns and caissons complete, with more than one hundred artillery and cavalry horses, fell into our hands. Our loss was considerable, including the lamented Gregg, the dashing commander of Hood's old Texas brigade.

By the 12th a new line of works had been constructed between the exterior and interior lines, the right resting on Fort Gilmore and the left on the Darbytown road, and the same occupied by Fields and Hoke. At daylight on that day the enemy in heavy force moved up the Darbytown road and attacked Fields's division. His several assaults were gallantly met and repelled by Gen. Perry, and he finally withdrew. Gen. Longstreet having recovered from his wound received in the Wilderness, returned and resumed command, and Anderson returned to Petersburg.

On the 27th of October, early in the morning, the enemy again made a formidable demonstration in Longstreet's front, while Wietzel's division of infantry and Kautz's division of cavalry were sent through the forests to turn the Confederate left and sweep our lines from the Williamsburg and Nine Mile roads. This movement was discovered and Fields's division sent to meet it. Hoke with a heavy skirmish line held the works in front, while Fields attended to the flanking column. Wietzel and Kautz attacked with considerable bluster, but could not overcome the fury of Fields's determined defense. They came up to within three hundred yards of our lines, but could not stand the fire. They threw themselves flat on the ground and remained until Capt. Lyle of Bratton's staff with a small squad went out and captured about five hundred of them, while the rest broke and scampered from the field. During the night the whole Federal force fell back to their fortifications. Thus ended the active campaigning of 1864 on the north side of the James.

On the same day, forty miles from Fort Harrison, on the Confederate right, Heth and Mahone had met and defeated Hancock's corps and two divisions of the fifth corps at Hatcher's Run, west of Petersburg. McGowan's brigade was not engaged, but moved to and fro along the works under a good shelling from the enemy's guns, ready for action. This movement by the enemy against Hatcher's Run, though unsuccessful, resulted in the extension of our lines to the right. Our brigade moved some distance to the right and settled in line in front of the Dr. Boisseaw house. Here the men were again set to building and strengthening our works.

The order of the regiments was as follows: The first regiment on the right, then the twelfth, then the thirteenth, then the fourteenth, and then the rifles on the left. Heth's division was on our right, with McRae's brigade touching the first regiment, and Lane's brigade next on our left. Brigade headquarters were established in the Boisseaw house, and the regiments were ordered to construct winter quarters in rear of their respective positions on the line, which was done; and this became their home for the winter.

To economize men and shorten the line of his defense, Gen. Lee constructed a huge dam across —— Run, two miles west of Petersburg, on the Boydton plank road, just below the confluence of two branches which came together from opposite directions, and which ran along immediately in front of the Confederate lines. These branches rippled in perpetual flow down the sharp valleys between prominent hills. The dam was some 300 feet long, fifty feet high, 100 feet thick at the base and thirty feet at the top. When filled, the water covered the valleys to a depth of from five to thirty feet for more than half a mile on either side of the dam; and was an effectual bar to Federal attack for that distance. Hence no troops were needed on this part of our line while the dam lasted. The weight of water which collected above the dam, and lay against the unsettled earth heavily, eventually broke the dam with a disastrous flood, which swept the valley of coons and cabins out into the roaring Appomattox; and the lines thus vacated had again to be manned with troops.

CHAPTER XVI.

CLOSING INCIDENTS OF 1864.

> "Dreary east winds howling o'er us,
> Clay lands knee deep spread before us;
> Mire and ice and snow and sleet;
> Aching backs and frozen feet;
> Knees which reel as marches quicken;
> Ranks which thin as corpses thicken;
> While with carrion birds we eat,
> Calling puddle water sweet.
> As we pledge the health of our general, who fares as rough as we:
> What can daunt us, what can turn us, led to death by such as Lee."

To meet the expedition sent out under Warren to destroy the Weldon railroad at Jarrett's Station, the three divisions of Wilcox, Heth and Mahone, under A. P. Hill, were withdrawn from the lines soon after dark of the 8th of December, and took up the line of march westward on the Boydton plank road. Passing through the town of Dinwiddie Court House about midnight, we turned southward, and after marching several miles went into bivouac.

We resumed the march at dawn the next morning and hurried forward in the direction of Jarrett's Station.

The weather was intensely cold, the ground frozen hard, and the heavens were dark with clouds, portending a snowstorm. We made good time over the solid earth and accomplished one of our best day's marches. We went into bivouac about dark in a skirt of timber where wood was abundant. The threatened storm burst upon us, and already the sleet and snow was descending in blinding showers upon the frozen ground. We built huge log fires and prepared as best we could for the night. After eating our scant rations and smoking our pipes, we wrapped ourselves in our blankets and gum cloths, and stood, sat or lay around our camp fires in a semi-conscious, half freezing condition until morning. We resumed the march early next morning, and in great distress wended our weary way, thinly clad and half shod, through sleet and snow, mud and slush, to Jarrett's Station. Heavy skirmishing and considerable artillery firing was heard in front as we neared the station, but ceased on our approach. Warren kindly retired before Hill's column, and generously maintained his distance as Hill pursued him. We followed on his track until night overtook us, some six miles beyond the station, when we went into bivouac. We continued the pursuit early next morning for three or four miles; but finding that Warren had made good his escape to the Federal lines, we halted and began to retrace our steps. We recrossed the railroad at Jarrett's and pressed on towards Petersburg. We bivouacked that night on the banks of the Nottaway river; the night following near Dinwiddie court house; and on the 12th reached our winter quarters in a somewhat dilapidated condition. A few days of comfort and rest, however, restored the spirits and physical energies of the men, when they were again employed in building and strengthening the line of breastworks.

A strong picket was kept up about half a mile in advance of the main line, the sharpshooters occupying the front alternately with regimental details made from the brigade. The year closed without any further movement on the part of McGowan's brigade.

On the 28th day of December, when the eventful campaign of 1864 with its sanguinary record had evidently closed, and the two great armies which confronted each other before the beleaguered cities of Petersburg and Richmond had settled down into the repose of winter, Gen. Wilcox, by the advise and with the consent of the brigade commanders, published an order to the four battalions of sharpshooters of the light division, containing (*inter alia*) this proposition: "That whenever they should place the rifle pits on the picket line in first class condition, and report the fact to division headquarters, the sharpshooters might retire from the front and go into winter quarters until the campaign of 1865 should open." The conditions of the order were met by noon of the 30th, and the fact reported. The report was accompanied with a request on the part of the two battalions of McGowan and Scales, asking permission of the major general to make a requisition on their blue coated neighbors in front for such articles of camp equipment as might be necessary to render them comfortable during the winter; which report was received as satisfactory, and the request granted upon terms.

Hence, in the evening twilight of that cold and murky December day, the commandants of the two battalions named, sallied forth without attendants, and were soon lost to sight in the thickening darkness and dense skirt of woods lying between the lines. The enemy's outposts and picket lines were closely scrutinized and the point where the sortie should be made definitely determined. The two officers now returned to their respective commands and issued the necessary orders and instructions. Accordingly, about 4 o'clock the following morning, some two hours before daybreak, the two battalions met at the point designated—which was between the lines, some distance east of the Weldon railroad—and formed at right angles with the line to be attacked, about twenty paces apart, back to back. Eight men of superior courage and activity were selected from each battalion and formed at intervals of five paces across the forward flanks of the two battalions, facing the enemy. R. M. Plexico, Silas Perry, R. J. Fields and Press Watson were four of those selected from my battalion; the names of the others I am unable to recall. At the command the sixteen men, with their center well advanced, moved forward slowly upon the rifle pits directly before them, and which had been designated as the point of attack. The two battalions followed closely, Young taking intervals by the right flank and Dunlop by the left, as the movement progressed. Silently and stealthily, as a tiger would skirt a jungle, this double transverse line with spike head in front, slipped along through the darkness upon the unsuspecting enemy. A treacherous ditch lay directly across our path about a hundred yards in front of the Federal rifle pits, into which every man fell as his turn came; but each recovering, moved on in his place. When the front had nearly reached the point where the plunge should be made, a man in the rear of my line tumbled into the ditch and accidentally discharged his gun. (The plan was to capture the entire line without firing a gun.) This aroused the enemy, and they poured a harmless volley from the length of their line into the bleak darkness in front. At the same instant the battalions charged and drove their spike head squarely through the Federal lines, capturing half a dozen rifle pits with their occupants. When the battalions had moved half their length through the gap, the right battalion faced to the right, the left battalion to the left, and throwing forward their wings so as to form a sack, swept the lines for nearly a mile on either side, capturing a large number of prisoners with all the supplies needed. The wounding of private Carter in the back by the accidental discharge of the gun referred to, was the only casualty reported on our side, whereas the enemy lost not less than three hundred, in killed, wounded and captured. The success of the expedition was promptly reported to division headquarters, and approved, with generous commendations by Gen. Wilcox.

An incident occurred at the moment of encounter, which illustrates the personal courage of this daring command.

When Sergt. Plexico scrambled out of the ditch, into which all had fallen, and rubbed the mud and water from his eyes, he discovered that he had lost his bearings, as well as his connection with the spike head, but made for a rifle pit—which he supposed to be the right one—some distance to the left of the point on which his comrades were bearing, and charged it single handed and alone, capturing a corporal and four other prisoners, whom he marched off to the rear. Of course the concussion produced at the instant of encounter paralyzed the corporal and his men for the time, otherwise Plexico would have failed.

We secured all the supplies necessary to our comfort for the winter and returned to camp about sunrise, a happy command, resumed our duties at the front; and continued to alternate with details from the brigade until sometime about the middle of January, before the order for our retirement was carried into effect.

To give the eventful campaign an appropriate closing, a substantial Christmas dinner was prepared for the Army of Northern Virginia by an organized effort of the dear, good ladies of Richmond and Petersburg, and sent to the front. This treat was forwarded through the commissary department for distribution, and was intended to be given out, share and share alike, to both officers and men. The rights of all were equal, from the commanding general down to the lowest private. The conception was generous and lofty, the sentiment patriotic and tender. Of these we all received our share. But when it came to the grub itself, we received only an intimation of the generous donation, and were glad to get even the smallest reminder of "the substance of things hoped for, the evidence of things not seen."

More than six months had elapsed since the investment of our capital city, and yet our lines were intact. Not a breach had been made, save at Fort Harrison, on the banks of the James, notwithstanding assault after assault had been made, and scarce an hour had passed when the roar of hostile guns was not heard in front of Petersburg.

And thus the year of 1864 closed.

CHAPTER XVII.

DASH BY THE SHARPSHOOTERS; PEACE NEGOTIATIONS.

"Shall we upon the footing of our land
Send fair play orders and make compromise,
Insinuation, parley, or base truce
To arms invasive."

About 11 o'clock p. m., January 8, 1865, when the sharpshooters were on duty at the front, the following order from Lieut. Gen. Hill, endorsed by the division and brigade commanders, was referred to me on the picket line to the right of the Jones house:

HEADQUARTERS THIRD CORPS.
JANUARY 8, 1865.

It is represented that the enemy intends renewing their attack upon Wilmington, and that troops have left here to that end. Can not you ascertain whether or not any troops have left your front, or any changes occurred.

Respectfully,
(Signed) A. P. HILL, Lieutenant General.

In passing the order down to the brigade commanders the major general says, in his endorsement: "The attention of brigade commanders is invited to Gen. Hill's note. They will try to obtain the desired information, and communicate the same promptly to these headquarters. Capture a prisoner, if it can be done without risking too much, and question him as soon as captured."

Gen. McGowan referred the order to me with this endorsement: "You will comply with the instructions of the corps and division commanders, as far as practicable."

We knew quite well that a prisoner could be captured "without risking too much," and determined to "comply with the instructions" of the several commanders at once. Accordingly B. K. Benson and R. M. Plexico were directed to go to the front, crawl up on the enemy's outposts, and, "if practicable," to capture a vidette and return without delay. These scouts returned about 4 o'clock without a prisoner, and reported that the vidette posts were so near the Federal picket lines it was impossible to capture a vidette without arousing the picket, and thus "risking too much." The failure of these two men to "capture a prisoner" settled the question, in so far as success by strategy was concerned, and it now became necessary to extract the information desired by force. It was therefore determined to withdraw two companies of the battalion from the lines, cover the vacancy by extending intervals with the third company, and attack the enemy's line before daylight. Hence at 5:20 o'clock on the morning of the 9th, the first and second companies under Hasell and Brunson were assembled on the left of our line, and formed in front at intervals of five paces. We advanced slowly and cautiously until we reached a point not exceeding thirty yards from the Federal lines, when a vidette discovered our approach and fired. Instantly we sprang forward and measured our full length on their rifle pits, routed their line for some distance on either flank, captured fourteen prisoners and returned to our position before daylight without losing a man. The prisoners were promptly sent under guard to brigade headquarters for examination.

We were relieved about 9 o'clock and returned to camp, where we received the compliments of Gen. McGowan for the information secured for Gen. Hill, by our successful dash on the enemy's line; then retired to rest.

We continued to take our turn on the picket line until the 15th of January, when we were relieved from the front and went into winter quarters in rear at the brigade, according to the terms of the order of December 28th.

The position selected for our winter home was in rear of the center of the brigade, in the head of a hollow which penetrated the ridge occupied by the brigade to within one hundred yards of the line of works. Our camp was laid off in the form of a square, three sides of which were occupied by the three companies of the battalion in comfortable shanties covered with tents, facing inward. The second or center company running parallel with the line of the brigade; the first and third companies in reverse order on the two sides of the gulch, running back their full length and facing each other across the square. The foundation for each shanty was made level by digging into the face of the hill and drawing the earth back on the lower side. Chimneys were cut into the wall on the deepest side of the excavation. The lower side was built up to a level with small timbers and a fly tent stretched over the whole. The openings or doors of entrance were all on the inside, looking out upon the square, which was our parade ground. We were soon as confortable and happy as soldiers could be, with nothing to do but drill, drill, drill.

The battalion was mustered for roll call, inspection or drill several times during the day, and for roll call occasionally at uncertain hours during the night, that the men might always be ready for duty when called on. Between drills during the day, and after the duties of the day were ended, the men were allowed to ramble, forage or visit their neighbors of other commands; only they must be on hand at emergency call, day or night. They were always on hand when needed.

For a period of six weeks or more the enemy remained quiet in our front, which gave us the opportunity to cast about us and consider the attitude and possibilities of the struggle. We looked—and lo! the clouds of impending disaster were gathering dark and ominous about our darling Confederacy.

Early, after a short and brilliant career in the Shenandoah valley, had been beaten and routed by a vastly superior force under Sheridan. Sherman, with a magnificent army, was marching in triumph through Georgia and the Carolinas. Charleston, Mobile and Wilmington had been evacuated, and the entire southern coast, from the Rio Grande to the Potomac, had been given up. And the Army of Northern Virginia, drawn out to a thread over a crescent shaped line of earthworks nearly forty miles in length, with an effective roll of not more than forty thousand men, confronted by an army of little less than one hundred and fifty thousand veteran soldiers, was the sole surviving hope of the Confederate cause. Gen. Johnston, with all his splendid generalship, could not with his remnant of an army withstand Sherman's victorious columns as they pressed onward through the Carolinas to a junction with Grant. Nor was there any other source of possible relief to the great Lee and his war worn veterans. The fate of the Confederacy rested alone upon the shoulders of this incomparable leader; to whom all looked, both soldiers and citizens, for deliverance He calmly bore this great responsibility, as well as this vain confidence—in which he did not share—determined to do his duty to the end. We glanced sadly at our proud banner, the Southern cross, as it floated defiantly here and there along our thin lines, and could dimly trace in lines of blood "Ichabod," written over that significant motto, "*Deo Vendice*," where lay our strength and trust; and for a moment our hearts sank within us. Nevertheless the undaunted Confederates stood to their colors, ready to meet the enemy on any part of the ground.

When not on duty we spent the time in social pleasures, visiting and entertaining friends, dining and giving dinners, perpetrating practical jokes, and discussing politics, tactics and religion. The study of military tactics was enjoined by general orders upon all officers—commissioned and non-commissioned—with schools of recitation established at company, regimental and brigade headquarters, in which at stated periods lessons in the school of the company, battalion and evolutions of the line, were recited to the commanding officers and discussed. Drills were kept up daily, with marked improvement in the ease and accuracy with which the more difficult evolutions were performed. Examining boards were also established, before whom every applicant for promotion was required to appear and pass his examination before his commission was issued.

On the 28th of January, Capt. Hasell, of the first company of sharpshooters, was granted leave of absence to visit his home in Charleston, S. C., and Lieut. Ballinger was assigned to duty in his place. Ballinger was wounded on the 25th of March, and Lieut. N. G. Dicen took his place. Capt. Hasell was due to return the last of February, but Sherman's army cut him off from Virginia, and he took service on Gen. Hardee's staff in Johnson's army, for the time, and did not reach his command until after the lines were broken at Petersburg in April.

On the 30th of January, at the instance of Mr. Francis Blair, a distinguished citizen of the United States and confidential friend of President Lincoln, President Davis commissioned Messrs. Alexander H. Stephens, Hunter and Campbell to meet President Lincoln and Secretary of State Seward at Fortress Monroe, to negotiate the suspension of hostilities with a view to the establishment of peace between the divided sections. The meeting, however, partook more of the nature of a private interview than of a diplomatic council. When the purpose of the conference was introduced by Mr. Stephens, Mr. Lincoln at once announced that any proposition short of unconditional surrender of the armies of the Confederate States would not be entertained. Such an ultimatum the Southern commissioners had neither the power nor disposition to consider; hence withdrew in disdain, returned to Richmond and reported the result. The report was received and the action of the commissioners sustained. Thereupon, President Davis uttered (impromptu), according to information, one of the grandest speeches of his life. A copy of this address I endeavored to obtain, for months, for the adornment of these sketches, but failed.

The secretary of the Southern Historical Society, at Richmond, Va., after an exhaustive examination of the files of his office and of the Richmond daily newspapers of that period, reported that he could find nothing. The secretary of the West Virginia society; a Canadian editor, whose staff correspondent was stationed in Richmond at the time; Senators Kenna of West Virginia and Reagan of Texas—all made similar reports. Senator Reagan, however, said that his speech was delivered in the

African church in Richmond; that he was present and heard it; and that it was the most thrilling and patriotic address he had ever heard fall from the lips of man; but that it had never been published. I then awaited the publication of the "Life of Jefferson Davis" by his widow, hoping that in the privacy of his home he might have confided to her an extended epitome of this great speech, which she might, with propriety, incorporate in the memoirs of his illustrious life; but not so. Not one word was published.

When the results of the conference were made known to the Army of Northern Virginia, the troops were mustered by brigades and regiments, and the question of submission, according to Mr. Lincoln's terms, was referred to them for determination. The poll was taken, and every mother's son of them voted to fight it out to the bitter end.

The pickets now consisted of about 200 men detailed from the brigades, and commanded by a captain.

The picket line of McGowan's brigade was about 600 yards in front, protected by a strong line of rifle pits. The Federal pickets were about 300 yards beyond. This arrangement was substantially maintained until about the last of February, when the sharpshooters were ordered to resume their duties at the front. In the meantime the enemy had become somewhat insolent, and betimes amused themselves by firing at our details and forcing them to hug their rifle pits for safety. This annoyance was exactly to the taste of the sharpshooters, and hence, as soon as they took the front, set about to silence their cheeky neighbors. They responded cheerfully to every shot, and assuming the offensive, proceeded to blister every blue coated gentleman that dared to expose himself in the least degree above his rifle pit. A few hours only were necessary to convince them that they were dealing with willing experts who could beat them at their own game, and hence proposed a truce, which was granted; and henceforth peace and good fellowship prevailed between the picket lines.

On Sunday, the 12th day of March, the Sacrament of the Lord's Supper was administered in camp by the Rev. Dr. Theoderick Prior, assisted by the Rev. Messrs. Dickson and

Douglas, in which all denominations of professing Christians participated—a touchingly solemn scene in which many joined for the last time.

CHAPTER XVIII.

GORDON'S ATTACK ON FORT STEADMAN; STORMING OF McILWAINE'S HILL.

> "War is honorable
> In those who do their native rights maintain;
> In those whose swords in iron barrier are
> Between the lawless spoiler and the weak;
> But is, in those who draw th' offensive blade
> For added power or gain, sordid and despicable
> As meanest office of the worldly churl."

The Army of Northern Virginia now mustered scarcely thirty-five thousand muskets. Longstreet commanded the left, covering the Confederate capital and the interval between the James and the Appomattox; Gordon the center, covering Petersburg; and A. P. Hill the right, extending from Petersburg to Hatcher's Run; while our wretchedly mounted cavalry guarded our flanks. Our lines were drawn out to their utmost attenuation, and although we injected into the winter's campaign a good deal of pleasurable amusement, let me assure you it was no holiday parade. The small force at Lee's command had to do guard and picket duty, and cover the entire forty miles of works, passing almost continually from one duty to another. No reserves were available to relieve those who broke down, and the men were shifted again and again from point to point to meet the divers demonstrations of the enemy. Sherman with his magnificent army was rapidly pressing back the skeleton of an army under Johnston to a juncture with Grant's forces in front of Petersburg. If these two grand armies were permitted to unite, it would give Grant an effective roll of more than two hundred thousand men; whereas, the addition of Johnston's troops to the Army of Northern Virginia would give Gen. Lee scarcely fifty thousand. The Confederates, though half clad, bare footed, gaunt and famished, with unswerving devotion stood to their colors and defied the embattled legions of Grant and Sherman as they closed around them. Gen. Lee, however, had determined to escape so fearful a combination by evacuating the lines of Petersburg and Richmond, and falling back to the hills in the interior before it was too late. Hence pontoon trains were made ready and a large supply of provisions was ordered to be collected at Amelia court house; and Gen. Johnston was directed to so manœuvre as to connect his left with Lee's right, whenever and wherever such a union could be consummated. To divert the attention of the Federal commander from his left near Hatcher's Run, which was dangerously near the Cox road, along which alone the Confederates could safely retire, Gen. Lee prepared to attack the Union lines just south of the Appomattox river and at their strongest point.

Fort Steadman was selected as the point of attack. This formidable castle, with its cordon of supporting redoubts and connecting parapets on each flank, armed with the heaviest metal and defended by the bravest of men, and withal protected by a perfect labyrinth of entanglements in front, was to be carried by an assault *coup de main*. Batteries 10, 11 and 12 on the left were to be swept out, and Fort Haskell on the right was to be reduced. Then the high ground in rear was to be gained, the City Point railroad seized, and Grant's main line of communication broken up and destroyed. Gen. Gordon, with two of his best divisions, was to make the assault, while the rest of the army was to stand to arms in readiness to support the movement. If Grant assaulted to recover his lost ground, Lee would be ready to meet him; if he hastened toward City Point to re-establish his communications, the Southern army would withdraw over the Cox road. It was a reasonable presumption that Gordon would, in some measure, succeed; that the Federal left would be withdrawn to meet Gordon, and thus the line of retreat be opened.

A little before daybreak on the morning of the 25th of March, 1865, Gordon's two divisions moved up and confronted Fort Steadman. Young's battalion of sharpshooters preceded the assaulting column and cleared the way of obstructions. Then came the main lines, as silently as spectres, slipped across the interval, bounded into Fort Steadman and quietly captured garrison and guns before the bewildered Unionists understood what was up. The guns of the captured fort were immediately turned upon the adjacent supporting fortifications, numbers of which were abandoned, leaving in Gordon's hands nine pieces of heavy artillery, eight mortars and five hundred prisoners, including a brigadier general. The initial movement was thus completely successful, with a prospect of greater and more brilliant successes; but unfortunately the leading division was not sustained. The troops set off to attack Fort Haskell did so in a hesitating, half hearted manner, and were repulsed. Others refused to advance at the critical moment, and hence the movement was stayed and the great opportunity lost. The Federals at once concentrated a heavy fire upon Fort Steadman from front and flanks, and Gordon was caught in a frightful trap, from which his high courage and masterly leadership could with great difficulty extricate him and his daring command. So completely were they encircled by the ring of consuming fire that nearly two thousand Confederates surrendered on the spot, which added to the killed and wounded made a total loss of nearly three thousand men, against an aggregate loss on the other side of twenty-five hundred in killed, wounded and missing. The remainder of our forces succeeded in getting out and returned to our lines.

Our repulse at Fort Steadman was followed by an advance of the sixth Federal corps, which after hard fighting succeeded in capturing our picket lines for several miles west of the Weldon railroad. The pickets in McGowan's front made a gallant fight for their position, but were overwhelmed and driven in. About 2 o'clock p. m. the sharpshooters, who had been off duty, were thrown out and engaged the enemy at a range of about two hundred and fifty yards, which caused them to hug their works with amusing tenacity. The Federal artillery played upon our lines with but little effect, save the destruction of a few of our shanties and the explosion of an ammunition chest, which killed two men and wounded two or three others.

About 3 o'clock two regiments of Thomas's brigade on our left were sent forward to drive the enemy from McIlwaine's Hill, a commanding position east of the Jones house, which had been seized from the Georgians in the morning, and which was necessary to the comfort and security of our lines at that point.

A battery of artillery assisted Thomas in the assault. The Federals also advanced two or three regiments from their main line to meet the Confederates. The two lines met about the crest and grappled. For a time the contest was furious and deadly, but the Federals yielded at length to the determined Georgians. Other reinforcements were sent forward from each side, and the contest renewed, with a manifest determination on the part of both to recover and hold possession of the hill at whatever cost, or involve much larger forces in the contest. Hour after hour the conflict raged back and forth across the consecrated hilltop, until the mantle of darkness interposed and closed the contest—leaving the crest in possession of enemy. The sharpshooters in the meantime with merciless accuracy were peeling the topknots from every Federal head that peered above their rifle pits in McGowan's front; for be it remembered, " they never touched a trigger without drawing blood." Two companies of sharpshooters were relieved about 9 o'clock the next morning, but the third could not be relieved until after dark the following night, on account of its proximity to the Federal lines and the dangers besetting every approach to their advanced position.

About 10 o'clock on the night of the 26th, while I was busily engaged in establishing a new line of rifle pits for our pickets, I was summoned to appear *instanter* at brigade headquarters. The order was promptly obeyed, and I was informed by Gen. McGowan that Gen. Lee with our corps and division commanders had been in conference at his headquarters; that it was determined that McIlwaine Hill must be recovered from the enemy at all hazards, and *that* before daylight in the morning; that the four battalions of sharpshooters of the light division had been selected and assigned to that disagreeable duty; and that he was authorized by Gen. Lee to say that, in the event of success, every man who survived the action should receive as a reward for the service a leave of absence for thirty days to visit his home and family, to begin at once and continue as rapidly as the exigencies of the service would permit, until all had received their reward. We were only to take and hold the hill until other troops could be brought from the line, when we should be relieved.

The Forefront of Battle. 251

The persistent gallantry of the Georgia brigade in their efforts to recover and hold the hill, and the heroic and successful defense of the Federals to retain its possession, which we had witnessed, together with the conditions of the order of our assignment, impressed us with the importance and peril of the undertaking, and we felt that the crisis was upon us, when every man, with all his muscle and nerve, was called upon to do and to dare for the honor of his country, or ground his arms in ignominious defeat; and we stood for our country, determined to take the hill or impale ourselves on the enemy's bayonets which bristled along the crest in solid mass.

Accordingly, at 1:30 on the morning of the 27th the battalion was formed, the order read and explained, the enormity of the job in hand discussed, and men and officers put upon their metal for the desperate adventure. We moved out on the Boydton plank road directly in front of the McIlwaine Hill, where in a short time the several battalions assembled. Upon consultation of the several commanders, it was determined to make the assault in solid order of battle, with Wooten's North Carolina battalion on the right and Dunlop's South Carolina battalion on the left in front, covered and supported by Young's North Carolina and —— Georgia battalion, on a second line immediately in rear of the first. The center of the hill was to be carried by storm. The two leading battalions were then to wheel—the one to the right and the other to the left—and sweep out, while the two supporting battalions should move up and occupy the summit as a basis of further effort to hold the position, should the enemy attempt to retake it; and upon whose right and left the leading battalions, as soon as the hill was cleared, were to return and form.

The lights on our picket line in front were gradually extinguished and every precaution taken so that our movements might not be discovered, and thus the chances of success placed at less hazard. Orders and instructions were given in detail to each and every man. At 5 o'clock the column began to move. The troops of the line stood to arms, and in breathless suspense gazed out into the bleak darkness in front, eager to catch the first sound when their champions should strike. The stars of heaven refused to shine, and the stillness of death settled down upon the dark valley which intervened between the lines, as this little band of devoted Confederates sallied forth with undaunted courage to encounter a foe five times their number, in a strong position well fortified, and the arena of a deadly yet unsuccessful combat of the day before.

Slowly and steadily, and with the most perfect order of alignment, the column advanced. When within 100 yards of the Federal breastworks we encountered a deep ditch, densely hedged on both sides with briars and thorns, into which, without hesitation, each and every man let himself down and crawled out on the other side and took his place in line. With but a moment's delay to adjust the lines and see that none stuck in the ditch, the advance was continued until the leading battalions were within thirty paces of the enemy's lines, when we were discovered and their vidette fired. We awaited not the murderous volley which we expected to crash through our ranks at this moment, but with all the energy of a desperate determination we sprang upon them. In the "blackness of darkness" as at midnight we throttled them in their stronghold, and the crest of McIlwaine Hill blazed with the flashes of a thousand muzzles spurting death. The fury of the struggle was but for a moment. We wrenched from their grasp the *eclat* of their dearly won victory of the preceding day, and hurled them reeling and bleeding from the summit back upon the main lines. The right battalion changed direction to the right upon the center, and the left battalion to the left, and swept the hill of every solitary blue coat—tooth and toe nail—from center to circumference; while the supporting battalions, as soon as unmasked, moved up and took position on the summit, and continued the fire upon the broken ranks of retreating Federals. The leading battalions, having cleared the hill for half a mile on either side, returned and formed upon the right and left of the other two, and squared themselves for a counter attack, should one be made.

At three several times during the day the enemy organized strong columns of assault and endeavored to retake the hill, but as many times were broken and driven back upon their main line before they got within two hundred yards of our position. We had been promised relief early in the morning, but none came; so we held the position against every assault and all odds, and without asssistance, save a few shots by one gun from the main line, until 9 o'clock the succeeding night, when other troops took our places and we retired to rest. The enemy lost heavily in killed, wounded and prisoners, and sued for a truce of three hours to bury their dead, which was granted; while the four battalions only lost ten or fifteen men all told. The storming of McIlwaine Hill was unquestionably one of the most daring and successful engagements of its dimensions ever witnessed upon any field during the great struggle, and our generals did not hesitate to so declare.

In the history of McGowan's brigade great credit is given by the author to the twelve pounder which assisted the sharpshooters in repelling the assaults made by the enemy to recover the hill after it was taken. Of course the shells fired by this gun did some good, but in comparison with the effect of the deadly aim of these trained riflemen, which punctured their courage as well as their carcasses at every step, was but as "a drop in the bucket" in this contest. We repudiate "the faint praise" accorded to the sharpshooters by Comrade Caldwell and appeal to the facts of history for our dues.

CHAPTER XIX.

LAST BATTLE OF HATCHER'S RUN.

"Firm paced and slow, a horrid front they form,
  Still as the breeze, but dreadful as the storm;
  Low murmuring sounds along their banners fly,
  Victory or death—the watchword and reply.
  Then pealed the notes, omnipotent to charm,
  And the loud tocsin tolled their last alarm."

The enemy made no further demonstrations in our front and we lay quietly resting all of the 28th and 29th, closely observing their movements and listening to the incessant roar of artillery in front of Petersburg.

The meteoric display of hostile mortar shells as they vaulted high over the lines, and with their blazing trains came crashing down into hostile ranks, gave us night scenes of rare excellence and beauty, but somehow or other we were not then in the mood to enjoy them. The last desperate effort was about to be made to overthrow our armies and destroy our government, and we felt that nothing short of the interposition of the Almighty could save us from the dreadful catastrophe; and we were not happy.

Late in the afternoon of the 29th orders were received at brigade headquarters to be ready to move at 10 o'clock that night. Accordingly about 10 o'clock the brigade moved out of their winter quarters and marched off rapidly to the westward along the Boydton plank road toward Hatcher's Run. The rain was pouring down and the roads were heavy with deep mud. We halted on this side of the Run and went into bivouac for the night. We built huge log fires and made ourselves as comfortable as possible. Early the next morning we crossed the Run at Burgis's Mill, and the brigade went into position on the White Oak road, with its left resting at or near a small redoubt on the hill and just beyond the forks of the road. The sharpshooters were ordered to the front and went into line about three hundred yards in front of the brigade. Our right occupied slightly rising ground near the outer edge of a pine thicket which had been felled in front of the brigade nearly out to our line, and formed into a formidable abatis; while the left, after passing a skirt of heavy timber which passed through our left center and terminated in a sharp point about a hundred yards in rear of the line, was drawn out on a plateau of comparatively open ground. The belt of timber where our line crossed was low and wet, and opened out in front into an impenetrable jungle, through which it was impossible to move an organized body of troops. To the right of the jungle and in front of our right there was an open field of about four hundred yards in width, whereas our left fronted on a dry flat covered thinly with small timber and underbrush. In the absence of the enemy the sharpshooters spent the day in active preparations for the impending conflict—adjusting our lines, digging rifle pits, etc.

The enemy appeared in our front late in the afternoon, but made no demonstration. Shortly after our line was established, and Brunson's company was withdrawn and assigned to duty in a different part of the field; and Capt. Parker, of the twelfth regiment, with a detail of 100 men reported for duty; whereupon, the remaining companies of sharpshooters were closed to the right, and the detail under Capt.

Parker placed in position on the left of the line; and we were ready.

Early on the morning of the 31st a heavy column of Federal infantry, in solid order of battle, was seen to be advancing on the east side of the marsh against our left. The ringing peel of Watson's rifles and the clatter of Parker's muskets announced the advance of the enemy, and we knew at once that the temper of our metal was again to be tested in the furnace of battle "seven times heated." Watson and Parker opened at long range the instant the movement began, and continued the fire with increasing vigor and effect until forced to retire before the superior weight of the assaulting column; which they did inch by inch, swinging back upon the center and assembling as they retired, until the entire left wing assumed a solid form in the skirt of timber before mentioned, and facing the left flank of the Federal line as it attempted to pass on to the attack of the main line. After a silence of a few minutes to allow the enemy to reach the point where we could strike them well in flank, the charge was sounded, a raking volley poured into their naked flank, and with the ominous cry of a rebel countercharge we rushed forward in full breast, struck and crushed their exposed left, and rolled it up in muddled confusion; then pressing our advantage with such irresistible energy, that the whole line gave way and fled the field in utter route, leaving their killed and wounded in regular windrows behind our rifle pits.

The detail under Capt. Parker behaved with marked gallantry and clung to their lines with such dogged pertinacity that for a few minutes a number of men fell into the hands of the enemy, Capt. Parker himself escaping by a feat of daring which but few men would have undertaken. All were recaptured, however, and our lines reoccupied.

In the afternoon of the same day the right wing was attacked in like manner by an overwhelming force on the west side of the jungle. This attack was met by Hasell's men with great gallantry. Receiving the charge with a galling fire, they yielded with vindictive obstinacy to the Federal column and swung back upon the center as they retired. The enemy pressed forward toward our breastworks until their right flank stood midair before the center of Hasell's line, now assembled in solid order of battle in the timber to the rear of our center. As in the attack upon the left, Hasell's men struck the enemy squarely in flank with a direct and converging fire that shriveled their ranks as the lightning blasts the tender foliage in early summer; then with a rousing cheer and a headlong charge, we swept the enemy from the field in inglorious defeat, and re-established our lines. The killed and wounded were left in rear of our lines and a number of prisoners fell into our hands. Between assaults the sharpshooters kept up almost a continuous fusilade upon the Federal lines in the distance, day and night; and killed many a Federal sharpshooter between the lines, even up to the very rim of our rifle pits, as they lurked in the bushes and crawled about to pick off our men. This gallant corps maintained their position against every assault and all odds, without assistance, to the end.

McGowan's brigade was not idle during these several eventful days; but with steadfast heroism met and defeated every assault made upon it, here and there, as it was shifted from one position to another on the lines. On the first day of April, assisted by Gracy's brigade of Johnston's division, it moved around the Federal left, struck and crushed the left wing of Warren's corps, drove the two divisions of Ayers and Crawford pellmell through the woods for more than a mile, and was only checked up when Miles's division of another corps reinforced Warren and was thrown against McGowan's flank. The brigade then fought its way back with comparatively slight loss; thus adding new lustre to the roll of its brilliant achievements.

On this first day of April, 1865, Gen. Grant, having massed the flower of his vast army against the Confederate right, with one last grand masterly effort overwhelmed Pickett and Fitzhugh Lee at Five Forks and put them to flight, and the succeeding night with another column broke through our lines in the neighborhood of Fort Gregg and Battery Forty-five; thus severing the two wings of the army the one from the other, and necessitating the giving up of both Petersburg and Richmond and the long lines of Confederate fortifications which had been our home for more than nine months. Here tons of powder, rivers of blood and millions of treasure had been wasted in the vain effort to break our lines. Here Grant's most furious onsets were made, and broke and fell flat, like the puny demonstration of human effort against the granite walls of destiny.

Our lines between Battery 45 and Hatcher's Run had been thinned out to a mere skirmish line, in order to meet the massive array of Union forces confronting the Confederate right beyond Hatcher's Run, when Sheridan with 10,000 cavalry and two full corps of infantry overwhelmed and crushed the divisions of Pickett and Fitzhugh Lee at Five Forks; immediately another Federal column broke through our lines at Jones's farm—their thinnest point—swept eastward and attacked forts Gregg and Anderson on Hill's left. A column of more than 5000 men closed upon these two little forts, which were occupied by small detachments—of perhaps equal numbers from Lane's North Carolina and Harris's Mississippi brigades—of some 250 men, with a few pieces of artillery to the fort; but the weight of the assault fell upon Fort Gregg. The little band of heroes stood to arms, raised a shout of defiance—that shrill slogan with which the Confederates were wont to utter their passion in battle—and with a withering blast of consuming fire swept their assailants back beyond the range of their rifles. Rallying, the enemy lengthened their lines in deeper curve, and on they came again. Again they are hurled back reeling and bleeding, leaving a large contribution to the fallen, which had dotted the ground on the first assault. To this point Fort Anderson had materially assisted in the heroic defense of Fort Gregg; but realizing the futility of further effort, the men abandoned its defense and retired to our main lines, leaving the little garrison of Fort Gregg with the "bag to hold."

The assault was again made, and repeated again and again with longer lines and increasing determination, until the little band of Spartan heroes was completely enveloped in a ring of Federal musketry, which poured into the fort a concentrated fire. Half the garrison had already fallen, but the survivors stood to their guns, and yelled and fired and fired and yelled, until their ammunition was exhausted. Then the Federals crowded upon the fort, scaled the walls and poured in upon the Confederates from all sides in overwhelming numbers, when a hand to hand struggle with bayonets and clubbed muskets ensued. Up and down, back and forth, like so many wounded tigers throttled in their lair, they wrestled with their assailants with the energy of despair. The Federals continued to pour into the fort until the enclosure became so packed that men could scarcely breathe, much less fight, when the little band of thirty survivors, overpowered and exhausted, yielded the contest and surrendered.

The artillerists did their part faithfully and well throughout the contest, and equaled in valor and effective service the best of the infantry. E. K. Culver, of Little Rock, is an honored survivor of that desperate encounter.

For the 220 killed and wounded and 30 captured Confederates, there lay in front and around Fort Gregg more than 500 Union soldiers killed and wounded.

But the time had come when this little band of dauntless heroes must yield to the inevitable and give way to the relentless blows of overwhelming numbers.

Gen. Lee drew in his lines closely around Petersburg, and successfully met and repelled every assault during the next day, then quietly withdrew after dark of the 2nd to the north side of the Appomattox, whence he took up the line of march to Amelia court house; whereas the troops of the right wing had withdrawn from the lines of Hatcher's Run and Five Forks early in the day.

The commandant of the sharpshooters was never officially notified of the disasters which had overtaken our arms in other parts of the field, nor of the purpose of the commanding general to withdraw from Petersburg and Richmond, but was left as a necessary and unsuspecting sacrifice to the safety of the army, while it made good its escape to the interior. Hence this gallant corps stood to arms in the breach, like a bristling hedge of burnished steel, between the victorious columns of Grant and Sheridan and the broken ranks of retreating Confederates—to cover the movement as long as might be, and when driven (if perchance any should escape capture) to hang upon the advance guard of pursuing Federals, to harass and detain as much as possible, while Gen.

Lee should fall back into the hills of Prince Edward or elsewhere, there to rally and concentrate his scattered forces and continue the struggle.

The sharpshooters therefore held their position on Hatcher's Run until the last Confederate regiment had filed out of the trenches west of Petersburg, when, at about 9 o'clock a. m. of April 2, 1865, they withdrew in good order to the breastworks, pursued by a heavy line of Federal infantry, and by a few well directed shots checked the pursuit. Then slowly retiring from the works, the sharpshooters covered the retreat back to Southerland Station on the South Side railroad.

Capt. Brunson reports the operations of his company on the lines of Hatcher's Run, after his withdrawal from the battalion, as follows: "I was piloted by Lieut. Caldwell of McGowan's staff to the extreme right of our works, which extended to Hatcher's Run, to recapture a skirmish line left vacant by Gen. Wise's brigade. Before getting over the works the order was countermanded, and I was instructed to hold the works instead. It was soon discovered that the space to be occupied and held was about three-quarters of a mile in length; and after covering as much ground as possible, I reported the situation and awaited further instructions. At daylight on the morning of the 31st my company was assembled at the works where the White Oak road passed through, when a company of Federal cavalry, mistaking us for their own men, rode up within twenty yards of where we stood. A single volley from my line unhorsed nearly the last man of them, and in a few minutes a number of my barefooted crowd were up to the knees in cavalry boots. I now received orders to move to the left and rear to guard a bridge on the Run, while the brigade crossed at the ford below. I had barely time to form for defense of the bridge when a large body of the enemy was discovered on the same side of the Run to the left and rear of my position, and I at once prepared to meet them. Fortunately just at this time I was ordered to rejoin the brigade, and hence retired. I had gone but a short distance, however, when I met Gen. McCombs, whose brigade had been overwhelmed and driven from the works to our left on the night before, and was in a demoralized condition;

and who requested assistance in restoring order in his brigade. I consented and deployed at once in front of his brigade, and between it and a body of Federal cavalry which could be distinctly seen in the pine thicket deploying for a charge. Gen. McCombs by this time was on the march, retreating. Without exposing the weakness of our force by moving into the open ground in front, we delivered a few volleys from the thicket with a rousing yell, which sent them flying in beautiful confusion into the timber behind them. We then fell back beyond Gen. Pickett's hospital, a sufficient distance to not endanger the sick and wounded, to an old apple orchard, and made a stand. Here, assisted by a piece of artillery posted on an eminence, we easily succeeded in repelling the enemy by another game of bluff. We made one or two other stands successfully before we reached Southerland Station, where we fought with McRae's brigade on the extreme right."

Capt. Brunson modestly forbears anything like a minute report of his operations on the lines of Hatcher's Run and Southerland Station; but, knowing his skill and daring as an officer, the character of men he commanded, and the exigencies of the service at the time, I am persuaded that the simple truth, definitely detailed, would constitute a chapter of thrilling adventure and achievement performed by his daring command, which would brighten the pages and increase the interest of these sketches.

CHAPTER XX.

SOUTHERLAND STATION, APPOMATTOX AND THE END.

"All that the mind would shrink from, of excesses;
  All that the body perpetrates of bad;
All that we read, hear, dream, of man's distresses;
  All that the devil would do, if run stark mad;
All that defies the worst which pen expresses
  All by which hell is peopled, or is sad
As hell—mere mortals who their power abuse—
  Was here (as heretofore and since) let loose."

When we reached Southerland Station we found McGowan's and two other brigades of the "light division" in position on a commanding ridge, further to protect the retreating army, and delay pursuit as much as possible. We had no orders and might have passed on and escaped the hazards of this stand; but appreciating the compliment paid the trustworthy valor of the brave Carolinians and their gallant leader, we disdained to pass our comrades by in this the hour of their greatest peril;

and hence took our position about 200 yards in front of the brigade. The line occupied by the brigade was in an open field, on the crest of the hill south of the South Side railroad, with the left resting on or near the Southerland church; the other brigades were formed to the right of McGowan. The position was somewhat strengthened by a slender line of earthworks, hastily constructed of fence rails and what earth could be dug up with bayonets and shoveled with the hands. The ground in front gradually declined into a low valley, which was covered with a dense growth of young pines, then rose again to a wooded hill of equal height beyond. A deep ravine, running out from the valley below, headed immediately in front and about the center of the brigade, across which the sharpshooters were formed. The enemy soon made their appearance on the opposite hill, and after a short artillery introduction, moved down into the valley and formed in the pines.

The sharpshooters opened fire at once. In a few minutes a heavy column emerged from the pines and moved up the ravine against McGowan's front. The sharpshooters continued their fire with spirit and effect as the Federals advanced—opening in the center and assembling on the flanks upon the high grounds on either side of the ravine, facing inward. When within easy range of the main line the brigade rose and delivered volley after volley into the face of the assailants, while the two wings of the sharpshooters closed upon each flank, driving home with fearful accuracy every discharge of their deadly rifles. The enemy hesitated, then broke and fled the field, pursued by the merciless sharpshooters and a perfect stream of lead from the brigade, which piled the ground with killed and wounded. The conflict was short, sharp and deadly.

In a little while, with heavier columns and greater energy, the assault was renewed at the same point and was met by the same men, with the same steadiness and determination. This time pressing up to the immediate front of the main line, the enemy fought with the desperation of veterans with minds made up to succeed. But they had met their match in this gallant little brigade, and when they saw their ranks writhing under the storm of lead which crashed through them from front and flank, and their men falling by scores and hundreds on every hand, they broke in wild confusion and yielded the field again to the Confederates, with a large number of prisoners, which the sharpshooters gathered up as they swept down the face of the hill in pursuit. I never saw finer fighting *anywhere* than was done by the three little brigades at Southerland Station. I stood upon a stump on the hill to the eastward of the Federal column where the left wing of sharpshooters were contending with the Federal right, and great tears of overwhelming admiration flowed down my cheeks in streams, as I contemplated the grand courage of that glorious little band of unfaltering heroes, fighting to the very death for a cause already lost. I could hardly stand it.

A third demonstration was made against our front, but amounted to but little. The enemy had become convinced that the position could not be carried by direct assault, and hence inaugurated a movement to turn our flanks. In order to counteract this movement as far as possible, the sharpshooters unmasked the brigade, dropped back to the top of the hill, and extended intervals away to the left. In overwhelming force the blue columns of the enemy were discovered advancing from all directions, and as some one has said, "O'er our embattled ranks the waves return and overwhelm our war." Our lines opened fire in full chorus at long range, and as the enemy closed upon us the vigor of our defense increased, until the entire line was enveloped in one living cloud of blue coats, whose muskets spurted fire and smoke and death, and here they came rolling up from the valley in front and along the hills on either flank; then, with one last, desperate, fruitless effort, the Confederates dashed the contents of their faithful rifles into the very teeth of their overpowering assailants, broke and fled the field, leaving our dead and wounded, with a number of prisoners, in their hands. A perfect bedlam ensued. Officers and men mixed together in wildest confusion, fled before the withering blasts of consuming fire which swept the hill, until the point of danger was passed, when they came together, were assorted out, formed into some sort of organization, and continued the retreat. Those who inclined westward made good their escape to the main army, while those who fled directly to the rear found themselves cut off by the roaring Appomattox.

The Federal commander now urged forward his deeply curved lines until each wing stuck hard and fast to the south bank of the river, whose surging waters rushing through her deep cut channels defy escape and complete the cordon which now enclosed these unfortunate Confederates. Worn out, overwhelmed, bagged, these proud spirited sons of the South accepted the only alternative, laid down their arms, and forever closed their connection with the Army of Northern Virginia, but not with the Lost Cause.

Three out of five of our regimental commanders, the commandant of the sharpshooters, and about the same proportion of line officers and men were captured either at Southerland Station or on the banks of the Appomattox, April 2 and 3, 1865.

Capt. Brunson reports that his company sharpshooters was the last on the right at Southerland Station to break. He fell back across the railroad, passing on a bridge over a deep cut, and made a stand. The enemy came rushing forward in pursuit, and when they crowded on the bridge he gave them a blizzard, and "feeling lonesome, departed." He soon overtook the brigade and such sharpshooters as had escaped, and they struggled and struggled along the south bank of the raging Appomattox the livelong night. Early on the morning of the 3rd they encountered "Deep Run," a tributary of the Appomattox, and attempted to construct a bridge across it. Before they had succeeded the cavalry pickets were charged and routed by the Federal cavalry and came rushing down to the stream in a perfect mob. To avoid capture, Gen. McGowan and his entire force plunged into the stream, swam across and escaped. Brunson was so exhausted when he crawled out on the opposite bank, that he was compelled to lie down and rest under a sharp fire from the Federal cavalry.

On the morning of the 4th, when they had reached the north bank of the Appomattox, the brigade fell in with a part of Longstreet's corps from Richmond, and halted and organized. Capt. Hasell here reported for duty and resumed command of what was left of his company. Capt. Watson was taken from the battalion—now but a skeleton of its former self—and assigned to duty on Gen. McGowan's staff, and Hasell and Brunson took charge of the sharpshooters.

"From this time forth," Brunson writes, "the army was but little more than a mob. We fought night and day without much system, surrounded by Yankee cavalry. The sharpshooters were ordered from one flank to the other, and from front to rear, as occasion required, until—Appomattox and the end;" adding, "The sharpshooters were deploying for another advance when the white flag was seen to meet Gen. Longstreet."

It is impossible to describe the anguish of the troops when it became known that the Army of Northern Virginia had been surrendered. Of all their trials this was the hardest to endure. There was no consciousness of shame; each heart could boast with honest pride that its duty had been done to the end, and that its honor remained unsullied still. When, after his interview with Gen. Grant, Gen. Lee again appeared, a shout of welcome instinctively ran through the army. But instantly recollecting the sad occasion that brought him before them, their shouts sank into silence, every hat was raised, and the bronzed faces of the thousands of grim warriors were bathed in tears. As he rode slowly along the lines, hundreds of his devoted veterans pressed around their noble chief, eager to take his hand, touch his person, or even lay their hands upon his horse; thus exhibiting for him their great affection. The general then, with head bare and tears flowing down his manly cheeks, bade adieu to the army in the following farewell order:

HEADQUARTERS
ARMY OF NORTHERN VIRGINIA.
April 9, 1865.

After four years of arduous service, marked by unsurpassed courage and fortitude, the Army of Northern Virginia has been compelled to yield to overwhelming numbers and resources. I need not tell the survivors of so many hard fought battles, who have remained steadfast to the end, that I consented to this result from no distrust of them; but, feeling that valor and devotion could accomplish nothing that would compensate for the loss that would have attended a continuance of the contest, I have determined to avoid the useless sacrifice of those whose past services have endeared them to their countrymen.

By the terms of agreement, officers and men will return to their homes and remain there until exchanged.

You will take with you the satisfaction that proceeds from the consciousness of duty faithfully performed; and I earnestly pray that a merciful God will extend to you His blessing and protection.

With an increasing admiration of your constancy and devotion to your country, and a grateful remembrance of your kind consideration of myself, I bid you an affectionate farewell.   R. E. LEE, General.

On the morning of the 12th day of April, 1865, the battalion of sharpshooters of McGowan's brigade laid down their arms, and in the afternoon of the same day marched through the Federal lines and took the road for their distant homes.

THE CONQUERED BANNER.

BY FATHER RYAN, THE POET PRIEST OF THE SOUTH.

Furl that banner! for 'tis weary,
Round its staff 'tis drooping dreary;
  Furl it, fold it, it is best:
For there's not a man to wave it,
And there's not a sword to save it,
And there's not one left to lave it
In the blood which heroes gave it,
And its foes now scorn and brave it—
  Furl it, hide it, let it rest.

Take that banner down! 'tis tattered,
Broken is its staff and shattered,
And the valiant hosts are scattered
  Over whom it floated high.
Oh! 'tis hard for us to fold it,
Hard to think there's none to hold it,
Hard that those who once unrolled it
  Now must furl it with a sigh.

The Forefront of Battle.

Furl that banner! furl it sadly—
Once ten thousands hailed it gladly,
And ten thousands wildly, madly,
    Swore it should forever wave;
Swore that foeman's sword could never
Hearts like theirs entwined dissever,
Till that flag would float forever
    O'er their freedom or their grave.

Furl it! for the hands that grasped it,
And the hearts that fondly clasped it,
    Cold and dead are lying low:
And the banner, it is trailing,
While around it sounds the wailing
    Of its people in their woe.
For, though conquered, they adore it,
Love the cold, dead hands that bore it,
Weep for those who fell before it,
Pardon those who trailed and tore it,
And—oh! wildly they deplore it—
    Now to furl and fold it so.

Furl that banner! true 'tis gory,
Yet 'tis wreathed around with glory,
And 'twill live in song and story,
    Though its folds are in the dust;
For its fame on brightest pages,
Penned by poets and by sages,
Shall go sounding down the ages,
    Furl its folds though now we must.
Furl that banner! softly, slowly,
Treat it gently—it is holy—
    For it droops above the dead;
Touch it not, unfold it never,
Let it droop there, furled forever,
    For its people's hopes are dead.

REPLY.

BY SIR HENRY HOUGHTON, BART., ENGLAND.

Gallant nation, failed by numbers!
Say not that your hopes are fled;
Keep that glorious flag which slumbers,
    One day to avenge your dead.
Keep it, widowed, sonless mothers!
Keep it, sisters, mourning brothers!
Furl it with an iron will;
Furl it now, but keep it still—
    Think not that its work is done.
Keep it till your children take it,
Once again to hail and make it
All their sires have bled and fought for;
All their noble hearts have sought for—
    Bled and fought for all alone.
All alone! aye, shame the story!
    Millions here deplore the stain;
Shame, alas! for England's glory,
    Freedom called and called in vain!
Furl that banner sadly, slowly,
Treat it gently, for 'tis holy;
Till that day—yes, furl it sadly;
Then once more unfurl it gladly—
    Conquered banner! keep it still.

CHAPTER XXI.

MUSTER ROLL OF THE BATTALION.

He who in such trying times does his duty faithfully
 and well
Is a hero indeed, be he high or low, great or small.

The following list of honored names *only*, can now be recalled from a complete roll of more than two hundred officers and men, which constituted the battalion of sharpshooters of McGowan's brigade. I seriously regret my inability to name the others—even after the lapse of thirty years.

N. Ingraham Hasell, captain first company, Charleston, S. C.

Wm. H. Brunson, captain second company, Edgefield Court House, S. C.

Charles E. Watson, captain third company, Greenville Court House, S. C.

Berry Benson, orderly sergeant first company, Augusta, Ga.

—— Dougherty, orderly sergeant second company, unknown.

M. A. Terrill, orderly sergeant third company, Westminster, S. C.

B. K. Benson, sergeant, Austin, Tex.

W. N. Bolding, sergeant, Prater, Pickens county, South Carolina.

—— Corley, sergeant, unknown.

W. L. Cunningham, sergeant, Madden's, S. C.

M. F. Hawthorn, sergeant, killed September 30, 1864, Petersburg, Va.

J. G. Love, sergeant, Wilkinsville, S. C.

David Moore, sergeant, Columbia, S. C.

R. M. Plexico, sergeant, Blacksburg, S. C.

Abner Stewart, sergeant, Pickens, S. C.

George W. Abbott, private, Weatherford, Tex.

William T. Abbott, private, died May 23, 1884, Weatherford, Tex.

J. B. Adams, private, died June 7, 1888, Lancaster, S. C.

Henson Alexander, private, killed at Southerland Station, Va.

—— Anson, private, unknown.

Gus Ashley, private, Abbeville, S. C.

—— Bedford, private, unknown.

Henry Belk, private, unknown.
Thomas Belk, private, unknown.
Andrew Bell, private, Walhalla, S. C.
George Bell, private, Walhalla, S. C.
Redding Bethea, private, killed at McIlwaine's Hill, Va.
—— Boals, private, unknown.
—— Bobo, private, unknown.
—— Burnett, private, unknown.
—— Bundricks, private, Lexington, S. C.
Oscar Bookman, private, killed August 25, 1864, Ream's Station, Va.
Millage Bartlett, private, killed at Petersburg, Va.
Samuel Carter, private, Rock Hill, S. C.
J. N. Carwile, private, Abbeville, S. C.
Oscar F. Chappel, private, Winsboro, S. C.
A. J. Clegg, private, unknown.
—— Coates, private, unknown.
—— Cohen, private, unknown.
Benjamin Cole, private, unknown.
David Cothran, private, unknown.
Henry Cook, private, Winsboro, S. C.
Lawrence Courtney, private, unknown.
John Crossland, private, unknown.
Samuel Crossland, private, unknown.

Kie Crenshaw, private, Walhalla, S. C.

Isaac Daily, private, Lexington county, South Carolina.

—— Dale, private, killed at Petersburg, Va.

Frank Day, private, Abbeville, S. C.

Thomas Davenport, drowned in June, 1865, off Cape Hatteras, North Carolina.

John Davenport, private, unknown.

J. W. Denton, private, scout, Craigsville, S. C.

—— Dix, private, unknown.

—— Dodges, private, unknown.

—— Duke, private, unknown.

John Elmore, private, died November 3, 1880, South Carolina.

R. J. Fields, private, Bryant, Ark.

John Fuller, private, unknown.

—— Fraser, private, unknown.

—— Gassett, private, unknown.

John Gambrell, private, Texas.

John Gilliam, private, unknown.

H. H. Gray, private, Anderson Court House, S. C.

Tillar Havard, private, unknown.

Luke Haynie, private, Anderson Court House, S. C.

Henry Haygood, private, died November, 1890, Florida.

Rufus Harling, private, Clark's Hill, S. C.

—— Hathcock, private, Columbia, S. C.

Elisha Hellams, private, last heard from in Illinois.

Crockett Henderson, private, Texas.

—— Hinson, private, unknown.

James W. Hood, private, unknown.

John E. Hurst, private, Bryant, Ark.

Simeon Hurst, private, died May, 1874, at Bryant, Ark.

James Hutchison, private, unknown.

Z T. James, private, died in 1898, Mississippi.

T. A. G. Jaynes, private, Jefferson, Tex.

John D. Kell, private, Blairsville, S. C.

B. E. Kell, private, Blackstock, S. C.

Wm. Kennedy, private, killed June 24, 1864, Petersburg, Va.

—— Kizer, private, unknown.

John Killgore, private, Abbeville, S. C.

Thos. J. Leak, private, killed May 6, 1864, Wilderness, Va.

John Land, private, Cartersville, S. C.

—— Lee, private, unknown.

Manning Lewis, private, killed March 25, 1865, Petersburg, Va.

John W. Martin, private, Brayles, S. C.

John T. Massey, private, died 1872, Ola, Yell county, Ark.

Henry J. McCormick, private, died October 31, 1892, Charleston, S. C.

Neill McInnis, private, Carolina Post Office, S. C.

John McCullough, private, killed at Spottsylvania Court House, Va.

W. T. McGill, private, Anderson Court House, S. C.

Jack McLaughlin, private, Abbeville, S. C.

Davis M. Miller, private, Abbeville, S. C.

Brit Medlin, private, killed at Chafin's Farm, Va.

William Mills, private, Seneca, S. C.

R. J. Moore, private, Columbia, S. C.

—— Norris, private, unknown.

J. Wesley Norton, private, Conway, S. C.

John Outz, private, killed at Petersburg, Va.

Warren Oxendine, private, killed May 21, 1864, at Spottsylvania Court House.

W. S. Pearson, private, Clinton, S. C.

Silas R. Perry, private, Gaston, Lexington county, S. C.

J. B. Porter, private, Union Court House, S. C.

C. W. Parish, private, killed June 24, 1864, Petersburg, Va.

Walter Pool, private, Kinard Post Office, S. C.

John Parrott, private, Kaughman, Edgefield county, S. C.

Benj. Powell, private, scout, Lancaster, S. C.

—— Powell, private, killed May 6, 1864, Wilderness, Va.

Elmore Price, private, unknown.

—— Putnam, private, unknown.

—— Rhodes, private, unknown.

L. K. Robertson, private, Parks Post Office, Ark.

—— Rogers, private, unknown.

Silas W. Ruff, private, Winsboro, S. C.

—— Russell, private, unknown.

R. S. Rutledge, private, Walhalla, S. C.

John Scott, private, Marion Court House, S. C.

—— Seigler, private, unknown.

James Sharpton, private, Clark's Hill, S. C.

Frank Sheely, private, drowned April 2, 1865, in Appomattox, Va.

Clark Short, private, killed at Petersburg, Va.

Thomas Simms, private, Rock Hill, S. C.

John C. Squier, private, Morganton, N. C.

William Staggs, private, unknown.

Jacob Swarts, private, unknown.

W. H. Smith, private, Pelzer Post Office, S. C.

Hiram Tinsley, private, Edgefield, S. C.

—— Thompson, private, unknown.

Wm. Vanderon, private, unknown

—— Vinson, private, unknown.

Press Watson, private, Texas.

Gus Walters, private, Greelyville, S. C.

Ed. Wallace, private, Hickory Grove, S. C.

James Williamson, private, killed in railroad wreck in 1892, at Florence, S. C.

Charlie Wilson, private, Lancaster Court House, South Carolina.

Sim Worts, private, Johnson, Edgefield county, South Carolina.

J. C. Whiteside, private, killed May 6, 1864, Wilderness, Va.

Robert W. Williams, private, Pelzer Post Office, South Carolina.

—— Williams, private, unknown.

James Wood, private, Jacksonville, Ark.

James D. Young, private, unknown.

Most of those whose whereabouts are marked unknown, and those whose names are omitted from the list, as well as those marked "killed" and "dead," long since

> "On fame's eternal camping ground
> Their silent tents have spread,
> Where glory guards with solemn sound
> The bivouac of the dead."

∗

After the foregoing roster of immortals—living and dead—the author closes the story of McGowan's sharpshooters, with the following rare bit of rehearshal, to be followed by a short sketch of his capture and prison life, and other sketches.

∗

Dreamily, dreamily, the years come and go, and slowly the old Confederate soldier counts them, as one by one they drop into the "invisible glass of time." He can almost see the grain drop that shall mark the point when time, to him, shall be no more. His comrades nearly all have "crossed the river and are resting under the shade of the trees."

The sound of the bugle, the tread of marching columns, "the pomp and circumstance of war," which mark the movement of modern armies, are mere suggestions of the mighty past, in which he and his comrades withstood for four inexorable years the combined armies and resources of the world. The spectral armies of the great Lee and Longstreet, Jackson and the Hills—aye, of Beauregard, Bragg, and the Johnstons—pass before him as terrible yet familiar phenomena of that greatest and most vicious of all national tragedies.

His heart beats time to the inspiring music, and the principles of the past for which he fought loom up before him, richer in memory and high admiration, yea, richer to the world in sacrifice and military achievement than any former struggle that ever graced the annals of war. The long gray lines of the past grow shorter and thinner as the years roll by. "Close up! close up!" is the language of each resounding clod that drops into the tomb of our departing comrades, inviting us to a closer union. It is no new sound to the Confederate veteran; he heard it amidst the "sulphurous siroc" of a hundred battles. It touched his nerves at Bethel and Bull Run; in the seven days struggle before Richmond, at Manassas, Sharpsburg, Fredericksburg and Chancellorsville; he heard it above the roar of more than two hundred thundering cannon at Gettysburg; again at the Wilderness, Spottsylvania, Hanover Junction, Atlee's Station and Cold Harbor; yea, at Petersburg, Ream's Station, Hatcher's Run and Five Forks; and, when rushing to the last death grapple at Appomattox, he heard it again and for the last time. It is a familiar sound to him, but the memory of it makes him sad and lonely, now that soon none will be left to "close up" the gaps, and none to cover the graves.

The battle scarred veteran who followed the Southern Cross under our great leaders in Virginia and Tennessee, Georgia and the Carolinas, as well as those in the trans-Mississippi and other subordinate departments, is beginning to feel that his day is done. That his deeds of valor and heroism at Oak Hills, Prairie Grove, Helena; at Shiloh, Chickamauga, Atlanta; at Cold Harbor, Gettysburg and Appomattox, are no longer objects of attention and admiration, now that the dapper soldiery of a mock struggle are flecking the earth with the hues of unused uniforms, unfurled flags and unfired guns, and monopolizing the attention of a thoughtless public, to the exclusion of these grizzly patriots who stood in the breach, staked all and lost all in the great conflict for Southern rights.

The embryo hero of the rifle range and rendezvous returns home on leave of absence and struts through town. The people gaze and admire. The city fathers go into executive session and devise ways and means to give eclat to the occasion and honor to their distinguished guest.

The old Confederate comes into town on his crutches, or with halting step and empty sleeve; and none deign to notice or regard the care worn, poverty stricken old hero, but pass by on the other side.

The young soldier, fretting under the restraints of army regulations, falls a victim to nostalgia, or dies of some other disease superinduced by ignorance or disregard of the laws of health. His remains are brought home under military escort, the community turns out en masse and crowds around his open grave to do him honor, and the newspapers commemorate the sad event in columns of fulsome obituary.

The old Confederate dies, after a hard struggle for existence, is laid to rest in the Confederate Cemetery, "unwept, unhonored and unsung."

He who for four years had borne upon his musket (that was burnished brighter by the battle's fury and the attrition of "merciless disaster") the fortunes of the Southern Confederacy, receives this parsimonious notice: " A. B——, an ex-Confederate veteran, died at the soldiers' home, at ——, and was buried in the Confederate Cemetery "—that was all.

Lee's veterans! Johnston's heroes! ex-Confederates all, think of it! Had you not better have died on the field of battle and been buried with your fellow comrades, having for your requiem the roar of battle and the shouts of victory, than to have lived to see the day when the living generations know you not, regard you not, but grudge even the time it takes to fill your graves with scanty dust? Sad reflections! painful realities!

Now I do not complain of the honor paid our dear young men of the South who patriotically entered the army to defend the honor of our flag on foreign soil; nay, I myself will never fail to do them honor. But I do contend for a fair distribution of honors to the dear old veterans of the Lost Cause, who not only stood for the honor of our flag, but had to feed and equip themselves largely from the enemy's stores, and even wrenched from them the very ordnance of war with which to expel them from our borders.

This little volume is designed to counteract, as far as possible, this tendency, and to "stir up your pure minds by way of remembrance," that you may appreciate the self denying services and patriotic deeds of these grand old heroes of the South.

To that end, I have endeavored to set forth in systematic detail the story of "Lee's Sharpshooters," as exemplified in the operations of a single battalion, which I had the honor to command.

This little band of two hundred veteran soldiers, who for twelve long and weary months stood in the "forefront of battle;" saw war and experienced war in all its horrors; who met on many a field, not only the Federal sharpshooters in equal numbers, but whole regiments and sometimes brigades and divisions in solid lines of battle, and met them successfully; and when the days grew darker and the cause more hopeless, dared even then to mass themselves against entrenched lines, pierce them like a lance, or shiver them like a thunderbolt, and drive them from the field. They bore the brunt of battle where danger was greatest and fighting fiercest; made a record and earned a fame worthy of eternal preservation in the annals of our struggle. They saw the conflict and carnage of battle as no general saw it, and as no historian did who was not in the line; and therefore they, and such as they, who pulled the trigger and drove the bayonet must at last give the true story of every battle. They watched the "ebb and flow of the crimson tide," and rallying upon the hard pressed line, hurled themselves against the opposing column, and wrung victory from impending defeat.

They fought for principle and not for pay—for home rule, local self government, constitutional liberty—against agression, paternalism and Federal domination. And while their cause went down under the "arbitrament of the sword," no court of justice or equity has ever adjudicated against their claims. They were grand soldiers, and they were right.

Notice what Swinton, the Northern historian, says of them: "Nor can there fail to arise the image of that other army, that was the adversary of the Army of the Potomac, and which who can forget that once looked upon it? That army of tattered uniforms and bright muskets; that body of incomparable infantry, the Army of Northern Virginia, which for four years carried the revolt on its bayonets, opposing a constant front to the mighty concentration of power brought against it; which receiving terrible blows, did not fail to give the like; and which, vital in all its parts, died only with its annihilation."

And again, in another place and on another occasion, he says: "That incomparable Southern infantry, which tempered for two years in battle and accustomed to victory, equalled any soldiers that ever followed the eagles to conquest."

Out of such material as this Lee's sharpshooters were selected and organized, and were the *creme de la creme* of that "incomparable

Southern infantry"—the refinement of perfection in all soldierly qualities.

And now, my dear old comrades of the sharpshooters, I have given as best I could the story of your heroic deeds. I have gone again with you through the battle's red glare; have heard again the sharp crack of your rifles; have seen you scale the enemy's high entrenchments and drive back twice, thrice, yea, five times your numbers; have seen you strike at the dead hours of midnight, break and sweep out the Federal advance lines for miles, capturing hundreds of prisoners, without losing a man. Your martial tread, your soldierly bearing, your devotion to duty, your uncomplaining sacrifice, and your matchless courage, have all passed in review before me. Your headlong charges and shouts of triumph ring again in my ears, as I drop my pen, close my eyes and call up in memory your many deeds of personal daring as well as your splendid achievements in combined action. I tramp again with you along the valleys and over the hills of Virginia, and in a short retrospect see you in your respective original commands plunge into the blue, rolling Potomac, and in water to your waists keep step to the inspiring strains of "Dixie Land." I see your good conduct as you march through the "promised land," and witness your high courage as you scale the rugged heights of Gettysburg. I return with you again to dear old Virginia, and on the banks of the Rapidan bind up our wounds and prepare for more determined and more deadly work.

Here I notice your organization, your movements in drill, rifle training and splendid equipment for the coming struggle. I then follow you through the Wilderness, Spottsylvania, Hanover Junction, Atlee's Station, Cold Harbor, Riddle's Shops, Deep Bottom, Fussell's Mill, Petersburg, Ream's Station, Jones's Farm, Jarrett's Station, McIlwaine's Hill, Hatcher's Run, Southerland Station, and then again in the last sad scene of Appomattox. Then all were before me. But when I opened my eyes and the sad realities of the present confronted me, where, oh! where are the members of that gallant band? Echo answers, where? Scores lie scattered along the track of that matchless campaign from the Wilderness to Appomattox, their bodies sleeping in unmarked graves, or their bones bleaching and crumbling into dust again, there to await the sounding of the last trump, when the dead shall come forth to their final and everlasting reward. The survivors scattered here and there throughout the land for which they fought—no longer side by side in the struggle for existence, which to some of us has been more lasting and just as fierce as that terrible conflict of which we write.

Soon the last one will be left standing alone, facing the celestial army of patriots gone before. The last gap he must close, and then like a bird for whose feet the sands have become too warm, he will spread his wings and soar away to join our comrades who await our coming in the land beyond the skies.

I have registered as best I could your martial exploits, your chivalrous deeds. But no peer of man could properly portray your splendid qualities and high achievements as Confederate soldiers. You were overwhelmed, not conquered, and yielding to the demands of inevitable necessity, laid down your arms and returned to your homes "with the consciousness of duty well performed." And doubtless the recording angel above, under the touch of your great leaders, will give you at last a richer and far more enduring victory than earth could give. Peace to the ashes of our fellow comrades! We may not fire a soldier's salute over your dust, but the pulses of our hearts beat like muffled drums, and every deep drawn sigh breathes a low and passionate requiem. Earth venerate your memories and history preserve the record of your noble deeds. Heaven bless the living, and crown your declining years with comfort and peace; and may God's abundant mercy and the benedictions of his grace abide with you both now and forever more.

Heroes of the lost cause! Champions of constitutional rights! Martyrs for regulated liberty! Faithful, dauntless soldiers! Dear old comrades of the sharpshooters! Farewell!

> "Enough of valor had each honored name
> To shine untarnished on the rolls of fame,
> And add new lustre to the historic page."

CHAPTER XXII.

MRS. DUNLOP AND MYSELF BOTH CAPTIVES.

Mrs. Dunlop, my young and faithful wife, arrived in Petersburg from South Carolina at 8:30 p. m. February 13, 1865, on a visit, and took rooms beneath the hospitable roof of Prof. Charles Campbell, superintendent of public schools of the city. Prof. Campbell was a Virginia gentleman of the old school, of genial manners, broad culture, and pure and lofty patriotism; and his good lady, though of Northern birth and education, was intensely Southern in all her views and feelings—a fitting counterpart of such a character. Their two young daughters and little son added no little to the attractiveness of this charming home.

The paralyzing effects of the siege and the depreciated value of the Confederate currency had reduced them from a condition of ease and abundance to that of almost absolute penury and want; hence, the arrival of Mrs. Dunlop, with her large stock of supplies, was received as a godsend, and gratefully attributed to the direct interposition of Providence for their relief. For it will be remembered that we formed a sort of joint stock company, by the terms of which each family was to contribute to the common fund according to ability, regardless of numbers or relative obligations, and with no thought of anything like an accurate accounting of expenditures or adjustment of dividends. The congeniality of our religious faith, a common cause, and the fellowship of suffering, at once united all hearts, and we became one harmonious and delightful family association.

The constant clatter of musketry along the lines and the perpetual roar of hostile guns—at first so shocking to the nervous structure of the delicate ladies—soon became as monotonous as the melody of an old song, and fell upon their ears like the story of one's own exploits—worn threadbare.

Day after day the Federal commander lengthened his lines and strengthened his stakes about the beleaguered city. The disasters which had overtaken the Southern standards in other parts of the field naturally resulted in the concentration of forces around the Confederate capital; and although Gen. Lee held his ground and never failed to deliver his adversary a blow at every opportunity, yet in the intervals of rest he felt more and more sensibly the grip of the anaconda as he tightened his coils around him and his little band of Confederates. The clouds were gathering and the ominous mutterings of the impending storm were heard and felt as sensibly in the ranks as in official circles. Men gathered in groups and discussed the situation, but determined to stand to their colors to the bitter end.

The visiting ladies were advised to pack their baggage and escape to the interior, or return to their homes in South Carolina, without delay. Charles, my faithful body servant, was therefore ordered to get his mistress ready for the morning train of March 29th. For some reason the omnibus failed to call by and the madam failed to get off; and this was the last train out of Petersburg until some time after Lee's surrender. Majors Wardlaw and Hammond, our brigade quartermaster and commissary, however, sent an ambulance Sunday morning, April 2d, and had the ladies and their trunks conveyed across the river; put them on the train and sent them to Richmond, where they arrived, with about 500 wounded, at midnight of the 2d of April, ready for the next morning's train, southbound. Mrs. Brailsford, of the company, the young wife of Maj. E. D. Brailsford, of the first South Carolina regiment, kindly invited Mrs. Dr. Huot and Mrs. Dunlop to her father's house for the remainder of the night, which invitation was gratefully accepted, and the ladies were soon sheltered in the hospitable home of Mr. —— Hill of Richmond. But President Davis and cabinet had vacated the capital and boarded the last southbound train early in the morning, and the rear guard of Longstreet's corps was filing through the streets in full retreat to the mountains. Immediately after the passage of the troops to the south side of the James, the bridges were blown up with an explosion that shook the staid old city to its foundations; from the effects of which, or other cause, the city was set on fire in a number of places. Owing to the paralyzed condition of the population, the fire fiend swept away many buildings and a large amount of valuable property before an adequate force could be organized to resist the progress of destruction. The flames were at length brought under control and finally extinguished, and thus the city was saved.

The ladies being cut off from their line of retreat, were therefore forced to accept the generous hospitality of Mr. Hill and his excellent family for a period of some ten days or two weeks. When the city had become somewhat quiet, the ladies—Mrs. Dr. Huot and Mrs. Dunlop—appealed to Gen. Mumford, who kindly furnished them transportation and other substantial aid, which enabled them to return to Petersburg, which they did by way of the James river and City Point railroad.

They reached Petersburg about midnight of the 17th of April, and were received with tears of joy into open arms by Prof. Campbell and his dear family. They had passed through many dangers and had had a number of thrilling adventures since their exit from Petersburg, but had incurred no loss or damage to person or property, save and except the taking of a disabled sabre from Mrs. Dunlop's trunk, where-it had been strapped for safekeeping, and which was held in high esteem by its owner, the commandant of the sharpshooters, on account of its valuable services and the severe wound which it had received on the 29th of August, 1862, in the second battle of Manassas.

It was ascertained, upon inquiry, that Dr. Huot had been placed in charge of a Confederate hospital in the city, and was safe. Hence he and his accomplished young wife were soon happily re-united in their former winter home. Mrs. Dunlop also learned that her husband had been captured at Southerland Station, ten miles west of Petersburg, and had passed through the city unhurt on his way to some Northern prison. Assured now of his safety, as far as the dangers of the battle field were concerned, Mrs. Dunlop set about to discover his destination, that she might cheer him in his lonely confinement with tokens of her sympathy and abiding affection. She wrote to every Federal prison that she could hear of, but for weeks could evoke no response. This ominous silence led to renewed apprehensions of distress, and so she sought a personal interview with the commissary general of prisoners, that she might enlist his sympathy and official aid in her search for the lost one, both of which were readily accorded. The general was true to his word, for the letter delivered to him that afternoon was received on Johnson's Island in the very shortest possible time required to compass the distance; and not only so, but all her letters were promptly forwarded from the different prisons, and were joyfully received in a very few days.

The purpose and failure to take the last train out of Petersburg, and the subsequent purpose and failure to take the last train out of Richmond, had disconcerted all our plans; so that, while Mrs. Dunlop's letters were wandering about over the country in search of her lost husband, he was writing regularly to South Carolina, supposing that, according to the second plan, the ladies had made good their escape to their Carolina homes. But Sherman's march through the Carolinas had disrupted all lines of postal communication in that direction, hence my letters did not reach their destination until the railroads were rebuilt and Mrs. Dunlop had reached home, some time about the middle of June. Meanwhile she was in an agony of suspense.

Upon her return from Richmond to Petersburg, Mrs. Dunlop found that Charles, who had been playing the role of courier between herself in the city and myself on the lines of Hatcher's Run, had been captured on his last trip, and had just made his escape and returned to Petersburg a few days before her arrival. He at once engaged to work in the gardens and truck patches in the city for wages, and loyal to the last, turned over to his mistress a good part of his earnings every night, which he continued to do until the railroads began to operate, when he put her on the train and saw her safe at home in South Carolina.

When our lines were formed at Southerland Station, the sharpshooters were instructed that, when they were driven—which was inevitable—to make clean heels for the rear and incline westward as much as possible—the direction the army had gone; as for myself, I should make directly for the rear, swim the Appomattox and rejoin them on the north bank.

As many as obeyed instructions made good their escape, while those who disregarded instructions and followed the example of their commander were hemmed in on the banks of the roaring Appomattox and captured the next day. The river was too full and turbulent to swim. Only one man, Frank Sheely, tried it and he found a watery grave ere he reached the middle of the stream. We put a vidette on the hills to watch, while we set about to construct a raft on which to ferry ourselves across to the other shore. We impressed into service a number of negroes, who were cutting wood for the city, with their axes, and had gotten our work fairly under way, when the videttes ran in and reported the Federal cavalry approaching. We dispersed in amusing haste and concealed ourselves in a dense thicket of switch cane and underbrush along the banks of the river; where, once hidden, we were afraid to show our heads above the cane, lest our hiding place might be discovered and ourselves made prisoners. Hence, we remained in the thicket, as quiet as mice, until after dark, when search began for some friendly craft to convey ourselves to the opposite shore. First up and then down the rushing river, we peered into every nook and corner of her rugged banks for some means of escape, but nothing could be found. We then took the Federal lines which were drawn around us and industriously scrutinized every inch from the river below to the river above, hoping to find a gap, but the lines were solid and the circle complete. This search was continued until daylight, when we again hid ourselves in a dense cedar brake. All our efforts to evade capture proved fruitless. So about 9 o'clock a. m., April 3, 1865, a heavy skirmish line combed out the fatal *cul de sac* and took us in. I surrendered my sword to an officer of the twenty-sixth Michigan regiment, United States infantry. We were treated with marked courtesy by our captors, and were marched off with the Federal column, under guard. After marching in rear of Grant's army for several days we were returned, several hundred strong, to Petersburg; thence to City Point; thence by steamer to the old capitol prison, Washington, D. C.; thence, after a delay of some ten days, to Johnson's Island, Ohio. We reached Washington City on the 10th, and thirty Confederate officers were crowded into room No. 16, on the third floor of the old capitol building—a room about

18 x 18 feet square, without the least semblance of furniture—a gaunt and forlorn looking, yet a jolly and spirited crowd. The next day we heard of the surrender of the Army of Northern Virginia, but refused to believe it until the report was confirmed.

The regulations of the prison were: Roll call at 8 o'clock in the morning; breakfast at 9 o'clock; dinner at 3 o'clock in the afternoon; roll call again at 7 o'clock p. m.; no supper, and lights out at 9 o'clock—two meals a day on scant rations. We spent the time in smoking our pipes, washing clothes and discussing the cause and results of the war, the conditions of the country, and the methods and consequences of reconstruction likely to follow.

On the 13th of April, the fourth anniversary of the fall of Fort Sumpter, the American flag was formally rehoisted in triumph with appropriate ceremonies, upon the battered ramparts of that historic old castle, and the occasion celebrated at the Federal capital by the grandest convocation of citizens ever held in the city of Washington. Men and women of all grades of human society, and almost every nationality, participated in the grand demonstration. Military parades, music and oratorical harangues were the order of the day; while at night, amid the blaze of the finest pyrotechnic display ever witnessed on the continent, the assembled thousands vied together in unrestrained manifestations of joy and exultation over the triumphs of their armies, the prospects of peace and a reunited country. With stolid indifference we heard and beheld, nor felt the faintest emotions of pleasure, even while gazing out upon a gorgeous panorama of almost dazzling brilliancy.

On the night of the 14th, Abraham Lincoln, President of the United States, was assassinated, and the nation's joy was turned into mourning. John Wilkes Booth, of Virginia, was the assassin. Intense excitement prevailed for several days, and no Confederate soldier, or even friend of the South, would have been safe on the streets of Washington during this period. Indeed, so shocking was the crime against enlightened humanity, and so stunning the blow to public conscience, that the spirit of revenge clamored for blood; and but for the interposition of military authority every prisoner confined in the old capitol building would have been murdered in retaliation. A large mob of infuriated citizens was organized for that purpose, and was only restrained by a strong guard placed within the halls and corridors of the building, and a perfect wall of United States bayonets stationed around the square.

On the 15th the decapitated nation, in one immense throng, assembled at the capital, and increased from day to day while the body lay in state, to pay their last respects to the distinguished dead. From the windows of room No. 16, which commanded full view of Capitol Square, we could distinctly see the ceaseless stream of sorrowing citizens as they crowded through the capitol building to take one last sad view at the remains of the murdered President. As far as the eye could reach the city was clad in the habiliments of mourning. A sad day to the people of this country, and especially so for the unfortunate citizens of the South.

When the excitement had sufficiently abated, and it was considered safe to remove the prisoners, rolls were made out and we were marched down to the Baltimore depot and took the train for Johnson's Island. After a tedious and tiresome trip of several days, passing through Baltimore, Harrisburg, Pittsburg, Mansfield and Sandusky, we reached our prison home on the 27th day of April. We were discharged from the trains at Sandusky and immediately boarded a steamer for Johnson's Island, where we arrived in a somewhat dilapidated condition the same afternoon. After examination and enrollment we were dispossessed of everything valuable or contraband of war, and marched through the great prison gate into the courts of the vast enclosure, where we were assigned to quarters in different parts of the prison. Myself and Lieut. James A. Watson, of the twelfth South Carolina regiment, were assigned to room No. 13, block No. 7, south side of the street and second floor of the building. Here we made ourselves as comfortable as circumstances would permit. We were received by our comrades who had preceded us with great cordiality, and were joyfully welcomed to the freedom and hospitality of that noted prison (whose commissariat and latchstrings were always on the outside), not that they took pleasure in our misfortunes, but because of our common cause and fellowship of suffering, and they loved us.

The prison on Johnson's Island was located safely above the water line on the south side of the island, at the nearest point to the city of Sandusky, about three or four miles distant, across an arm of the beautiful Lake Erie, and covered an area of ten acres, laid off in the form of an oblong square, running east and west. It was enclosed by a solid wall of heavy timber, twelve feet high, about three and a half or four feet below the top of which, on the outside, were constructed the platform and sentry boxes where our sleepless guardians were wont to stand or pace their weary rounds, day and night, to hold us harmless and secure until by official authority our liberties should be restored. Two lines of two story, oblong boxed buildings, with double rooms above and below, about 16 x 22 feet square, with ten foot walls, constituted our quarters. These barracks were built on either side of a broad street, some two hundred feet in width, running lengthwise through the center of the enclosure, and facing inward. The entrance to the rooms below was by a single door to each room, located in front, near the corner, and on either side of the partition which divided the rooms ; the rooms above were reached by a stairway and balcony built on the outside of the front wall, with doors of entrance similarly situated to those below.

Beginning at the great gate, the blocks and rooms were regularly numbered, 1, 2, 3, 4, etc., the odd numbers on the south side and the even numbers on the north side of the street. There were six blocks on either side of the street, and one block (No. 13) in the center of the street at the east end, facing the great gate at the west end. The kitchens and mess halls were in rear of the barracks, and the sinks and closets in rear of these buildings; one of the mess halls on the north side being used for a hospital for the sick. Back of all the buildings, and some twenty or thirty feet from the prison walls, were the dungeon and dead lines, beyond which no prisoner was allowed to pass. In addition to the chain of sentinels which girded the balustrade, and as further security against insolence or insubordination on the part of the Confederates, a single 12-pound smooth bore was mounted on the front wall near the prison gate, charged with grape and canister, and trained upon the broad street so as to rake it from end to end in the event of any formidable disturbance.

The garrison and officers' quarters were on an elevated plateau of beautiful grounds, a hundred yards or more west and northwest of the front gate, where there was also stationed a full battery of artillery, frowning down upon us with gaping muzzles, ready to demolish the prison and all it contained should there occur anything like a conspiracy or rebellion against the restraints of Federal authority. But, as Gen. Toombs said to Senator Morton, "we had worn ourselves out whipping Yankees," therefore did not care to have any further trouble with them, and hence behaved ourselves like pretty boys. Johnson's Island was specifically designed and set apart for the accommodation of Confederate officers, of whom there were at this time something like three thousand here confined, ranging all the way from major general down to junior second lieutenant. They were to a large extent educated, intelligent, grave and dignified, and for the most part behaved themselves with the utmost propriety and decorum. Our rations were painfully scant, and but for the acute gnawings of hunger we would have been reasonably comfortable.

Col. Hill, commandant of the garrison, was a clever gentleman and good friend to the prisoners, all of whom esteemed him very highly for his kindness of heart and other excellencies of character. He always manifested due regard for our comfort and protection as well as for our good behavior and safe keeping. He frequently entered the pen in person to inquire into our condition, and occasionally addressed the prisoners on questions of moment relating to themselves, such as the adjustment of war issues, the restoration of peace and good will between the divided sections, etc. He invariably received a cordial welcome, and his speeches were well attended and heartily enjoyed by all.

When it became known that Congress was considering a bill of amnesty for the liberation of prisoners, which involved many questions of important detail requiring time and careful consideration, the necessary delay caused much anxiety and impatience on the part of many of the inmates of Johnson's Island. Others, however, made the best of the situation by jests and merrymaking, to the annoyance of our less buoyant comrades. Day after day, for weeks, these lovers of fun played upon the credulity of their home sick associates, by publishing bogus dispatches on the bulletin board relating to their discharge. The bill was finally passed about the last of May, and President Johnson's amnesty proclamation was promulgated immediately.

Hence, about the 1st of June, beginning with the oldest captures, the discharge of prisoners began, and was continued from day to day as rapidly as rolls could be made out and transportation furnished, until all were set free.

I passed out at the great gate with a class of something over two hundred, about 7 o'clock a. m., June 18, 1865, henceforth a free citizen of the United States. By 8 o'clock we were in Sandusky, where all trains leading out of the city were utilized in the transportation of prisoners, and where, by distribution, we took different routes for our Southern homes. Myself and a goodly number of others took the train for Cleveland, thence to Pittsburg, thence to Harrisburg—where further distribution was made—and thence to New York, where we arrived about 10 o'clock on the morning of the 21st. When discharged from Johnson's Island we were furnished with free transportation and (only) one day's rations. With this scant supply we anticipated distress from hunger ere we should reach the half way point to our distant homes. But thanks to a kind Providence, who put it into the hearts of very many good people of the North to supply all our needs abundantly, we had no occasion whatever to use our one day's rations of hard tack and bacon.

The courtesy and kindness extended to us all the way from Sandusky to New York were as amazing to us as they were grateful to our feelings, and reminded us more of the treatment due a victorious army returning from the conquests of a formidable foe than of a remnant of defeated Confederates released from captivity and returning to their homes under grace and amnesty of their victors. The instant we landed in New York I hurried to the transportation office, that I might secure passage without delay to South Carolina. A gentleman whom I had seen on the train, a resident of the city, and whose dainty appearance for some reason I did not fancy, proposed to accompany and assist me in my purpose. His proposition repeated, was twice declined but accepted the third time. Under his guidance I was presently ushered into a large brick building and into the very presence of the chief of the department. My good friend now assumed the role of advocate, and presented my request for transportation on the first steamer southbound, which was promptly denied upon the ground of inconvenience and delay; the officer stating that there were hundreds of released Confederates in the city awaiting transportation to the South Atlantic states; that he could not issue a *single* pass, when the same time and work would set forward on their homeward journey hundreds from the same section; and that I would have to await the enrollment of an entire class. This failure did not in the least disconcert my friend, who said as we passed out of the office, "Come, walk into the next office and let us see what can be done with the first deputy." Our request was again presented and urged, this time receiving more favorable consideration. The deputy, however, honestly but kindly detailed the difficulties to be overcome, while my friend recounted the premises of our plea and enforced the facts with such skill and power, that had we been in a court of final resort our prayer would have been granted *sine conditiones*. But the signature of the chief was absolutely necessary, and upon this alone our success depended.

We retired from the office with the assurance that everything that could would be done for our relief, and we were requested to call again at 1 o'clock, when we should know the result. At the door a carriage was called, and we entered. For two hours we drove about the city, taking in the more salient points and beholding the sights of this wonderful metropolis, meanwhile enjoying a good luncheon at a fashionable restaurant, donning a new suit of clothes and replenishing our exchequer with a small roll of United States currency—all at the expense of our advocate and friend, who was urging us all the while to remain over in the city for some time and rest up, at his expense; which, of course, I gratefully declined. At 1 o'clock we returned to the office, and sure enough our transportation was ready, and we had nothing to do but board the steamer for Dixie, which was billed to sail at 4 o'clock that afternoon. By 3 o'clock we were aboard the rolling Clyde, which lay at the wharf making preparations for the voyage. My unnamed friend was still with me, and introduced me to the officers of the steamer and bespoke for me a good birth and the courtesies of the ship, which were accorded. I was also introduced to a number of citizens who had come down to see the rebels embark. Among others I met H. P. Clark, who resided in Brooklyn but did business in New York. Mr. Clark proved a friend indeed, showing marked courtesy and offering further financial assistance, which I declined with thanks. He gave me his autograph, on request, which I still have, and cherish for the pleasant recollections associated with his name. I also requested the autograph of my anonymous friend, but he declined, stating that my desire was a mere matter of sentiment and would soon pass away, as would the memory of the fact and circumstances of our meeting, but if I wanted a sermon preached or marriage solemnized he was at my service. I then requested his influence on behalf of my comrades, numbers of whom I had seen in the city awaiting transportation, to which he readily consented, and we bade each other farewell. In a very short time here came about four hundred Confederates from Carolina, Georgia and Florida, numbers of whom were of my acquaintance and some of my own command. Greetings and congratulations were now in order, and we spent a few hours in a most delightful reunion on the decks of the stately Clyde. The Clyde was a heavy and somewhat clumsy but seaworthy craft, single decked, with a small block of state rooms, narrow cabin, store room and kitchen for the accommodation of her officers and crew, and an immense hold, in which the Confederates were quartered, with the privileges of the deck during the day. I was comfortably quartered in a reasonably well furnished state room, with free access to the cabin and all its appointments.

After some delay we weighed anchor, unthrottled the engines and set sail for Dixie Land. We spent a comfortable night and rose early to note progress and take bearings. We found that we had cleared the harbor and, under full head of steam, were bounding along over the heaving bosom of the broad Atlantic. After breakfast the men were called together for the purpose of organization, that order and discipline might be maintained, rations distributed, etc. I was unanimously elected commander of the four hundred, and proceeded at once to perfect the organization by the appointment of quartermaster, commissary and other necessary staff assistants. At the outset the officers and crew were somewhat disposed to exercise authority over the Confederates, but they were very soon given to understand that twenty-five Yankees, upon the high seas, and separated from the protection of their government, could not control four hundred Confederate veterans, and that orders and commands issuing from any other source than their own chosen commander would be regarded as insolence and treated as such. Hence, thereafter the issuance of orders and the administration of discipline were given into my hands, and I became commander-in-chief of the entire expedition thence to Savannah, Georgia. We were eight days on " the dark, blue sea," skirting our eastern coast, sometimes in and sometimes out of sight of land, and enjoyed the trip intensely. As we rounded Cape Hatteras, off the coast of North Carolina, we encountered a gale on the night of the 25th, resulting in a turbulent sea, in which considerable apprehension was felt on the part of some of our men for their safety.

Many of us slept soundly, however, all night and knew nothing of the storm until morning, when we awoke to find the ship rolling and plunging in a boisterous sea. The storm had passed and the sun rose in unclouded splendor; but Old Ocean was furious still, to have had her repose between suns so ruthlessly disturbed by a miserable night squall. After awhile her wrath abated and she sank back into her wonted complacency. Reveille was sounded and the men summoned to roll call. The sergeants reported "all present or accounted for," except one who could not be found. It was then discovered, and not till then, that Thomas Davenport, one of my most gallant and esteemed sharpshooters, had been lifted from the deck, where he slept, by one of those immense waves which swept over the ship, and dashed into the depths of the sea. Poor, brave fellow! he had escaped the dangers of a hundred bloody battle fields to find a watery grave, where his body now sleeps and shall continue to sleep until summoned to roll call on resurrection morn in the courts of glory. We passed in distant view of Fort Sumpter on the 28th, and reached Savannah, Georgia, on the 29th. Here all were discharged except the South Carolina boys, who after a detention of one day and two nights, returned to Charleston via Hilton Head, where we arrived on the 1st day of July. We spent the night with friends in the city, took the train next morning for Orangeburg; thence marched twenty-five miles to Columbia; thence marched thirty-five miles to White Oak Station, ten miles above Winsboro; thence by rail to Rock Hill, my South Carolina home, where I met in tears of joy, among other rejoicing friends, my own darling wife. Amen.

CHAPTER XXIII.

PROMISCUOUS ANECDOTES, ETC.

ROLL CALL.

The orderly sergeant was calling the roll. "Jehoshaphat Jenkins!" "Here!" promptly responded Jehoshaphat. "George Squib!" "Here!" in a firm voice responded the heroic Squib. "Ebenezer Meade!" No answer. "Ebenezer Meade, what do you mean by standing there staring me in the face, and not answering when your name is called?" said the sergeant impatiently. "You didn't call my name," gruffly answered the private. "Isn't your name Ebenezer Meade?" "Nary time." "What is it then?" "Eben Meade." "What's the difference?" "A heap." "I can't see any." "Now, sergeant, your name is Peter Wright; isn't it?" "Yes." "Well, would you answer to the name of Peternezer Wright?" "Of course not." A laugh from the company, and after roll call a mutual smile between Eben and Peter, at the latter's expense, settled the matter in a manner satisfactory to all concerned.

THREE DAYS WITH NOTHING TO EAT.

Said a hungry Confederate to the lady who met him at the door, when out foraging one day: "Madam, will you please give me something to eat? I haven't had a mouthful to eat for three days—today, tomorrow and next day."

FOUR YEARS TO REACH RICHMOND.

City Point, on the James river, was the landing for transports with soldiers released from Northern prisons on parole. One day a most woebegone and emaciated "Johnny" sat swinging his shoeless feet from a barrel, awaiting his turn, when a pompous Federal major remarked, to no one in particular, "It isn't far to Richmond?" "Reck'n it's near unto three thousand miles," drawled Johnny, weakly. "Nonsense! you must be crazy!" replied the officer, staring. "Wal, I ent a-recknin' edzact," was the slow reply; "jest thought so, kinder." "Oh, you did! and why, pray?" "'Cause it took'n youens nigh onto four years to git thar from Washington," was the settled retort.

NEGRO FOR BREASTWORKS.

Said a Federal soldier the other day: "A Johnny Reb got away with me entirely one day after we captured him at Resaca. He said to me that they had found out how to fight us without getting fired at in return. They simply stood a negro upon the breastworks and fired at us from behind him. The result was that we did not fire back for fear of killing the negro."

AN OFFICER'S WIT.

A gallant soldier and distinguished politician, who commanded one of the regiments, perpetrated an "Irish bull" one day, which the other regiments of the brigade never suffered his men to hear the last of. Having halted on the march, and the men not falling in with sufficient promptness when the order to move was given, the gallant colonel exclaimed: "Fall in there, men! Fall in quickly! If you don't fall in I'll march the regiment off and leave every man of you!" At the battle of Winchester, in June, 1863, this same officer (now a brigadier general) was very deliberately forming his line of battle when the division commander grew impatient and sent an aid, who came galloping up to the old hero to say, "General! Gen. —— wants to know if you are proposing to have dress parade down here?" The instant retort was, "Go back and tell him yes; we are going to dress on the enemy." "Dress on the enemy" at once became a slang phrase among the men.

WIFE'S LETTER.

Just before the battle of the Wilderness, Sergt. Billy Bass received a letter from his wife. She said there was to be a big battle, and she did so much wish to see him before it was fought. When Billy read the letter he said he would also like to see her before the battle, but would a great deal rather see her after the battle.

COMMISSARIES' DINNER.

A column of infantry was one day marching along a dusty road under a broiling sun. Close by, under some trees, was discovered a cluster of sleek commissaries seated at dinner. A tall, raw boned and dust begrimed North Carolinian went up to the fence and, putting his chin upon it, stared long and earnestly at the tempting table. At last, bursting with envy, he yelled out, "I say, misters, did any of ye ever hearn tell of the battle of Chancellorsville?"

TRUE COURAGE.

In all ages, courage on the battle field has been the theme of orators and poets, yet the courage of the warrior is not only a common and a variable quality, but has often been surpassed by that displayed by women. Native valor, too, is sometimes inferior to that which is acquired. Frederick the Great ran like a coward out of his first battle. Flying on the wings of fear, he went a great distance from the field, and, coming to one of his own strongholds, reported that his army was destroyed. What was his surprise and mortification to learn that his men had gained a great victory. He never forgot the lesson taught, and ever afterwards was conspicuous for steady courage in action. Many instances might be given of soldiers in the last war who in their first fight were "lily livered," but who afterward faced with dauntless front the gleaming steel; and, on the other hand, of some who were lion hearted till taught by the pain of wounds the perils of a battle, and who then became notable cowards. Bravery in action, though more admired, is really not so great as that displayed in passive suffering. The woman who sticks to her post in the pestilential chamber is far braver than Alexander charging at the head of his cavalry.

ELECTION OATH.

The following oath was administered to the members of a volunteer company during the war: "You solemnly swear to obey, fight for and maintain the laws of the Confederate government and constitution, and support John W. Dean for captain of this company." Upon inquiry it was learned that the reason that the last clause was inserted was because he had been quite active in getting up a company before, and when they elected their officers he was left out; so this time he was determined to make it sure.

CONFEDERATE UNIFORM.

At the outbreak of the war between the states, Capt. Reynolds raised a company of Mississippians, and in the enthusiasm of the occasion made some rash promises to the parents of the boys. Among these was one to keep his company well uniformed. Years passed, and one of the anxious fathers, visiting the Army of Northern Virginia, was mortified to see his boy in rags. He upbraided the captain for not keeping his company in uniform. The captain, for a moment, was stunned, but recovered himself and cried out: "Attention, company! About face!" And as the unconfined rags fluttered like so many banners of poverty from each of "Pope's Headquarters," Capt. Reynolds pointed to the company and said, "They are uni-formed, sir."

DANGERS OF WAR.

One of the best companies of the Stonewall brigade was composed of railroad men from Martinsburg, W. Va. In a charge at Manassas, the story goes, the captain offered a barrel of whisky to the man who first reached the guns. When the captain got there one of his men, already astraddle a cannon, cried out, "Don't forget that barrel, captain!" The next day an admirer of the hero asked him how war compared with railroading. "Well," said he, "the life of a soldier is pretty rough, but it has one advantage over railroading." "What is that?" was asked. "'Taint near so dangerous," said the man of the rail.

HARDEE'S TACTICS.

Gen. Hardee once came across a straggler and asked him why he did not travel faster and keep up with his command. The soldier wished to know what in the deuce he had to do with it. "Only that I am Gen. Hardee, the commander of this department," was the reply. "Oh, you wrote a book on tactics, did you?" "I did," said the general. "Well," said the soldier, "I have been taught, according to your rules, how to double column at half distance. Now I wish you would tell me how to double distance on half rations." Gen. Hardee stuck spurs to his horse and traveled on.

GRINDSTONE.

The following is given by an eye witness: "On Jones's West Virginia raid, one day there was a fight near a country store. The house was soon abandoned by the occupants, and when the enemy retired precipitately the store was plundered. It was first come, first served. In a twinkling the dry goods were gone; then the mob began on the miscellaneous articles. My most valuable capture was a jar of nutmegs. By the time I had them rolled up in a table cloth the store was about empty. I saw one poor fellow enter and look around for something to steal, but there was nothing left but a pile of grindstones. Uttering a volley of oaths at his bad luck, he shouldered a grindstone and marched off triumphantly."

WHAT FIGHTING FOR.

One day opposing pickets on the Rappahannock agreed not to fire. A brisk conversation arose between a Texan and an Irishman on the Federal side. "What are you fighting for in the Yankee army?" said the Texan. "I'm fightin' for thirteen dollars a month; I belave your fightin' for eleven."

CAPERING SIDEWAYS.

While in Virginia I witnessed a scene between two officers of my regiment—one a lieutenant colonel, the other the adjutant—which, if rather disgraceful for "officers and gentlemen," was redeemed somewhat by a little witty passage or two which occurred. Both were slightly "elevated," the adjutant being in fact in that state to which a stronger term would have been applied had he been a simple private; for, "what in the captain's but a choleric word, in the soldier is rank blasphemy." The colonel had mounted his horse and the adjutant made a scrambling effort to get up alongside of him. "Hold on," says the colonel, "don't you see that mark?" pointing to the "C. S." brand on his horse. "Yes," says the adjutant. "What mark is that anyhow? What's them letters stand for, kurnel? 'Cut with sabre?'" "No," replied the colonel, "that means 'carry single.'" Somebody assisted the adjutant on his own steed, which, when he had mounted, became very restive and shied about, owing to the rider's unsteady management. "Say, kurnel; see that mark on my horse? Know what it means? That means 'caper sideways.'"

THEIR TWO GIRLS MARRIED.

In the old first in 1861 two of the boys, whom we will call A and B, had left sweethearts in Richmond. One of them soon forgot the soldier boy who had left her behind, and married a gentleman named Point. At this time B was much pleased and joked A terribly. All day long he would ask him "if he could see the point?" etc. Soon after this B's sweetheart, whose name was Hurt, forgot the vows she had made, and got married also. This was A's sweet revenge, and he gave B no peace by constantly asking him, "What hurt him? where was he hurt?" etc. It was a case of diamond cut diamond.

CARRIED TO THE REAR.

It was at the second day's battle of Bull Run that a cannon ball carried off a poor soldier's leg. "Carry me to the rear!" he cried to a tall companion who had been fighting by his side;

"my leg is shot off!" The comrade caught the wounded soldier up, and as he was about to put him across his shoulder another cannon ball carried away the poor fellow's head. His friend, however, in the confusion did not notice this, but proceeded with his burden to the rear. "What are you carrying that thing for?" cried an officer. "Thing!" said he; "it's a man with his leg shot off." "Why, he hasn't any head," cried the officer. The soldier looked at his load, and for the first time saw that what the officer said was true. Throwing down the body, he thundered out, "Confound him! he told me it was his leg."

JACKSON'S ORDER.

In the war between the states, Stonewall Jackson ordered one of his colonels to attack a certain strong position. The colonel hesitated, and at last went to Gen. Jackson to expostulate. "General," said he, "to attack that position is madness; my regiment will be exterminated." "Colonel," said the commander, "do your duty; I have made every arrangement to care for the wounded and to bury the dead."

MAGRUDER'S DINNER.

On the Peninsula, the gallant and jolly general, J. Bankhead Magruder, had ordered a dinner for himself and staff. A hungry reb—and who ever saw one that was not hungry?—came up to the farm house, espied the nicely filled table, and without leave or license sat down and began to annihilate things. Just then the general and friends walked in, escorted by the host. All were surprised. "Hello!" said the fiery Magruder, in terms more explicit than polite; "do you know whose table this is you are eating at?" "No, sir," said Johnny Reb, with his mouth full; "whose is it?" "Gen. Magruder's, sir; the commander of this department." "All right, general"—with another big mouthful;—"these war times I ain't particular where I eat or who I eat with; sit down and make yourself at home." The foraging private was unceremoniously fired out, but not before he had gotten outside of a pretty square meal.

PRAYERS AND WHISKY.

When Gen. Gordon was about to lead an attack at Petersburg, he and Gen. Heth with some others went into a little school room on the lines to pray. Sol Heth, the general's brother and adjutant general, who was always on the lookout for something to drink, was standing a little way off, and Henry Peyton, one of Gen. Lee's staff, beckoned him to come to the house and join them. Sol did not understand the object, but totally misconstruing it, held up his canteen, and shaking it, said, "No, I thank you; I have just got hold of some."

STONEWALL'S BRIDGE.

During Jackson's brilliant campaign in the Shenandoah Valley, it became necessary that a bridge over a small creek should be built in great haste. One evening Jackson sent for his old pioneer captain, Myers, and pointed out to him the urgency of the occasion, saying that he would send him the plans of his colonel of engineers as soon as it was done. Next morning Jackson rode down to Capt. Myers's quarters, and saluting the veteran, said, "Captain, did you get the plan of the bridge from Col. ——?" "Well," said the captain, "the bridge, general, is built, but I don't know whether the *picture* is done or not."

FLAG AND WHISKY RECAPTURED.

One of the Alabama regiments was fiercely attacked by a whole brigade in one of the battles in front of Richmond. The Alabamians, unable to withstand such great odds, were compelled to fall back about thirty or forty yards, losing, to the utter mortification of officers and men, their flag, which remained in the hands of the enemy. Suddenly a tall Alabamian, a private in the color company, rushed from the ranks across the vacant ground, attacked a squad of Yankees who had possession of the flag with his musket, felled several to the ground, snatched the flag from them and returned safely back to his regiment. The bold fellow was of course immediately surrounded by his jubilant comrades and greatly praised for his gallantry. His captain appointed him to a sergeantcy on the spot, but the hero cut everything short by the reply: "Oh, never mind, captain! Say no more about it. I dropped my whisky flask among those Yankees and went to fetch it back, and I thought I might just as well bring the flag along."

BUNCE'S COFFIN.

An amusing thing occurred in the twelfth Tennessee. On one occasion a soldier, in passing to the lower part of the encampment, saw two others of his company making a rude coffin. He inquired who it was for. "Johnny Bunce," said the others. "Why," replied he, "Johnny is not dead yet. It is too bad to make a man's coffin when you don't know if he's going to die or not." "Don't trouble yourself," replied the others; "Dr. Coe told us to make his coffin, and I guess he knows what he gave him."

ASKING FOR PARDON.

Many amusing incidents might be reported of pardon seekers at the White House. Mr. Hilliard, of Georgia, former minister to Belgium, rushed up to President Lincoln, seized his hand, and hoped his pardon would not be delayed. The President quietly remarked to the ex-reverend gentleman that "hope is the reward of the righteous," and vouchsafed no other reply. On another occasion a Confederate of some notoriety raised quite a laugh by saying, "I thank you, Mr. President, for my pardon; I am now a good Union man—am emphatically one of you; but didn't Stonewall Jackson give us h—l in the valley."

PEACE OR WAR.

Some people cry "Peace, peace," while there is no peace. Let us cry "War, war," while there is war. While you are crying "War, war," George, your old brandy scorched stomach is crying "War-ter!"—*Rebel.*

FRYING PAN.

A soldier being on picket reserve, went to a farm house, as he said, to borrow a frying pan, but for what purpose none could imagine, as there was nothing to fry. However, he went to the house and knocked at the door, which was opened by a lady who asked what he wished. "Madam, could you lend me a frying pan? I belong to the picket down here." "Yes, sir;" and forthwith came the pan. He took it, looked at it, turned it over, and looked again and again at it and in it, as if not certain it was clean. "Well, sir," said the lady, "can I do anything more for you?" "Could—could

—could you lend me a piece of meat to fry in it, ma'am?" and he laughed in spite of himself. He got the meat.

LAYOUT AND SHEBANG.

It will be remembered that a curious habit prevailed among the soldiers in the latter part of the war, of designating their respective companies and battalions by the queer names of "outfit" and "layout," while they would call a brigade a "shebang." The story goes that Gen. Polignac, the noble Frenchman who so generously espoused the cause of the South and served her with distinguished bravery to the last, was once accosted by a bright eyed Creole boy, who announced to the general that he had just returned from a furlough and wished to know where he could find Col. Ceusir's "layout." "Col. Ceusir's what?" shouted the general, his eyes bulging with astonishment. "Col. Ceusir's 'layout,'" repeated the lad; "it belongs to your 'shebang.'" "Well, I hope to land in h—l," ejaculated Polignac, who when excited sometimes became profane; "if I know what ze little diable mean! I have been educate all my life in ze armee. I have hear of ze campaignie, ze battalion, ze brigade and ze division; but I agree to be hanged if I ever hear of ze 'layout' or ze 'shebang' before!"

HUDDLE, DARN YE.

Immediately after the ordinance of secession had been passed, and it became apparent that there would be war, the attention of the Southern youth was directed almost exclusively to Hardee's tactics, and especially the drill of the company. A military company was organized in nearly every neighborhood all over the country, and the rivalry between them, as well as the interest elicited from their civilian friends and admirers, was immense. There was a very fine company organized in Memphis, which acquired a wide reputation for excellence in all the evolutions. It was commanded by a Mexican veteran who was a master of tactics and a martinet in drill. Every afternoon a throng of people would resort to the large vacant lot where this company was receiving instruction, to witness and applaud its performances. On one occasion, when an unusually large and appreciative crowd was collected, and many ladies present, the captain became so enthused that, after exhausting every recognized movement, be began to extemporize, and shouted out the command, " Company, right and left oblique; march!" The men gallantly essayed to obey the order, and diverging from the center toward the flanks, scattered widely. The captain racked his brain for a proper command to bring them together again, but the tactics provided no formula for such a dilemma. At length, when the boys had become strung out like a flock of wild pigeons and seemed about to separate forever, he yelled out, in desperation, "Huddle, gol darn ye!"

CONSECATED 'TATERS.

While the Confederate army occupied Bowling Green, the —— Kentucky regiment was encamped some two miles below town at Ennis & Dishman's mills, and while there one M. W. was detailed to go to the regimental commissary to assist in bringing rations for the company, and among his stores was a camp kettle of nice potatoes, not down on the requisition. Upon being asked where he got them, he said, in his natural, peculiar way, " I went to the cornersary to draw some 'visions, and seein' these 'taters, I consecated them." M. W. was, however, a good and gallant soldier, and could somehow manage to have a crosscut saw, maul and two wedges, and occasionally a frow carried, which were very useful in camp. He also carried, mostly himself, a four gallon jug, to bring water to the ditches, during the long retreat from Dalton to Atlanta. Adjutant Buchanan used to say he carried a sledge hammer and anvil in his knapsack.

OLD HUNTER'S TOAST.

Old Hunter was deaf as a post, and through his deafness and his shrewdness he managed to hide his sympathy for either Federal or Confederate. On one occasion a party drinking in his store, to test the old man's deafness, proposed the following toast: "Here's to old Hunter, the two sided old villain; may he be kicked to death by mules, and his body sunk in the sea a hundred fathoms deep. May no prayer be said over him, and his blind soul wander rayless through all eternity." The toast was drunk in great glee, in which the old man joined. "The same to yourselves, gentlemen," said he; "the same to yourselves." Of course, he had not heard a word that was said.

HOME GUARDS BURNED.

During the retreat of the Confederates through South Carolina, at the time of Sherman's advance, Sergt. McD—— of western North Carolina was sent on detail to the town of M——, where a regiment of home guards was stationed. These valorous heroes, seeing a soldier from the front, gathered around him, eagerly inquiring the news. "News?" says Mac, solemnly. "I believe there is none. Yes, there is a little, too, but it's not of much importance. Old Hardee burned up a regiment of home guards at Florence the other day, to keep them from falling into the hands of the enemy." No more questions were asked.

PROUD FLESH ON A HORSE'S BACK.

One day when the Army of Tennessee was on the move, the infantry column was halted and opened ranks to let the cavalry pass to the front. A young chaplain, full of conceit as well as consecration, came riding along on a good horse, with a high head and diked out in a new uniform, attracting the attention and exciting the ridicule of an infantryman, who, turning to one of his comrades, exclaimed, "Say, Tom, have you any borax or burnt alum in your pocket?" "No," said the other; "what do you want with it?" "I want to take the proud flesh off of that horse's back."

THE OTHER CHAP.

An Irishman was mortally wounded in one of the battles in front of Petersburg, and a Catholic priest was called in to counsel and comfort him in his last hours. But Pat did not seem to comprehend the meaning or force of the conversation of the man of God, and paid little attention to it. At last the priest, in deep concern for the dying soldier, said, "Pat, are you not afraid to meet your God, in your present regardless condition?" "No, indade," exclaimed Pat; "it's the other chap I'm afraid of."

FEED HIM.

A straggling Yankee soldier was in a squad that was captured and passed before Gen. Paul J. Semmes. One of the men remarked that this prisoner was hungry. "Feed him," said Gen. Semmes. "Shoot 'em in the line, but feed 'em on this side of it."

STONEWALL JACKSON.

(Our Sainted Corps Commander, who fell at Chancellorsville.)

All day the struggle had progressed between opposing foes,
And oft the brazen bugle's blast above the din arose.
In valiant charge and countercharge across the smoking plain
They grappled in a fierce embrace, regardless of the slain,
Till night her friendly mantle drew above the shattered lines,
And her refreshing breezes blew among the fragrant pines.

But not content to wait the dawn in perfecting his plans,
Our tireless chieftain's eager eye the foe's position scans.
With but a slender body guard out to the front he passed,
To find a salient where his troops in silence could be massed.
From his completed task he turns his charger to the rear,
To gain the shelter of his camp, nor dreams of danger near.

Mistaken in the deep'ning gloom for an advancing foe,
A bullet from his own command laid the great leader low.
A thousand soldiers of his corps would thankfully have shared
Their foeman's graves, if in their stead their idol's life was spared.
Ah! when that fatal volley rang out on the evening air,
Mars placed a wreath on Jackson's brow, and Clio leaves it there.

CAROLINA—1865.

(Our Own Darling Carolina.)

Pale, fainting from the battle field,
Carolina leaned on dented shield.
Her broken sword and shivered spear
She laid aside to wipe a tear.
Sob choked, I heard her feebly say:
"My sons! My sons!—Oh, where are they?"
The evening breeze, soft whispering, sighed:
"On Freedom's battle ground they died;
Fame's loudest trump shall proudly tell,
How bravely fought—how nobly fell."
Loyal, true hearted men were they;
They sought no portion in the fray;
But Sunny South they could not see
Bow down to Northern tyranny.

BIVOUAC OF THE DEAD.

The muffled drum's sad roll has beat
    The soldier's last tattoo;
No more on life's parade shall meet
    That brave and fallen few.
On Fame's eternal camping ground
    Their silent tents are spread,
And glory guards with solemn round
    The bivouac of the dead.

No rumor of the foe's advance
    Now sweeps upon the wind;
No troubled thoughts of midnight haunt
    Of loved ones left behind;
No vision of the morrow's strife
    The warrior's dream alarms;
Nor braying horn, nor screaming fife
    At dawn shall call to arms.

Their shivered swords are red with rust,
  Their plumed heads are bowed;
Their haughty banner, trailed in dust,
  Is now their martial shroud.
And plenteous funeral tears have washed
  The red stains from each brow;
And the proud forms, by battle gashed,
  Are freed from anguish now.

The neighing troop, the flashing blade,
  The bugle's stirring blast,
The charge, the dreadful cannonade,
  The din and shout are past.
Nor war's wild note, nor glory's peal,
  Shall thrill with fierce delight
Those breasts that never more may feel
  The rapture of the fight.

APPENDIX.

CHAPTER XXIV.

A story of Mississippi sharpshooters, by their commander, Capt. Robert F. Ward, interpolated by an exhaustive description of the battles of the Wilderness and Spottsylvania court house by the correspondent of the London Morning Herald, and published in the Richmond Daily Enquirer immediately after the battles in 1864, is here inserted, and is as follows:

MARION, ARK., December 30, 1898.

MAJ. W. S. DUNLOP, Little Rock, Ark.

DEAR COMRADE: Your having asked me to contribute a sketch of the operations of the company of Lee's sharpshooters which I had the honor to command, it affords me much pleasure to comply with your request, and the more so because you grant the esteemed privilege of incorporating in my contribution the letters of the correspondent of the London Morning Herald, cantaining an account of the battles of the Wilderness and of Spottsylvania, as witnessed by the correspondent with Gen. Lee, and as he learned the facts from other general officers. The letters appeared in the Richmond Enquirer, in May, 1864, and the papers containing them have been in my possession ever since, and so far as I know have never been republished in any form.

I have desired ever since the close of the conflict between the Federal and Confederate armies, that I might enjoy the privilege of making a statement for publication of a part of what came under my observation, especially during the campaign of the Wilderness, which, as historically known, embraces the battles of the Wilderness, Spottsylvania and second Cold Harbor, from the 3d of May to the 3d of June, 1864, one month. The company of sharpshooters which I commanded covered the front of the forty-second Mississippi regiment, of Davis's brigade, which was in Heth's division, A. P. Hill's corps, and protected the flanks exposed to the enemy when moving in line of battle to the right or left.

Early in April, 1864, while Gen. Lee's army was encamped along the Rapidan, near Orange court house, I was notified by Col. Feeney, of the forty-second Mississippi regiment, that I had been selected by Gen. Davis and himself to command the sharpshooters of that regiment; that the company was to be composed of select men from the various companies of the regiment, one sharpshooter for every ten men present for duty; that they were to be relieved from all camp duty, guard duty and fatigue service of any kind; that they were to be drilled six hours a day in skirmish drill and in the estimation of distances, until the opening of the approaching campaign.

I had entered the army from Senatobia, Miss., at the age of nineteen years, with the first regiment that left the state, March 27, 1861, the ninth Mississippi regiment, Col. Chalmers commanding. We were stationed at Pensacola, Florida, with Gen. Bragg, under whose strict discipline and continuous drill for nearly twelve months we were thoroughly seasoned and ready for business before re-enlist-ing in the forty-second Mississippi regiment, under Col. Hugh R. Miller. Col. Feeney was at the close of our first year's service a first lieutenant of Company I, ninth Mississippi, while I was orderly, or first sergeant, of the same company.

He had doubtless observed then my fondness for skirmish drill, and after re-enlistment in the forty-second Mississippi we had been tent mates and he was to me as an older brother; hence the appointment. In the further execution of the order of Gen. Lee as to the organization of sharpshooters, on the day of my appointment Col. Feeney directed the selection of the men to be made at once, and the regiment was called out in company quarters; and after the object of the organization was explained, volunteers were called for, and of the two hundred and forty men present for duty ninety men stepped forward, thereby announcing their desire to become sharpshooters, and out of this number we selected twenty-four men, as follows:

Company B—J. G. Coppidge, J. S. Moore, J. A. Moore, S. H. Leonard, De Soto county, Mississippi.

Company G—W. Hardin, —— Stroup, Calhoun county, Mississippi.

Company F—M. Austin, —— Davis, —— House, Calhoun county, Mississippi.

Company H—J. T. Saunderson, Joshua Smith, Yalaboosha county, Mississippi.

Company I—Tobe Harmon, Lee Campbell, Hub Campbell, Panola county, Mississippi.

Company A—Steve Lancaster, Mark Campbell, Carroll county, Mississippi.

Company C—Brit Jones, Steve Jones, J. M. Ham, De Soto county, Mississippi.

Company D—— —— Sowell, B. S. Strickland, T. M. Evison, Dan Yocumb, De Soto county, Mississippi.

Company B—J. N. (Dirk) Yarborough, De Soto county, Mississippi.

No doubt the desire to avoid the various duties from which sharpshooters were to be exempt influenced many of the ninety volunteers to seek a change, not realizing that they were offering to enter the most dangerous service incident to war. The next day the drill began and continued from day to day, skirmishing; the men seemed never to tire, the interest increased, and on the 17th of April, when I was furnished the following instructions for drilling and teaching estimation of distances, great earnestness was manifest and the drill each day was gone through as though they were contesting for a prize. The instructions read as follows:

HEADQUARTERS DAVIS BRIGADE,
April 16, 1864.

In order to teach the soldier to estimate distance by the eye, he is to be instructed in the following manner:

Men have to be placed as points for observation at the distance of 50, 100, 150, 200, 300, 400, and as far as 800 yards; standing at their ease and remaining in an erect position, facing the squad to be instructed.

These fixed points are to be thrown out in the following manner: The instructor is first to select a tree, house or any object in the distance and align two men thereon 20 yards apart and facing each other, and placed two paces to the right or left (as he may think proper) of the nearest man, and in the same line another man as a point for covering, after which he will march a squad of six men formed two deep on the alignment chosen and halted at 50 yards distance, when No. 3 of the rear rank will face about and cover the two men already aligned; the man 20 yards off will now be removed; the squad is then to make a half face to the right or left and march in an oblique direction for a distance of 50-5-6 yards, when it is again to halt and No. 3 of the front rank to face about three-quarters to the right or left and cover diagonally, moving to the right or left by the side step, as may be required, preserving his shoulders square to his present front. The squad is to continue so to march in an oblique direction, leaving a man at every distance of 50-5-6 yards, who is to act as before detailed, until every man is placed; when the points for observation are aligned diagonally the covering point is no longer required. It will be ob-

Appendix. 365

served that each man in the above formation is placed at a greater distance from the first line marched upon in proportion as he is distant from the point where the squad commences its instructions.

In order that each man may serve in turn as a distance point for the men of the party to make observations on, an officer or non-commissioned officer as assistant or squad instructor (if there is a sufficient number) is to be placed opposite the several points for observation, and the party formed to the left of the squad instructor placed opposite the first, 50 yards off.

The instructor should direct the men to notice the position of the sun, state of the atmosphere, and the back ground at the time they are making their observations, in order that they may be accustomed to the changes made in the appearance of the several objects under their altered condition. The squad instructor opposite the 50 yards post is then to proceed to indicate to each man in succession the different parts of the figure, arms, accoutrements and dress, which can still be distinctly perceived on the soldier before him, as also those parts which can no longer be perceived clearly at 50 yards, after which he will question him on the observations made, on what he can see, and enjoin him to try and impress upon his mind the appearance of a man at this distance, and pass him on to the next station. The squad instructor opposite the 100 yards post is to proceed in the same manner, and cause each man to make observations of the same kind as he did on the man at 50 yards, and direct him to make comparisons between the two men placed at this and the former distance, and then pass him to the next squad instructor, and so continue. At all points of observation attention must be called to the difference in the appearance of the men, as the distance increases or diminishes—at one point you can count the buttons or distinguish the features, complexion, etc. The men who are placed as points are to be relieved by others who have made their observations at the several distances, for which purpose the squad is to consist of at least double the number of men employed at points.

When the squad have made their observations on the different points, they will proceed to estimate the distances of men as follows: March the squad to a different ground and place a man at an unknown distance, and call on the squad to estimate the distance, cautioning them to remember their observations of men seen at known distances, each man to be questioned separately and his answer noted down in a register. Every man will adjust the sight of his rifle for the distance he judged; the squad will then pace the distance by marching towards the man judged from, to determine the distance. After having been drilled four days at three hundred yards (300) and under, they will then be drilled four days at 400, 500 and 600 yards. Instructors will take special pains to fix in the minds of the men the observations made at different distances, and make themselves acquainted with each man's capacity for acquiring a correct judgment of distances.

Regimental commanders will furnish the officer commanding the company of skirmishers or sharpshooters a copy of these instructions.

By command of

BRIG. GEN. J. R. DAVIS.

H. B. ESTES, A. D. C.

COL. WM. A. FEENEY, Commanding, etc.

On the 1st of May my last report attests the accuracy of their estimates.

Each successive day we were expecting marching orders and that the army would be put in motion for the field of battle. Marching orders came on the 4th, while divine service was being

---

* Report omitted.

held on a hill side in the open air by our beloved chaplain, T. D. Witherspoon. There was an unusual solemnity pervading that audience, each member of which was a soldier and doubtless thought that he might be hearing and did hear his last sermon; learning that hostile thousands were on the move southward. A strange sight to see an audience suddenly and silently vanish, but marching orders were announced.

Our division (Heth's) moved from Orange court house, east on the Fredericksburg plank road, and the forty-second Mississippi regiment camped at Verdiersville, continuing the march the next morning. The first guns of the enemy were heard on our right, about 9 o'clock, which caused a halt at short intervals. About noon the regiment was halted on the roadside and rested in place. We realized by sight and sound that the two armies were getting in position for battle. At the command the regiment came to attention and loaded, then awaited further orders.

Davis's brigade in the Wilderness, be it remembered, was commanded by Col. John M. Stone, of the second Mississippi regiment, the brigade at that time being composed of the second, eleventh and forty-second Mississippi, fifty-fifth North Carolina regiments and the first Confederate (Florida) battalion, and was assigned its position in the line of battle to the left of the plank road. About 1 p. m. Col. Stone indicated to Col. Feeney the position the forty-second would occupy, and Col. Feeney proceeded to the spot with his regiment on the crest of a ridge, which proved to be within the radius of what was about to become the storm center of battle, near the intersection of the plank road from Germania ford with that from Orange court house. Heth's division, supported by Wilcox's division, extended in full breast across and on both sides of the plank road. The storm was brewing in front, and away to our right the conflict was raging, the roar of battle approaching nearer and nearer as I was directed to form my company of sharpshooters, who up to this moment had remained with their respective companies in the line. At the word they stepped out quickly in double rank, in front of the right wing of the regiment, and counted twos. I gave the order to take intervals on the right group, but the rapid approach of the enemy's sharpshooters caused Col. Feeney to give a command sharply to take intervals as we advanced. This was his last command. We were in a forest thick with undergrowth, and the extent of vision was not more than eighty yards in any direction, and in places not thirty. The sharpshooters sprang forward down the slope, ascended the ridge in front and were halted half way up, about sixty yards from the Confederate line. The battle was now on between the sharpshooters of the opposing forces. Capt. O'Neil, commander of the battalion of sharpshooters of Davis's brigade, soon approached and said, "Lieut. Ward, take charge of the right wing of the battalion, and don't retire until you can see the enemy's colors." It was but a moment until the sharpshooting was terrific and I could see the approaching dark blue line of battle. About this time my anxiety to see the "old flag" rose to the high water mark.

The Federal line of battle was within seventy yards, as I thought, when I caught sight of a Federal color bearer, and the folds of the old flag clinging close to the flagstaff. The flag bearer did not flaunt his bunting to the breeze, and showed no desire to make his colors or himself conspicuous. Under the order I had it was not necessary that it should be unfurled so that I could count the stars and stripes. I was glad to see it in any shape, and promptly ordered a retreat. There was no straggling on that retreat. By the time we reached the ravine the opposing lines of battle had fired; before they could reload the sharpshooters formed on the left of their regiment in a vacancy left in the line for them. I found the line of battle lying down, and discovered that while I was watching for the enemy's colors the companies of sharpshooters on my right and left had already retired, and this caused the Confederates to think that the sharpshooters were all in, and they fired. If there had been no depression of surface between the two lines not one of us could have escaped death or wounds. By the time my sharpshooters had lain down and began firing in the line of battle there was one continuous unbroken roar from small arms, and an artillery duel going on, the width of the plank road. An army of drummers beating the long roll could not have made a more continuous sound.

The Confederate line of battle lying down, when the enemy came in range the movement of the sharpshooters into their place in the line of battle was the more conspicuous, and must have drawn a concentration of fire from the Federal line of battle, for while Company B of of the regiment lost ten out of twenty-four killed and wounded during the four and a half hours, there were nineteen of the twenty-four sharpshooters killed and wounded within the first hour of battle. They were in double file, twelve men abreast, and occupied a space to the left of their regiment of not more than fifteen steps. What time my duties did not demand my presence elsewhere I made my headquarters behind a white oak sapling within a few feet of the sharpshooters. The sapling was quite large enough near the ground, but grew distressingly small further up, so that little protection was afforded, yet it had stopped six Federal bullets, the last count I made, during a lull in the firing, while three balls had cut through my clothing.

Early in the battle Saunderson was shot fatally through the body, and I tried to hear his dying message, but the roar of battle was too great; not a syllable could be heard, although I held my ear close. He was a sincere christian and a faithful soldier. Leonard received a ball through his thigh and Evison lost an arm. Memory fails to note the other casualties. During a lull in the battle our adjutant, Oliver C. Carr, approached and told me that Col. Feeney was killed before I had retired with the sharpshooters, that Lieut. Col. Nelson was wounded, also other officers, and suggested that I take charge of the left wing of the regiment. I then directed the four or five sharpshooters who had survived to go to their respective companies in line, and by the time I had taken position near the center of the regiment I noted the absence of Adjutant Carr and learned that he was wounded. Very soon I saw that Capt. Donaldson, of Company G, was the only captain present. Donaldson was small, red headed and florid, particularly so in battle, and possessed staying qualities in battle worth a premium.

It was perhaps 4 o'clock, when our regiment had been much reduced, that our ammunition was nearly exhausted. At this period in the action Col. Stone was giving special attention to our part of the line of battle; he said he had sent for cartridges repeatedly, but the men who were sent were killed or wounded. The forty-second had almost ceased firing for want of cartridges. Col. Stone had dismounted and was passing back and forth along the line seeing that every man did his duty.

The situation had developed a crisis. The Federal line became more aggressive as ours became weaker, but there was no change in Col. Stone. His voice rang out firm and clear, as if on dress parade, without the least sign of agitation; his magnetic presence and his gallant but quiet, dignified bearing amidst the storm of battle was holding the weakest part of the line of battle steady, with empty guns. I thought then, as now, that the presence of no other except Gen. Lee could have held the men in line during such a crisis. So long as I live and memory survives I shall never forget the order Col. Stone gave. It was given in cold blood, and made me chilly, and given as calmly as if it was meaningless. "Lieut. Ward, a brigade is forming in the rear of our line and will charge over you; follow with fixed bayonets." The words "follow" and "fixed" were slightly emphasized. The regiment was quickly informed and awaited the expected charge. It was a brigade of Wilcox's division. Thinned almost to a skirmish line, with empty guns and bayonets fixed, we were to rush on a Federal line from four to six men deep. It was only sixty or seventy yards to a hand to hand encounter. The brigade never charged over us, and I have ever felt thankful that it did not. At the time we thought they refused to make the charge, and did not know until after the battle why the failure. When you reach the point in the correspondent's account where "Heth's division bore at first the whole brunt of the Federal onslaught," read slowly until you pass where "Wilcox formed his second brigade in the rear of the left flank of Heth's division," and you will note a very good reason why the charge was made in the opposite direction from that intended.

About dusk I could see the Federals creeping through a gap, worn through our line by

Federal bullets, to the left; and to meet that movement I placed the left wing of our regiment at right angles to the original line of battle, behind the trunk of an old tree that had fallen up the hill—the regiment thus forming two sides of a square, facing outward. Having received cartridges we continued the firing in both directions until about dark, when the regiment assembled near the root of the fallen tree. The only officers present that I can remember were Capt. Donaldson, Lieuts. Godfrey, Mears, Wilburn and myself. We decided to remain quiet, without firing, and watch for a place to go out. The enemy kept firing on three sides of the square, and we made a rush for the dark belt where there was no firing, toward the plank road, and went out through the gap that did not appear more than thirty yards wide. When we reached the open road where it was not so dark we found Col. Stone mounted and looking for us. We were never so glad to see him. We crossed into the woods a short distance only and halted for the night. It was too dark to straighten lines in a wilderness. Col. Stone directed me to post videttes. The detail was made and directed to take position thirty or forty yards in front. It was only a few moments before one of the videttes returned and whispered to me, "The Yankees are right out there." I reported to Col. Stone, and the result was that the videttes stood along the line over their sleeping comrades, who sank down on the bare earth without unrolling their blankets, with their trusty rifles encircled in their arms, clothed and accoutred as they had stood in battle, expecting that they would have to rise at dawn fighting.

Heth's division may have been ordered during the night to go to the rear as a reserve, as the correspondent states, but that part of it under command of Col. Stone did not move until an irresistible tidal wave of retreating Confederates struck it as day dawned, and before Davis's brigade could rise and form in line it was borne backward amidst the struggling mass, some of whom were firing toward the enemy through their own ranks. This was the beginning of the struggle on the second day of the Wilderness, May 6th, on our part of the field.

The twenty-sixth Mississippi being a little farther from the stampede, formed in line and became partly disorganized by the wave that struck it, but rallied and reformed, and was immediately borne back in confusion and became absorbed in the rush to the rear for a hundred yards or more, when the wave struck a stone wall in the person of Col. Stone, where the force of the stampede was broken and confidence much restored by the well known voice of command which rose above the tumult as clear and calm as on the day before, "Steady, men! steady! form on your colors." He drifted with the tide a short distance and the brigade came to a halt. The appearance of Col. Stone on his battle horse, as he rode from color bearer to color bearer, locating them on a line and calling on the men to form on their respective regimental colors, has never been effaced from my memory.

It was but a few moments until Davis's brigade was once more in line ready for action, and covered in front by a line of sharpshooters, a majority of whom were new men. The Federal sharpshooters had not ceased firing during the reformation of the brigade. We advanced upon them only a short distance until we reached a line of Federal dead and wounded. When our sharpshooters began to reply spiritedly to the Federal sharpshooters, shot for shot, Col. Stone directed me to try to stop the sharpshooting, and at the command the Confederates ceased firing; but the enemy did not recognize the truce, but continued to fire. I called on our sharpshooters to lay down their arms and place a wounded Federal on the Federal side of the respective trees behind which had stood a Confederate sharpshooter. We selected those who were the most slightly wounded and laid them at the roots of the trees. They plead against the experiment, as inhuman, but we replied that their own men would certainly not fire on them, and that the object in view was to stop the firing. When Sergt. Perry, of the one hundred and twenty-fifth New York regiment, was laid at the root of a tree, he asked me if I knew Col. Reynolds of the twenty-sixth Mississippi. I told him I did. He requested to be sent to him, which request was granted, and as he was being borne back within the Confederate lines he offered me his watch, which I declined, and told him that he might need it, or the value of it, in prison; he then desired to present me his testament; this I accepted, and it is still in my possession as a souvenir of the battle of the Wilderness, and a beautiful volume. The Federal sharpshooters seemed to have understood at once the object, and ceased firing, and not a single man was wounded afterwards, while in that position. After the battle it was asserted by those who followed Col. Stone, that he fought the battle "on his own hook;" not being able to communicate with either Generals Heth, Hill or Lee, he struck the enemy when and where he thought the brigade could be made most efficient. I never heard the assertion denied, and so far as my observation extended, there were no couriers nor aids carrying orders to or from him, and he was rarely out of sight. Reinforcements having arrived and formed, aided in checking the stampede. A charge was made, and as the line swept by Davis's brigade joined in and the enemy was borne back across and far beyond the road from Germania ford. The field was strewn with knapsacks, small arms, etc. In this charge two men of the sharpshooters were wounded— J. S. Moore received a scalp wound, and J. A. Moore was partially paralyzed by the explosion of a shell. After this there was a lull in the firing and Davis's brigade was not engaged for an hour or so, when Col. Stone moved to another point on the field, but not in connection with other troops. The brigade was resting in place, when to our left firing began; and the Federal officers could be heard distinctly urging their men forward, begging, pleading and threatening, trying to make their men charge. Col. Stone started off in that direction, and in a few moments returned and commanded the brigade to face about; directed the sharpshooters to form on the left of the brigade and deploy; this done, he commanded the whole to wheel to the right, and when the brigade swung around sufficiently to face the object of attack, he ordered a charge and led it himself. The tumult was silenced at once and the enemy routed, and a dead calm ensued. This is the movement, I think, which was referred to when the correspondent mentions the critical position of Gen. Perrin, "when Davis's fine brigade of Mississippians came sweeping up to complete, by connecting with Harris's right, the protection of the whole transverse front, Harris and Davis having thus saved by a timely movement the three brigades on the left, the artillery trains. etc., on that highway, and the line of the plank road." Immediately after this charge Col. Stone moved the brigade two or three hundred yards to the left behind a log breastwork and closed a gap in the Confederate line of battle, and ordered the sharpshooters forward. We took position in a thicket forty or fifty yards in front of the brigade, and in a short while had to retire under a terrible fire from a Federal line of battle. This was within two hours of sunset, and the battle raged until dark, but the brigade repulsed the enemy. I remember distinctly that the sun seemed to stand still, as if a Joshua had commanded it, as of old. Our chief desire was for sudden and thick darkness. At the point where I crossed the log works there was not sufficient room, and I took refuge behind a sapling which forked about eighteen inches from the ground, in rear a few feet, but the hill rose above the works and I was exposed to sharpshooters. The Federal sharpshooters here taught us a lesson, by firing obliquely up and down the line, away to the left or right, instead of firing straight to the front, and in this way they killed Lieut. Col. Boone of the twenty-sixth Mississippi, also Lieut. Godfrey to my left. Capt. Donaldson was down the hill to my right, and not so much exposed, behind a large tree. He succeeded in keeping his head against the tree, or near it, but the Federal sharpshooters kept his body in motion from right to left; a ball from the right would move him to the left, and vice versa, but Donaldson smiled all the same, seeing that I and others were kept on the move, likewise. Col. Stone was sitting on the ground about twenty steps in the rear of Donaldson, holding his horse, in open woods. I approached him the second time before I got his consent to move Lieut. Godfrey to the rear; he refused, saying the litter bearers would be killed, and to wait till dark. Lieut. Godfrey was the last of four young men of Company B who were originally from Greenville, S. C. Lieut. Ben F. Wham and Sergt. John G. Wham were killed at Gettysburg, and John Scott wounded and afterwards discharged. During the two days' battle we were all the time in the wilderness; there was no opening in sight of our brigade.

BATTLE OF THE WILDERNESS.

[Correspondence of the London Herald, May 18, 1864.]

The works occupied by Lee's army on the Rapidan extended on the right three miles below Racoon ford. Ewell's corps and Hill's lay behind those defenses, and stretched out on each side of Orange court house, along a line of twenty miles. Longstreet having returned some time ago from Eastern Tennessee, occupied the country around Gordonsville, thirteen miles southwest of the position on the Rapidan. Such had been the disposition of the Army of Northern Virginia during the latter part of April.

Grant having declined to assail Lee's front, determined to turn it by a movement on that officer's right. He marched eastwardly from his cantonments in the county of Culpepper, and having reached the river seven miles lower down at Germania ford, and also seven miles still lower down at Ely's ford, crossed the Rapidan. The campaign in Northern Virginia, fraught as it is with the fate of the Confederate States and of the United States, took thus its initial form on the 3rd of May.

From Orange court house two roads—the turnpike and the plank road—run on a line somewhat north of east to Fredericksburg. These two routes are in general parallel. The plank road consists of one track of worn planking and another of earth; its course, very irregular, vibrates in and out on the south side of the generally straight line known as the turnpike. A plank way runs from Culpepper court house to Germania ford; extending southeasterly, it crosses the turnpike, and after a route of four or five miles beyond that, terminates on the Orange and Fredericksburg plank road. Besides these main lines several others traverse the country around the battle field of the Wilderness—some pursuing a course parallel with these, some crossing them more or less transversely.

Grant's columns advanced from the Rapidan on the 3rd of May. That which marched from Ely's ford followed an earthen way leading to the junction of the Orange and Fredericksburg plank road with the plank road extending from Culpepper court house by way of Germania ford, while the other column moved down the latter route to the same point. That junction once gained, not only had the position of Lee on the Rapidan been turned, but several roads to Richmond would have been laid open.

Ewell's corps having been encamped on Lee's right, moved eastwardly on the 4th. A few of his brigades remained behind for a day guarding some of the fords across the Rapidan. Johnson's division, having the advance, followed the turnpike, and encamped for the night within three miles of a stream flowing northwardly—Wilderness Run. Rodes, next in order of march, lay in his rear along the same route; and Early, who had moved from Ewell's left at Somerville ford, encamped for the night a little behind a place called Locust Grove. The second corps had thus reached on the night of the 4th a position from which it stood ready to strike on the following morning the flank of Grant's column of advance.

Johnson moved with his division at the head of Ewell's corps on the 5th. Having thrown skirmishers out into the woods on either side of the turnpike, he discovered those of the enemy about six o'clock in the morning. The musketry on each side deepening, he pressed forward with Gen. J. M. Jones's brigade to gain a hill in his front, and having after a brief struggle driven back a heavy line of sharp shooters from that position, proceeded to form his troops in array of battle.

The thicket on all sides of the two armies excluded the use of artillery save only for the width of the turnpike. Jones's brigade had been formed but a moment across that road when the enemy advanced in what of order is practicable in a tangled forest. He approached with a heavy line of skirmishers, followed by a solid column extending across the whole Confederate front, four lines deep. Stewart's and Stafford's brigades proceeded to form rapidly on Jones's left. To guard against the danger of an overlapping breadth of attack, the brigade of Gen. Walker, which having nursed the genius of Jackson, is known as the "Stonewall," formed at some distance from Stafford's left flank, covering it by a front at right angles to that officer's line. In this position the division of Gen. Edward Johnson, of Ewell's corps, stood on the morning of the 5th to receive the enemy's onslaught.

Johnson's skirmishers were driven in. Those of the enemy took position in the advancing column. The fifth corps of the Federal army, accompanied by two pieces of artillery that came thundering along the turnpike, assailed the Confederate line at the intersection of that road. Receiving as it advanced a terrible fusilade without any sign of wavering, the rear ranks pressing forward those of the front, the attacking masses delivered from a forest of rifles a fast and furious fire upon Johnson's line. Closing in upon it with great spirit in front and threatening to envelope it on its right, they succeeded after a brief struggle in forcing back part of the brigade that had been formed across the turnpike—that of Gen. J. M. Jones. Two of his regiments—the twenty-first Virginia, commanded by Col. Witcher, and the twenty-fifth by Col. Higginbotham—holding their ground resolutely, Jones strove in desperation to rally his broken troops. Threatening, entreating, shaming were of no avail in arresting their disordered flight, and as he saw his men rushing from the field in hopeless confusion, he fell from his saddle a bleeding corpse. Capt. Early, of his staff, unwilling to desert him, had but a few moments previously wheeled his horse from its retreat, but only to share with his gallant chief while in the act the same red burial.

Stewart moved from his position in the line of battle to close the gap left in it by the brigade of Jones. As the Federal masses poured through, his men rushed forward with a cheer, and driving them back by the impetus of his charge, captured their guns.

Almost simultaneously with the signs of weakness in Jones's line Daniels's brigade of North Carolinians and Gordon's brigade of Georgians, both of Rodes's division, were placed rapidly in line upon the right. Ordered immediately afterwards by Gen. Ewell to charge, Gordon, holding command of the movement, crushed through the enemy's first lines and captured as he went forward a whole regiment, men, officers and colors. Driving onward furiously he struck back the Federal front in confusion upon its supports, and scattering both like leaves before a storm, forced them off the field in utter route for a mile and a half. His front thus cleared, Gordon found the enemy's lines firm on both his wings. Dividing his men into two bodies he formed them at right angles to the line of his original advance;

and, sending them both forward, back to back, took the masses on his right and on his left in flank. Pressing on them so energetically as to have prevented their formation across either of his lines of movement, he swept them in disorder from the Confederate front for a width of a mile.

At the moment of Gordon's brilliant charge the enemy attacked the brigade of Gen. Stafford. A deadly conflict on that part of the field raged for some time doubtfully. The marksmanship of Stafford's Louisianians, however, shot truly to the buckles of the Federal belts, strewing the field with death and agony. Reeling under its deliberate fire, the enemy finally fled, marking his route with his killed and wounded, and adding to his other disasters the loss of six hundred prisoners. In this repulse, however, the Confederates have to mourn the loss of Brig. Gen. Stafford. He fell mortally wounded. He had been a planter of Louisiana, but having gone through most of the battles in Northern Virginia had become an excellent officer, and was not more beloved by his men for his gentleness than he was admired by them for his daring.

Soon ofter the onslaught upon the Confederate front, the sixth corps of the Federal army advanced upon its left flank. Coming up at right angles to the line of movement of the fifth corps, its skirmishers were encountered by those thrown out in anticipation of attack in that direction from the Stonewall brigade. Sedgwick, commanding this movement on Johnson's flank, soon afterward threw the whole weight of his dense column upon those stout souls; but, though threatening to envelope it on the left, failed to force back the men who had learned heroic constancy from Jackson. Sorely pressed, however, Pegram's Virginians and Hay's Louisianians deployed rapidly on their left. Charging immediately upon the Federal right those fresh troops drove it back. The furious onslaught of Hay's men did not expend itself until they had forced the enemy to retreat in confusion for nearly a mile. In advance of all others on that face of the attack, these splendid troops—the heroes you will recollect of Winchester—having left nearly one-third of their number on the field, fell back with Pegram's gallant fellows to the general line of battle.

The enemy routed with great slaughter from all points of his advance, Ewell proceeded to select ground for the morrow's battle. Assisted by Gen. Smith, of the engineers, he reviewed his position, and proceeded at once to cover his front with a line of field works and an abatis of felled trees. Skirmishing continued murderously outside the lines; but the battle of the 5th of May, on Lee's left, appeared to have been lost and won. Immediately before the close of the evening the skirmishers of Gen. Pegram, on Johnson's left, came running in; and soon afterwards his sharpshooters sprang back from their rifle pits in his immediate front. A column three lines deep moved upon him from the depths of the forest, and, firing heavily as they came on, pressed towards his works furiously. His staunch Virginians, however, met the attack resolutely, and covered partially by their works, hurled volley after volley in withering blasts, breast high, into its serried ranks. Slaughtered by this terrible fire, the assailants paused, reeled, fled. The Moloch of the North had not, however, yet been sated. In five lines a column renewed the attack after nightfall, but did so without other result than to increase terribly the hundreds of men that, dead or dying outside the Confederate works, lay weltering in their gore. Pegram—who holds in his veins blood which a gallant member of his family declared to be thicker than water—fell in this last attack severely wounded. A dashing officer, this accident is deeply regretted by his brigade, but I am happy to add is not supposed to involve any danger of his life. The repulse, which he guided as he fell, closed the work of war for the day on the left, and witnessed the Confederates still in possession of their improved position and advanced lines, flushed with undoubted victory.

Hill was ordered to march on the 4th from Lee's left. Anderson's division having been left behind for the time to guard some fords in its front, Heth, followed by Wilcox, moved eastwardly through Orange court house, along the Fredericksburg plank road. The divisions of those two officers bivouacked for the night near a place called Verdiersville. Heth in advance, they resumed their march on the following day, still pursuing the line of the plank way.

The ring of small arms on the right announced in the course of the morning of the 5th a small cavalry affair near the route of Hill's column. The march still, however, continued, until it encountered at eleven o'clock some dismounted cavalry; but after a moment's pause, brushing those from its way, still went forward. At one o'clock musketry was again heard in front; and though at first thought to indicate the presence of merely a party of horse, proved after some skirmishing to have come from a large body of infantry. Kirtland's brigade of Heth's division deployed immediately on both sides of the plank road, and the whole column proceeded to form in line of battle on its flanks, while the sharpshooters of both armies kept up in front a desultory and somewhat languid fire.

Hill's advance followed, it will be recollected, the plank road, while Ewell's pursued the turnpike. Parallel lines in their general directions, these movements stood at the time of the deployment of Kirtland's brigade from three to four miles apart. The country intervening and round about for several miles is known as the "Wilderness;" and having very few clearings, consists almost wholly of a forest of dense undergrowth. The enemy, apparently bewildered by the character of the site and of the approaching conflict, sent out scouts and skirmishers in every direction from his front. Eight or ten of these having strayed in between the column of Hill and that of Ewell, came into an open field, in which they might have shot—as he sat with Gen. Hill and other officers on the ground—that idol of the army, Gen. Lee. Those adventurous blue coats finding themselves in front of two brigades of Wilcox's division, made a rapid retreat, ignorant, most happily, that a very precious life lay for a moment at the mercy of their rifles.

The interpolation of those skirmishers between his two columns suggested to Gen. Lee the necessity of opening communications with Ewell. Capt. Hotchkiss, of the engineers of the second corps, having come up immediately afterwards, indicated the route for that purpose; and Wilcox's division, moving accordingly to the left—having captured two hundred of the enemy on the way—effected after a march of a mile and a quarter a junction with Gordon's brigade on Ewell's extreme right.

The line of battle thus completed, extended from the right of the plank road through a succession of open fields and dense forest to the left of the turnpike. It presented a front of six miles, and with Flat Creek in its rear, occupied a very irregular plan along the broken slopes of a broad ridge that rises from the stream known as Wilderness Run. The thicket that lay along the whole face of the Confederate array is so impenetrable as to have excluded the use of artillery by the enemy, save only for the breadth of those openings where it is penetrated on the left by the old turnpike and on the right by the plank road.

The attack on Ewell having been repulsed, musketry began, at half past two, to deepen in volume in front of Hill. Large columns of the enemy, enveloped in clouds of dust, were seen at that time moving up from the rear in the direction of the deafening fire. Possession of the intersection of the plank road from Germania ford with that from Orange court house, opening as it would a favorable line for Federal advance southward, was shown by the enemy's movements to be about to become the subject of a bloody encounter.

Heth's skirmishers were driven in about 3 o'clock. They were followed closely by a heavy column, that appeared to move forward spiritedly. Firing with great rapidity as it advanced, its musketry, in the ears of a man approaching the field of battle, rolled through the depths of the forest like the roar of mighty waters. Resolute defense on the one hand, and on the other an attack that sought to force its way rather by constant pressure than by dashing enterprise, the struggle in Hill's front continued for two or three hours, unbroken in its terrible monotony by even any disturbance of the rapid regularity with which it added to its masses of grim death or of mortal agony.

Heth's division bore, at first, the whole brunt of the Federal onslaught. The heavy columns pressing so obstinately upon its front failed to break its heroic constancy. Thick and fast its men crept to the rear, bleeding, or dropped in the ranks, dead—but still it gave no signs of yielding. One half its number of the morning had been placed *hors de combat*. The weight of the immense masses hurled against it having excited in Lieut. Gen. Hill some fears for its solidity, orders were sent to Wilcox to come up with his division from Ewell's right, at the double quick. That gallant officer arrived at 4 o'clock, while the roar of the rifles in front, accompanied by the thunders of four or five guns on the plank road, declared the combat to be one of extraordinary fierceness.

Wilcox, guided by the heaviness of the fire, placed his leading brigade in rear of Heth's center, and deployed it to the right and left of the plank road. The conflict soon afterwards deepening in that direction he next formed his second brigade, as it arrived upon the field, on the left flank; but had no sooner drawn it up in line of battle than it became exposed to musketry so completely in reverse as to have wounded some of his men in the back. Changing front instantly to the rear, and swinging round his left, he found himself confronted by a Federal line of battle.

Reasoning from the crushing weight of musketry in Heth's front, Wilcox drew up another of his brigades in that officer's rear, on the right of the plank road. The hoarse roar of the fire extending, subsequently, in that direction, he placed his last brigade for the protection of that flank, in extension of Heth's array on the extreme right. Two of Wilcox's brigades lay thus in reserve in rear of the center, while another occupied each of the two flanks of the line of battle.

The losses in Heth's division had become so heavy that Wilcox's brigades in reserve were moved, at about half past five, to the front. McGowan's South Carolinians thus brought into action, their gallant chief, impatient of delay, leaped his horse over a rank that had lain down to let his men pass. Spurring forward, waving his sword as he went, he was followed by his brigade, with a cheer, and plunging immediately into the depths of the conflict drove back the enemy by his impetuous dash for several hundred yards. Wilcox, seeing the Federal lines on each side of the breadth of that charge of the fiery South Carolinians stand firm, became apprehensive for their safety; and, ordering them at once to fall back, placed them in the position assigned them in the array of battle. The murderous conflict raged in fierce monotony until night closed over the Confederate line in the position it had originally taken. The prisoners captured included men from the sixth corps, the

second and fifth corps; and this fact points to
the supposition that the gallant divisions of
Heth and Wilcox actually held at bay, from
3 o'clock until half past 7, three corps of the
Federal army.

Heth's division was ordered during the night
of the 5th to go to the rear as reserve. Lane's,
Scales's, McGowan's and Thomas's brigades,
constituting the division of Gen. Wilcox, occupied the front. Videttes were sent out, but
ventured only a short distance from the line of
battle. The two armies lay indeed so close to
each other throughout the night as to be within
easy earshot. A small stream on the Confederate left constituted their mutual supply of
water, and was so near both that men from
either side going to fill their canteens from it
were often captured by some from the other.
Col. Baldwin, of the first Massachusetts regiment, more thirsty than prudent, became in
that way a tenant of the Libby prison.

Longstreet's corps, it will be recollected, lay
on the 3rd thirteen miles southwest of the position on the Rapidan. Ordered forward by
Gen. Lee, it marched from the neighborhood of
Gordonsville on the morning of the 4th. On

the morning of the 5th it halted within twelve miles of the field of battle of that day. Intending to follow a road known as the Catharpen, with a view to a movement upon the rear of the enemy's left flank, it became necessary under the rapid development of Grant's masses of attack to call it to the support of the front. Its intrepid chief, informed after midnight of the danger of Hill's corps, was ordered to move up to the plank road with the view of meeting the renewal of the shock of the fifth upon the right. Breaking up his bivouac, Longstreet commenced his march about 2 o'clock in the morning to the field of battle.

Gen. Lee, concluding reasonably that feint upon the left would occupy sufficient time to delay the attack upon the right until the arrival and deployment of Longstreet's men, regarded the state of things on the dawn of the 6th without alarm. Wilcox had, however, looked anxiously throughout the night for the coming of the divisions of Anderson and Field, and disappointed in the delay of their arrival, began at daybreak to cover his front by an abatis of felled trees. The men employed for that purpose were immediately fired upon by the enemy's skirmishers, and in the next moment rushed to their rifles before the advance of an attack in heavy column. The Federals had spent the night in securing good positions for their onslaught of the morning, and coming now in great force from points threatening Heth's and Wilcox's envelopment, forced the gallant divisions of those officers to waver. Shattered in strength by the terrible struggle of the day before, and having already maintained a resistance for three-quarters of an hour against numbers absolutely crushing, they finally gave way. Continuing at first a desultory fire as they retreated, the right wing south of the plank road broke into disorder and finally fled in confusion before the enemy's overwhelming columns.

Wilcox seeing his lines shattered hopelessly, rushed back to report to Gen. Hill. The Federalists pressed forward so vigorously that he had but arrived at that point when he looked back to behold his disordered ranks surging already within 150 yards of the position of Gen. Lee. The head of McLaw's fine division of Longstreet's corps came up immediately under the command of Brig. Gen. Kershaw, and so outspoken was the augury of victory in its flashing eyes, that its appearance bound up at once the wounded spirits of Heth and Wilcox as they writhed in the presence of Gen. Lee under a reverse which that officer declared during the day had illuminated their previous struggle with unflinching constancy.

Apprehension was for a moment entertained that the rapid movement and heavy fire of the enemy's advance would prevent the deployment of the approaching columns in line. Kershaw's own brigade of South Carolinians and Humphrey's brigade of Mississippians, having the advance of Longstreet's corps, had the honor to be the first to form. Drawing up across the plank road—thus covering the trains, the artillery and the shattered retreat of Heth and Wilcox—they at once checked the enemy's advance, in the teeth of a fire, in which they stood firm, as though it were a storm of mere hail. Their resistance it was, however, feared at the time could not be maintained for many minutes. Their front swept by a tempest of bullets, they were threatened on their right flank with envelopment. Their heroic firmness triumphed, however, for the ring of their rifles had before long whirred its death rattle in so many Federal hearts that the assailants began after awhile to recoil. Other brigades having in the meantime begun to drop into line on the right, the enemy was soon afterwards checked at all points, and the tide of battle commenced after a short time to roll slowly back.

McLaw's division once in line, under Kershaw, Field's men formed on it as it came up. Anderson's splendid fellows, left by Gen. Hill to guard fords in the rear of the march from the Rapidan, soon came in a rush. Commanded by Gen. Mahone, they deployed immediately in array of battle. Breadth and weight thus given to Lee's front, the fortunes of the day quickly turned. The Confederate line moved majestically forward, and, in the teeth of a bloody and stubborn resistance, mowing down the enemy's ranks with its terrific musketry as with the sword of the destroying angel, drove him back for nearly a mile.

For about an hour the battle sunk into a lull of apparent exhaustion on both sides. The brigades of G. T. Anderson, of Wofford, and of

Mahone, were in the meantime directed against the enemy's left flank.

Having formed perpendicularly to his line, they struck it suddenly at about a mile south of the plank road, and giving it no time to fall into position in their front, drove it nearly up to that highway in a confused mass. The enemy carrying with him the debris of this route, retreated to the breastworks he had thrown up near the line of planking, along which he had advanced from Germania ford.

The flanking force thus having done their work triumphantly, halted within a few hundred yards of the Orange and Fredericksburg plank road. The Confederate line of battle on the left of their position, on learning of the enemy's route, broke into column, and, delighted at the complete success of their chieftain's strategy, moved forward amidst shouts of triumph. Longstreet rode up with his staff to take his place at the head of the advance, and was received as he passed along the moving mass with thunders of applause. Gen. Jenkins, spurring to his side, grasped his hand in a glow of pleasure, and the whole scene was one of universal rejoicing. Their faces glowing, their horses prancing, the cavalcade surrounding the lieutenant general had, however, not passed more than a hundred yards in advance of the column when their mood was sobered into profound regret. One of the brigades of the flanking force, heated with the work of destruction that they had executed so splendidly, mistook the glad group of horsemen that came prancing along the plank road for a party of the flying foe. It poured into them at short range a deadly fire. Poor Jenkins fell instantly from his horse with a bullet in his pulseless brain. An enthusiastic son of South Carolina, he was beloved by his troops for his fine qualities as a man and an officer. Longstreet received a ball that entered his throat and passed out through his right shoulder. Bleeding like an ox, he was helped from his horse so prostrated that fears were entertained of his immediate death. Major Walton, a gallant Mississippian on his staff, threw open his vest and shirt collar, and found great relief in discovering that he was mistaken in supposing that the ball had cut the carotid artery. Placed on a litter, the wounded general was removed from the field; but feeble though he was from the loss of blood, did not fail to lift his hat from time to time as he passed down the column, in acknowledgment of its cheers of applause and sympathy.

The column of advance deployed into line. Some of Field's and McLaw's men had already encountered and driven back the enemy on the left of the plank road, when Anderson's division of Hill's corps was ordered to their support. The brigade of Alabamians which had illuminated the name of Wilcox, having come up first in the order of march, was placed rapidly by its chief, Gen. Perrin, in the position of Law's brigade of Field's division, its right resting on the plank road.

It had hardly taken its place when the enemy, who had been previously driven back in fine style by Law, came up again, and under a terrible fire from Perrin's rifles retreated with precipitation. Renewing his advance, he once more emerged from the forest, but contented himself with quick and wild firing, as he lay down at a distance of a hundred and fifty yards from the front of the Confederate line. The Federal officers were heard at that moment urging their men to rise and charge. Their left pressed up to within a distance of seventy-five yards, but the deadly minnie cutting their close front into shreds, they fled after a struggle of ten minutes in utter confusion. Flinging away knapsacks, cartridge boxes, muskets and blankets the attacking party seemed stricken with terror, as well it might have been, in a field where its dead lay so thickly—sometimes one upon another—as to have traced out distinctly the line of the array in which they stood at the moment of their death.

A struggle equally sanguinary with that on the left of the plank road raged at the same time on its right. In the meantime, however, a force had been sent out with the design of turning the enemy's flank on that side. That movement was, however, found after a long march to be impracticable. Triumphant on both sides of the plank way, Lee decided on an attack in front. Perrin having just moved by the left flank sufficiently far to admit those troops between his right and the plank road, Benning's brigade of Field's division, and Kershaw's of McLaw's division formed upon his right. Their line extended from the roadway at right angles. Perrin and Law, drawn up in array of battle parallel with the road, lay at the moment of the advance transversely in the rear of Perrin's left. Right and left of the plank road the Confederates began to move forward. Kershaw, Benning and Perrin finding the enemy, pushed onward, freely swinging around their left somewhat adventurously into the unknown depths of the forest through which they moved.

In the meantime Federal skirmishers spring from tree to tree as they came on with a heavy fire, drove in those of Perry and Law. Followed in hot haste by a blue line of battle, the whole pressed back the brigades of those officers with great spirit towards the plank road. Alarmed by the firing going on during that movement in the rear of his left, Perrin sent his adjutant, Capt. Wynne, to communicate on the subject with Gen. Harris. That gallant fellow, seeing that no time was to be lost, rushed with his impetuous Mississippians on the face of the advancing attack and succeeded in driving it back handsomely for a sufficient distance to give protection to the rear of Kershaw and Benning. Perrin—on the extreme left be it recollected—stood still, exposed to imminent danger. As the whole breadth of the line from the plank way retired, he endeavored at the same time to swing back his exposed wing, but found it suddenly enfiladed by the fire of the enemy's skirmishers. His position became critical. Capt. Wynne led off two regiments from the exposed flank, and had placed them in position in the rear just as Davis's fine brigade of Mississippians came sweeping up to complete, by connecting with Harris's right, the protection of the whole transverse front, Harris and Davis having thus saved, by a timely movement, the three brigades on the left, the artillery trains, etc., on that highway, and the line of the plank road. The enemy foiled in this design, fell back, after a brief encounter, from the front. The symmetry of the Confederate line was restored subsequently in the day by the disposition of Hill's whole corps on Longstreet's left.

The forward movement progressed on the right of the plank road while events were thus threatening it on the left. Longstreet's men on that part of the field moved forward, went on for some distance without finding the enemy until G. T. Anderson's brigade of Georgians coming on, an array of battle in Federal blue rushed at it with such impetuosity as to have become almost immediately master of the field works. The single line of this attack was, however, too weak to hold what it had so handsomely won; and having been, as is too often the case in those apparently ill advised charges of the Confederates, unsupported, was compelled by the concentration of a crushing force in its front to retire.

The work of war on the right was done. So alarming had been the aspect of the field at one time that, fearing for the constancy of his troops, Gen. Lee had, as Field's division came under fire, placed himself at the head of Gregg's brigade of Texans. Ordering them, in that devotion which constitutes the great charm of his character, to follow him in a charge upon the triumphant line that came sweeping down upon him over the debris of Heth's and Wilcox's divisions. Longstreet protested against such an exposure of a life so valuable. A grim and ragged soldier of the line raised his voice in determined remonstrance; and was immediately followed by the rank and file of the whole brigade in positive refusal to advance until their beloved general-in-chief had gone to his proper position in the rear. Yielding to their touching solicitude, and thus terminating one of the most remarkable incidents in war, Gen. Lee retired; and well did Gregg's gallant fellows fulfill the promise with which they urged his withdrawal, by rushing forward, through a tempest of bullets, with a fury which nothing could withstand.

All the ground that had been lost was recovered, the enemy driven, routed, into his entrenchments, the Confederate lines advanced threateningly so far as to hem him closely in; and thus, almost helpless as its fortunes at one time appeared to be, the second day of the battle of the Wilderness terminated around the Southern Cross of the right wing in bloody triumph.

The 6th of May opened on Ewell's front with Rodes's division on the right of the turnpike, Johnson's on the other side of that road, and Early's still further to the left. In the morning a column of attack came up in front of Pegram's brigade and of part of Johnson's division, and attempting to force its way, pressed that part of the line heavily. Reinforced by a few regiments from Gordon's brigade, the Confederates with unflinching solidity hurled the onslaught back, mangled and bleeding. Again, however, and yet again, the obstinate masses renewed their advance, until the line of their movement, strewed thickly with evidences of the terrors in their way, they finally shrank from an encounter that had proved so disastrous.

The battle on the left appeared after the repulse of the morning to hang fire. Direct advance so sternly repelled, the enemy determined to make a movement on Ewell's flank. Wilcox's division having been withdrawn the day before for the support of Heth, the two wings of Lee's army continued still unconnected, and through the space thus open Burnside moved a force at about 2 o'clock, with the view of crushing our line from right to left. Ewell, who is gifted with the instincts of a military genius, stood, however, pressed at all points. As the flanking force of the enemy came up, moving perpendicularly to Rodes's line of battle, a battalion of sharpshooters from Ramseur's brigade of North Carolinians, following their bold commander, Major Osborne, had the audacity to charge a whole division of the Federal army. A whole division of the Federal army advancing on that handful of men, fled before Osborne's fellows at the top of their speed, leaving behind it in its flight all its knapsacks, and as many as fifteen hundred of its muskets. Burnside's movement against Ewell and Heth thus defeated by an amazing boldness, a repetition of such an enterprise was prevented by an immediate junction with the line of battle that had just been restored on the right wing.

The extreme left was held by the Georgians of Gen. Gordon. Our line at that part of the field extended beyond the enemy's right for the width of a brigade front. Gordon, anxious to employ this advantage, urged that he be allowed to use it for a moment against the Federal flank. Ewell and Early, yielding to his repeated representations, finally gave him the order to move. The sun was, however, at that instant about to set, and but a limited time remained therefore for the execution of an enterprise so important. But Gordon's men moved briskly out of their works; and forming at right angles to their previous position, moved forward in line of battle, supported by R. D. Johnston's brigade of North Carolinians. In complete surprise they struck the enemy's flank, and crushing his array as they swept forward majestically, drove everything before them like chaff before the wind. Brigade after brigade fled from the Federal works, and attempting one after another to wheel around into line in order to check the advance, was borne back under the rapidity of Gordon's movements before the seething mass that struggled down upon it in utter rout.

Gordon swept all before him for a distance along the enemy's line of two miles. The forest through which he advanced was so dense with undergrowth that by the setting in of nightfall he had become separated from his supports. Pegram's brigade paused, however, after nightfall upon his left. He paused before he had completed a movement that, if undertaken earlier in the day, would have completely routed at least the Federal right. The enterprise, notwithstanding its incompleteness, was crowned with brilliant success. The Confederate loss in that service numbered in killed and wounded but twenty-seven. To the enemy the results involved terrible slaughter. Four hundred Federals were buried next day in the ground over which that admirable movement had been made.

The field for two miles in extent was strewn with trophies flung wildly away—knapsacks, blankets, cartridge boxes, cooking utensils, and even large supplies of abandoned rations. The route was one of indescribable panic. The woods in front were alive with masses of men struggling to escape with life. The sixth corps of the Army of the Potomac was so completely broken up that, unable to restore its spirits, Gordon bivouacked for the night in its immediate front, in undisturbed repose. A brilliant stroke thus closed on Ewell's front the second day of the battle of the Wilderness in crowning triumph.

Victory smiled during the night of the 6th of May on the warriors that lay sleeping, from right to left, behind Lee's works. The losses of the Confederates in killed, wounded and missing do not exceed for the two days six thousand. The result to the enemy in some parts of the field cannot be described by any word less forcible than massacre. Eleven hundred and twenty-five Federal dead were buried in front of that part of Ewell's line lying to the left of the turnpike. Five hundred more were buried on the right of that road; and, in addition to about a hundred dead officers whose bodies must have been removed, the number of corpses lying on the field within range of the enemy's sharpshooters is estimated at fully three hundred. The Federals killed in the struggle on the right may therefore be declared positively to number as many as two thousand. I have no data on which to estimate the breadth of the slaughter in the fierce conflicts of the right; but from the stubbornness and volume of these, feel quite confident that they must have added to the slain as awful an account as that rendered in front of Ewell. With three thousand prisoners and four thousand dead, the usual proportion of six or seven to one for the wounded would show that the losses of Grant in the battle of the

Wilderness cannot have been less than twenty thousand men.

Gen. Lee, in attempting to lead Gregg's Texans into the jaws of death, has given history a striking proof of the attachment of his troops to his person. The world did not, however, want any evidence of his own devotion; and can hardly fail to pronounce judgment against his course, on that occasion, as one of rashness. His exposure during the present campaign has been so unusual, and apparently so unnecessary, as to have impressed his troops with profound concern. The explosion of a shell under his own horse, the killing of the horse of his adjutant general, Lieut. Col. Taylor, and the wounding in the face of another officer attached to his person, Lieut. Col. Marshall, have had the depressing effect of a deep anxiety on the morale of his army. The President, sharing the general apprehension in and out of the field for the safety of Gen. Lee, has, I am glad to say, written to him a touching letter of remonstrance. The relation, private and public, of the two men, will no doubt give great weight to that protest; notwithstanding that it comes from a man who, though charged in a struggle for all that is dear to a freeman with the fate of millions, had, under an error of his own devotion, but just returned from alarming exposure to the terrible missiles that screamed, and burst, and crashed in thunder claps around Drewry's Bluff.

CHAPTER XXV.

MISSISSIPPI SHARPSHOOTERS.
[Continued.]

On the 7th of May we lay on the battle field awaiting attack by the enemy, but nothing transpired worthy of note. During the day, and subsequently during the campaign, the gallantry of Col. Stone was frequently mentioned, and it was talked in camp that he had been complimented by Gens. Hill and Heth in person. Whether or not this was true is not known by the writer, but it is known that he was entitled to compliments and promotion. It is stated in the "Military Annals of Mississippi," page 32, that Gen. A. P. Hill said that he had earned stars as a general officer. The ranks of the army had been so thinned by casualties in battle that there was a surplus of officers, which fact operated against the promotion of many who were deserving.

Col. Stone's promotion finally came—during the reconstruction period, when Aimes, the carpetbag governor of Mississippi, was impeached, and he was chosen as governor in his stead. The veteran Mississippi soldiery of the Army of Northern Virginia have always rallied to the support of Col. Stone, and aided materially in electing him governor for the various terms he has served the state so ably and satisfactorily.

On the night of the 7th our part of the line manœuvred in getting into position from dark until about 11 o'clock. About that time a mighty cheer rose on our right and came along the line to the left, and every Confederate joined in as it approached, and it passed along to the left until it passed out of hearing. It was accepted as an assurance that all was going well on the right wing of the army. On the morning of the 8th (Sunday) Lee's army was moving by the right flank in column of fours towards Spottsylvania court house, and the Federal sharpshooters were more aggressive than before, and in stronger force, masking the movement of the Federal army to the left. There was a single occurrence of the day's sharpshooting which I think worthy of mention. Early in the day the Federal sharpshooters fired into Davis's brigade, and we advanced on them without meeting opposition for some distance and came in sight of the Federal line of works, when appearances indicated the presence of the Federal sharpshooters along the line; their small tents still standing. The unusual quiet that pervaded the wilderness at this point caused me to feel that the Federal sharpshooters were awaiting our near approach, withholding their fire. I must confess that to me this was a more trying ordeal than any event of the campaign thus far. I felt that each Federal sharpshooter had selected his Confederate; that his rifle was pressed against his shoulder; and that he was taking aim and had begun pressing the trigger gently. So I ordered my company to halt and assemble. I told them my fears, and called their attention to the advantage the Federals had (if there) behind breastworks, while we were in the open woods. I then told them that I wanted two men to go forward in advance of the main line of sharpshooters to draw the fire of the enemy, and called for two volunteers. Brit Jones and

"Hub" Campbell stepped forward, two of the remaining three originally selected and drilled. I directed them to go forward rapidly from tree to tree, and we would follow.

Experienced sharpshooters will at once recognize what a hazardous advance this was, for these two men especially. In my whole experience as a soldier I never looked upon any with so much pride as upon Jones and Campbell. Jones was nearly of middle age, Campbell a smooth faced boy. At the command the company, having deployed, rushed forward on the breastworks. The Federal sharpshooters waited until Jones and Campbell had advanced within thirty steps, when they fired on the whole line, and fled. We drove them from the field without the loss of a man, killed or wounded. By reference to a letter written by myself, dated May 29, 1864, in regard to this battle of the Wilderness, I find that I was on the battle field all day Sunday, the 8th, amongst the unburied dead, and drove the enemy's sharpshooters over two or three lines of Federal works. The carnage was fearful, and indescribable. The woods were thick, yet I stood at one point and counted around me fifty-four dead Federals. My estimate, as I then recorded it, was that I saw ten or fifteen Federals to one Confederate dead. In thick groves of saplings bullet marks on the Federal side showed that they overshot the Confederates, a large percentage of the balls passing from eight to fifteen feet above ground. Birds, squirrels and pheasants were found killed.

On the morning of the 9th we arrived on the field of the battle of Spottsylvania. Of course, the sharpshooters covered the front of the line of battle, but nothing occurred to vary the monotony of desultory sharpshooting. The next day, however, the 10th, when Gen. Early, in command of Hill's corps, "flanked the Federal flankers," as you will note in the correspondent's account of the battle, the sharpshooters played a conspicuous part. The sharpshooters of Davis's brigade crossed the Po on a foot log under fire of the Federal sharpshooters, above a mill on that stream. The fear of being drowned, if wounded, was equal to the fear of being burned to death if wounded, while charging through burning woods in the wilderness, where we passed several wounded Confederates brushing away the leaves around them with their ramrods to keep the advancing flames from closing in on them. Having crossed the Po we deployed up stream along the bank and moved on the enemy, and drove them. There was no line of battle supporting us; our deployment to the left was in extension of the line of battle. We captured several prisoners and drove the remainder off the field, when we halted to keep in line with the line of battle on our right. The Federals were fleeing across an open field, and the sharpshooters kept them moving until they passed out of sight and range. Up to this moment it had been a picnic with us. But soon grape and canister rained down in our midst. When there was a cessation of firing, a single sharpshooter appeared at the farthest point on a hill in front. He stood in plain view, the sky being the background to the picture. I called Brit Jones and told him to raise the thousand yard sight on his Enfield rifle and fire on him. He did so, taking rest and deliberate aim. There was no other firing going on. The Federal sharpshooter drooped. At first we thought he had dodged from the noise of the passing bullet. We kept our eye on the spot, and in a few moments his comrades came and bore him from the field. It was a thousand yards distant or more, and the best shot I witnessed during the war.

We were ordered to the right several hundred yards along the line, and were directed to drive out the Federals that had collected in a thicket in front. It was densely thick and not one of them could be seen. As we closed in on it a Federal captain's voice rang out, "Fire into 'em, boys!" I presume that the Confederate sharpshooter who killed him instantly, must have fired at the sound of his voice. He was directly in my front, and as I advanced I found his sword, and then the scabbard, several feet apart. It was Capt. J. B. Owen, of the one hundred and twenty-fifth New York regiment. Up to this date, from May, 1862, I had carried the Confederate sword of Lieut. Col. W. A. Rankin, who was killed at Shiloh while in command of the ninth Mississippi regiment; his sister, Miss Laura A. Rankin, being then my affianced, and at the time of this battle my bride. I had never drawn his sword from the scabbard nor returned it thereto, without a thought of the gallant Rankin and his sister;

the one a christian hero (see the enlarged edition of the "Old Guard in Gray," by J. Harvey Mathes), the other a perfect type of pure christian womanhood, a daughter of the typical ante-bellum Southern planter. I afterwards returned home the sword of Col. Rankin and carried the Federal sword of Capt. Owen, both of which I still have.

Returning to our position in line near the court house of Spottsylvania, the 11th was spent in sharpshooting without casualty or thrilling incident; but what shall I say of the 12th. Of all the days of the campaign, from the firing of the first gun in the Wilderness until the last, at second Cold Harbor, June 3rd, none was so awful to the sharpshooters of Davis's brigade. The correspondent will tell you that " at 4 o'clock in the morning of that day the hostile lines burst, as under the sudden bidding of an electric wire, into a fierce cannonade —an explosion in its suddenness, it raged from the first moment of opening in the full depth of its fury." "The suddenness of the thunders with which the artillery rent the air was not greater than the deafening storm which burst from the infantry. The musketry that followed immediately after the first gun was so great in its volume from the opening, that it bespoke clearly the presence of large masses of men. Rising in a deep roll, one and unbroken, its blended ringing declared that the hostile thousands from whom it rose must have met in conflict, hand to hand. The peals in quick succession of the artillery did not drown the voice, but on it went distinctly, a flowing roar that rose to heaven like the constant outcry of a rushing river." I have no remembrance as to how the sharpshooters scrambled over the breastworks in the fog and darkness to the front, through the tangled brush, over the abatis of fallen trees sixty or eighty yards deep in our front, with limbs sharpened towards the enemy; but I have a vivid recollection of that day's fighting in front of the fallen timber, under a constant fire from the sharpshooters, and sometimes from the line of battle, all day. We were in an open glade of pines; the enemy were in thick bushes. I took a central position along the line of my sharpshooters, and we all sheltered as best we could behind the pines. Early in the day the sharpshooters declared to me that the enemy's line of battle was not over sixty yards distant. I could not see the line and discredited their statement, but subsequent events proved that they were correct. I noticed soon after our line was posted that a Federal bullet passed the tree I was behind at unusually regular intervals. I stood with my left side to the tree, except when I moved along the line on duty. While I was standing, and leaning a little too far forward, a bullet passed in front of my eyes and lodged in the body of a tree a little in front and to my right, so near that I could lay my hand on it. It was not long before I was convinced that a Federal sharpshooter had chosen my head for a target. When duty called me to other points I left immediately after he had fired, and returned before he could reload. Gen. Davis reinforced our line from the line of battle during the day more than once, and the firing finally became so deadly that messengers could not go direct to our line and live.

After noon the commands were sent into our line on the right, at a point less dangerous, and passed from one to another of the sharpshooters until I received them. "Gen. Davis says,

'Forward the skirmish line!'" I knew that Gen. Davis could not know the situation, that we were so close to the Federal line of battle, and I further believed it would be certain death or wounds to almost every man. I made no reply and sent no message. In a short while the order came again in the same words. I never saw such a dreadful expression on the faces of men who never flinched in battle. It was not long before the order came down the line again, "Gen. Davis says, 'Forward the skirmish line!'" Under the circumstances I thought I had some right to exercise discretion in the matter, and that unless the line of battle was to advance with us it would be a useless sacrifice of life. I felt that a positive disobedience of orders would result in a court martial and dishonor, so I ordered the sharpshooters to go forward; but to my surprise not a single man moved. They looked at me but said not a single word. They had led me through the wilderness and all along down the line in every skirmish. It had come my time to work in the lead, and I must confess it was a mild mannered lead and ended abruptly. "Boys, we have to go; come ahead!" I passed the line ten feet or more, and they all moved as one man, and by the time they had closed up with me and gone ten steps, the very earth trembled under us from the shock of Federal musketry. The twigs, bark and leaves rained down upon us. As I turned to go back to our line of battle I saw that Jones and Campbell were both wounded, and it looked like nearly all the men were down.

It was as difficult for us to retreat over the abatis of fallen trees as for the enemy to advance over it. When we did reach our breastworks the greatest confusion existed, and some of the sharpshooters were wounded from our own line of battle. I walked up in front of a rifle aimed at the enemy; a moment later and I should have caught the ball. The firing ceased, except the sharpshooting, and as soon as a detail was made to replace the many that had fallen, we had to retrace our steps and establish our line where it was before. I went to my old stand. After awhile Dan Yocumb came and stood near me, looking pale and in dread. I directed him to take his place in line, and while he hesitated I said to him, "Dan, if you stay here a minute you will be killed; a sharpshooter has been shooting at me here all day." I had not finished the sentence before Yocumb's knee joint was crushed with a Federal bullet, and his comrades carried him back to the rear, to die next day. Not until I began this day's story of the sharpshooters have I ever thought of what might have been passing in young Yocumb's mind. Doubtless he had noticed that he was the only sharpshooter left of the original twenty four men who started in the campaign only a week before, and he could reasonably have concluded that his chance to escape death or wounds was slim; and so it was. The attention of the Confederate sharpshooters was attracted by this fatal result of the Federal sharpshooter's aim, and it was not long before he ceased firing, being either killed or wounded.

I do not know whether Jones survived the war or not. Campbell was killed by the Federals near Oxford, Mississippi, while at home wounded. Recently I met Sergt. Abner Myers, of Byhalia, Mississippi, who belonged to the eleventh Mississippi regiment of Davis's brigade, and who was a sharpshooter in front of that regiment on that day. In conversation touching our experience that day he asked if I knew what Gen. Davis said when we were driven in by the enemy's line of battle. I replied that I did not. Said Myers: "When I crossed our works Gen. Davis was sitting against them, and I said to him, 'General, their line of battle is coming.' He replied: 'D—n a line of battle; my sharpshooters can whip a line of battle. Forward, my sharpshooters!'" Abner Myers says that the sharpshooters of the eleventh Mississippi lost five commanders during the campaign, and one or two resigned on account of the hardships and fatality in that service, and a part of the time he, as sergeant, was in command.

The night of the 12th came on, finding Davis's brigade in the same position and the line of sharpshooters in front of the abatis in the same position as when the battle began in the morning. On this part of of the battle field, so far as my vision extended, the extra hazardous service of the sharpshooters was never more forcibly illustrated. All day long the sharpshooters were on the forefront of battle at close quarters with the enemy, under constant fire, without protection save trees and stumps, with a belt of sixty to eighty yards of fallen pines in the rear, which was a serious obstacle in the way of retreat; while the line of battle was not engaged save for a few minutes when the sharpshooters were driven in by the Federal line of battle. I here submit the correspondent's account of this battle.

BATTLE OF SPOTTSYLVANIA COURT HOUSE.

[Correspondence of the London Herald, May 25, 1864.]

On the morning of the 7th of May Lee's troops lay in line on the field of their victory of the Wilderness; Ewell still on the left and Hill in the centre. Longstreet's corps, under the command of Maj. Gen. R. H. Anderson, held the right. Some desultory skirmishing in front was the only evidence presented during the day that we were in the presence of the enemy. As I passed along the line of battle in a gear rather better than that of the soldier and somewhat worse than that of the officer, the men showed themselves in their amusing comments on my appearance to be in excellent spirits.

From the headquarters of Gen. Lee and of Gen. Hill I went on the evening of the 6th to those of Wilcox. I found the latter officer engaged with Gen. Smith, of the engineers, in an examination of the ground with a view to a revision of the line of field works. Changes decided on in my presence at some points of those improvised defences were immediately shown by stakes; and working parties actively at their execution. As I rode on to the left I observed revision going on at other parts of the line, new batteries being planted, epaulements for guns being thrown up, and other indications that the Confederates were determined to remain where they were. Gen. Ewell, Gen. Early and Gen. Johnson were in glowing spirits, and entertained clearly no intention of abandoning the great advantages of their present position. Everything along the front showed that Lee, judging doubtless from his knowledge of Grant's character, looked for a renewal of the attack; and far from any intention of moving from the field of his bloody triumph, awaited its delivery in confident preparation on the ground he then occupied.

The contest of the Wilderness presented to Grant on the evening of the 6th the choice of massacre, inaction or retreat. Two-thirds of his splendid army yet capable of duty, he determined on a movement by which, while not exposing the fact of his bloody defeat, he would be enabled to renew the struggle on open ground. From the point of conflict on the Orange and Fredericksburg plank track and earthen way known as Brock's road, follows the direction along which he would now seek naturally to move. The opening of that route was in fact one of the advantages sought from the attack on Lee's right. The employment of that road for his purpose having, however, been made impossible by the position of the Confederates at the close of the battle, he was obliged to adopt in its stead some of the inferior lines of movement in his rear. Under cover of his skirmishers he withdrew his right quietly on the evening of the 7th; moved it down behind its centre to the Orange and Fredericksburg plank road; and directing it along that track for some distance eastwardly, dropped it down by several minor roads still further to the south. The centre he next broke into column in the rear of heavy skirmishers, and marched it in the same direction behind the solid masses of the left. During the night that wing moved in like manner out of its works, and soon afterwards, followed by the sharpshooters that had been employed to mask the whole movement, took its position in the line of march.

The scene of the battle of the Wilderness is situated mainly in Spottsylvania. The court house of that county lies at a distance from the field of the 5th and 6th of May of nine miles, in a direction almost exactly southeast. The country around that village consists to a great extent of open fields, and watered by the heads of the Mattapony—those called, by a strange conceit, the Mat, the Ta, the Po, the Ny—presents excellent positions for the employment of artillery. The occupation of the village itself offering possession of a leading road to Richmond, became the first object of the new movement, and one that appeared very easy of accomplishment, seeing that the only obstacle in the way on the morning of the 7th was a brigade of Fitzhugh Lee's division of horse.

The scouting of the Army of Northern Virginia is, no doubt, a most active and efficient agency. But intuition of the very highest order can alone explain the rapidity with which Lee acts in reference to the movements of the enemy. Whether the cavalry conflict for the possession of that village, or some revelation from scouts or angels, may have appraised him of Grant's design, the army was directed by Gen. Lee on the night of the 7th to move rapidly towards Spottsylvania court house. Maj. Gen. R. H. Anderson, holding the right with Longstreet's corps, ordered forward the division commanded for the present by Brig. Gen. Kershaw. Wofford's brigade broke at once into column, and followed close up by Brian's, started with vivacity, at 11 o'clock in the night, to the support of Fitzhugh Lee. As these splendid troops began to move, the spirit with which they appeared to go forward shot like electricity from rank to rank, and found utterance in a cheer that, running back along the forming column for miles, rang like the roll of musketry from front to rear from the depths of the midnight forest, loud and clear.

The enemy in his race for Spottsylvania court hourt house had a start of a few hours. Having begun his movement, however, from a point opposite our extreme left, while we began ours from the extreme right, that advantage must have been nearly equated. There remained to us, however, no time to spare. We were obliged to push for the goal directly. Our shortest route lay, unfortunately, through a forest in which accident or design had, during the day, set the leaves on fire. The smoke of the burning continued still to hang in clouds upon the ground, threatening the troops as they went on with actual suffocation. Heated, blinded, choking, to a degree almost insupportable, they bore their sufferings patiently on their march through those smoking woods for a distance of seven miles. The ten thousand Greeks of Xenophon did not, when they saw the sea, feel more relief than the thousands of Lee's men did when they emerged from that forest pandemonium into the open country and untainted air.

Kershaw, having reached the high road, moved forward rapidly. Having on his way detached Humphrey's Mississippians and his own South Carolinians to the left, for the relief of Fitzhugh Lee, he pressed on with Wofford's and Brian's men to Spottsylvania court house. He succeeded in reaching that place in time— about sunrise of the 8th of May—to obtain possession of it without firing a shot. In the meantime Humphrey, in the command of the force sent to the left, turned from the road of Kershaw's advance to a point known as the Block house, about a mile and a half in front of the court house. Pressing up rapidly he had arrived at an opportune moment—on the morning of the 8th—to sustain an attack upon the position that had been for some time held against both cavalry and infantry by some of Fitzhugh Lee's horse. The defenses improvised at that point in front of the court house consisted of a rude barrier of dead trees; but, even feeble as they were, they, still worse, fell short in their extent of the breadth of Humphrey's front.

Robertson's and Griffin's division of the corps of Gen. Warren—the fifth—advanced with great spirit upon the Confederate position. The deadly marksmanship of the Mississippians and South Carolinains in their front, shot with terrible truth to their belt buckles. Though they dropped dead like deer struck down in a herd, still they came on. Volley after volley swept through their solid mass; but though finally showing signs of faltering, they continued to advance until they had actually crossed the Confederate barrier. The assailants having bayoneted some of the men who withstood them so fiercely, quailed before their unflinching firmness, and with the loss of a considerable number of prisoners and a large number in killed and wounded, fled. The South Carolinians behaved magnificently during the repulse, but held their ground as the enemy retired. The Mississippians sprang over the breastworks in hot pursuit. They had not advanced across the field more than a quarter of a mile when they were driven back in turn with the loss of many men, and two stands of colors captured, as was supposed at the time, by the enemy. That supposition, however, proved to be a mistake. Having after separation from their comrades found themselves free, they moved several miles through the woods around the enemy's left, and next day, to the great rejoicing of the whole brigade, came back safely, men and colors.

The assault upon Humphrey was repeated during the day several times, but in each instance without any other result to the assailants than defeat and death. Foiled thus in direct attack, Gen. Warren attempted to carry the position by a movement against its flank. Law's brigade of Alabamians were accordingly put in on Humphrey's left with the purpose of resisting the blow about to be struck from that direction. The Federal advance came up with great vigor, but after a brief struggle was flung back by the stubborn resistance of the fresh troops by whom it had been confronted. The combats of the 8th, brief and bloody as they were, had thus terminated for the day; and saw Lee in triumphant possession of all the positions covering the roads running southwardly from Spottsylvania court house. In the fights of the day, as in the race of the night previous, the Confederates had thus come off completely victorious.

Longstreet's corps continued to pour into the field during the early part of the day. The position of the divisions pointed out by Gen. Anderson as they came up, were immediately afterwards covered by a line of breastworks. At daylight on the morning of the 8th, the second and third corps still holding the field of the Wilderness, the former, under Ewell, broke into column, and moving behind the latter (Hill's) proceeded on its way to the scene of the impending conflict. Having arrived on the field, it drew up on Longstreet's left. Rodes's division having driven back the enemy in a charge for a mile, the whole corps spent the night after a very severe march, taking and strengthening its position.

Hill's corps, after having covered the left of Ewell's column, moved out of its works. Its leading division (Anderson's), commanded for the present by its senior brigadier, Gen. Mahone, was assailed on its march towards Spottsylvania court house, near a place called Shady Grove. Having, after a brief delay, repulsed the attack, it moved on; but the whole corps bivouacked only a short distance in advance of the scene of that passing conflict.

Appendix. 443

On the morning of the 9th it reached the field of the approaching battle, and taking its place on the right, proceeded rapidly to cover its front with a line of field works. The illness of the lieutenant general charged with the command of that grand division of Lee's army had unfitted him for the service when I saw him on the field of the Wilderness during the 6th of May. He remained, however, at his post; and the chafing of his spirit in impatience of his prostration at a moment fraught with such great events, appeared to me as I stood speaking to him in his ambulance on the field of the Ny, to have delayed his recovery. Gen. Early, of Ewell's corps, had accordingly been placed for the time in command of that of Hill at the approach of the bloody trial which appeared to hang over it on the 9th of May.

Our position lay in advance of the Po. Before it flowed the narrow and muddy stream of the Ny. Our lines wound in front along irregular slopes ascending from the latter branch of the Mattapony, and embracing within them the approaches southwardly from Spottsylvania court house, swept on the left back to the Po. The enemy's army stood partly in rear and partly in front of the Ny, and presented to the convexity of our alignment the general plan of a concave curve. The rainshed of the greater part of our position fell into the Ny, and the slopes looking down upon that stream witnessed the heat and burden of the battle. The approaches to Lee's works lay partly through forest, partly through field, but presented at many points excellent positions for artillery, while those open to the enemy for that purpose were generally much inferior. Such, in brief, was the attitude of the two armies when I bivouacked on the field, the Ny, with Gen. Ewell and his staff on the night of the 9th of May.

Field's division, resting on the Po, held Lee's left. A main road from Fredericksburg gave the enemy access to the rear of that wing of our army. The bridge on which we had crossed the river on our march from the Wilderness lay on the line of the detour that thus laid Field open to serious danger. Some cavalry having been said to be threatening that crossing of the stream, the brigades of Harris and Perrin—both of Anderson's division—were sent back with orders to hold it against all comers. They arrived there at 7 o'clock in the evening. Night had nearly come on, and they knew nothing of the position or force of the enemy. After consultation with Maj. Gen. W. H. F. Lee, of the cavalry—son of the commander-in-chief of the Army of Northern Virginia—the enemy being in present force, pickets were thrown out but a short distance in advance of the brigade, and a regiment placed for their support on a hill to the left of its immediate rear. The brigades of Perry, Wright, Perrin and Harris—all of Anderson's division—drew up in a favorable position for resisting any direct attempt of the enemy to obtain possession of the bridge.

Mahone had just made his dispositions when masses of men were heard moving down to the opposite bank of the Po. A thundering cheer from the midnight darkness which reigned around revealed that the Confederates on this side of the river lay in the presence of a host of armed men. Picket firing opened immediately in front of the bridge; but after a while subsiding, the thousands who stood on that part of the field confronting each other in deadly array, lay down to take a night of peace in the sleep of the battle bivouac.

Massing of the enemy in his front appeared to threaten Field on the morning of the 10th with serious attack. Gordon, who lay a reserve in rear of the second corps, was ordered up soon after sunrise to that officer's support. A heavy cannonade from both sides appeared to be the regular preface to an advance, and was followed by the appearance of the enemy coming forward in heavy column of five or six lines deep. That mighty mass came sweeping steadily on, and, absorbing its line of skirmishers, appeared of a volume sufficient to overcome all resistance. Field's sharpshooters inserted death in a hundred incisions through its solid front, and the lightning flash of his artillery cut through its living material in gashes broad and deep. Halting within two hundred yards of the works it retreated, leaving many a wretch behind in mortal agony or in the merciful repose of death. Again and again during the day the same demonstration was repeated, and on each occasion with the same result.

Masses of the enemy appeared collecting rapidly, in the afternoon, on the front of Gen.

Rodes. Gordon was at once ordered back to his support from the rear of Field. Eight or ten lines deep, a column of blue coats moved through the forest and hurled its immense weight against Dole's brigade of Rodes's division. Dropping its living and dead offal on all sides, under a well directed fire of rifle and gun, it still kept on its way, and by the heavy pressure from its rear burst a living torrent over the works held by Dole. Bearing like a mighty river everything before it, it swept surging to the rear of the Confederate position for several hundred yards, when it struck with a heavy recoil against the rocklike solidity of Gordon's front. He had just come up from the left, and charging, cheering as he went, hurled back the heavy masses in a terror as great as if the flash of his bayonets were the deadly light of the Gorgon's eye. His fire reserved until the enemy broke, he poured into him as he fled volley after volley with an aim and rapidity truly murderous. Twenty minutes having finished this stern work and restored the line to its original position, that valuable officer retired from the immediate front to his position in reserve.

The movements upon Field's lines during the morning of the 10th were designed, doubtless, to employ our attention during the operations against his rear. The Po follows a course generally parallel with the line taken up during the night of the 9th by the division under Mahone. Sweeping back, however, around that flank, at a short distance below his left, it exposed him from that part of the opposite bank to the fire of some guns, taking him even somewhat in reverse. Crossing the works they had thrown up during the night to protect their front, his troops sought shelter from the missiles of that battery by crouching on the outer slope. Under cover of the cannonade the enemy, not daring an attempt to force the bridge, crossed the river lower down, in full exposure to a well directed fire from some field pieces that had been planted on the Confederate left. Having driven in the skirmishers of Wright's brigade of Georgians, the Federal column began to form in line on this side, and, for a moment, war seemed about to subject to another fiery trial the well proved metal of Anderson's division.

Gen. Early had in the meantime crossed the Po at a bridge lower down than that in the front of the division of Anderson. With Heth's division and Mahone's superb brigade, he continued his march on the opposite bank up stream, until striking the flank of the Federal fiankers he drove them before him without encountering any resistance. The thundering of his guns, the shouting in wild triumph of his troops, came near and still nearer to Anderson's fellows, as they stood ready for a mortal struggle; and those welcome sounds as they swelled up from the woods heralded the arrival of a staff officer, who having dashed into the stream, rode up in full speed, his horse's flanks still dripping with water, to announce to Mahone that the enemy was withdrawing from the bridge in full retreat.

The Federal masses were seen by Mahone's artillerists moving across the open ground of heights on the other side of the Po. Shot and shell were immediately hurled into them as they rushed back hurriedly from Early's crushing advance. The division moved down at once to the bridge, and having crossed, formed on the opposite side in line of battle parallel

with the road by which the enemy had come—
that from Shady Grove. Wright's Georgians,
drawn up on Field's left, rested their right on
the river; Perrin's Alabamians came next;
then Perry's Floridians, Harris's Mississippians and Mahone's Virginians. Heth's men
as they came up with Early took position on
the left. The enemy had formed in line of
battle a half mile off. His front, covered by
breastworks, was further protected by four
improvised redoubts. The losses of his hurried retreat had been serious, and would
probably have been even more so had he not
embarrassed the pursuit by setting fire behind
him to the leafy woods, in which he had
dropped the dead and wounded of his flight.
The two arrays lay on the ground they had
just taken, and continued to look at each other
during what yet remained of the day, without
demonstration or attack save only to the
extent of occasional shelling.

Foiled by Early in flanking the left of our
position, Grant attempted to break it by direct
attack. Night had almost set in when the
heavy column that had threatened the left so
often during the day burst upon it at last in

terrible earnestness. Covering the whole front of the division, that tremendous attack came under the fire of the brigade on the left of McLaw's—Wofford's Georgians. Gen. G. T. Anderson's brigade received the shock in terrible force, but could be seen from the position of Maj. Gen. R. H. Anderson and Maj. Gen. Field to hold its ground as steadily as if it were on dress parade. Rapidly and regularly it threw up cloud after cloud of smoke, and the flashes of its fire burst along its front every few minutes in threadlike lines.

An angle in the line of the Confederate array—a salient, as it is termed by engineers—presented the weak point of the defence. The breadth of its fire necessarily contracted, and its sides exposed to enfilade, that part of the Confederate line was held by Gregg's brigade of Texans. Uncovered by traverses, his men, after the attacking column had swept up within a short distance of the works, encountered a fire from both front and flank; and finally, as the wave of the onslaught surged over headlong into their defences, were forced to fall back before its irresistible weight. That they did not yield in any feebleness of spirit was attested as they retired with their faces to the foe; by several of their comrades who lay in the trenches dead or dying under thrust of the stern bayonet. Stung with humiliation by their repulse, the gallant fellows paused in their retrogression, and springing furiously forward, drove the enemy—just as he began to quail before the terrible slaughter along other parts of the line—out of their works, that was followed by their unerring rifles for a quarter of a mile. The losses of Grant in that repulse of the 10th must have been very severe.

Two brigades of the right wing had been sent during the day to support Ewell, in anticipation of attack repelled so splendidly by Gordon. The sun had almost set when that wing of the Confederate army became itself subject of more or less serious threatening. Two lines of battle moved from the woods in front of Wilcox, but were met by the fire of a heavy line of sharpshooters, and by a thundering cannonade from batteries posted advantageously in that officer's immediate rear. Having contributed its victims to the carnage of the field, that threatening advance broke into a retreat. The attack on Field driven

Appendix. 453

back about the same time, night closed upon the two armies in a repose that was unbroken, outside the lines, save by the venomous whirring of bullets from the sleepless sharpshooters.

The morning of the 11th broke, unheralded by the shock of arms. A feeble demonstration against our left, and another against our center, deepened for a brief time the volume of the skirmish fire. During the weak show of attack made thus on Ewell's left, the country lost for a time the services of that gallant fellow, Brigadier General Hays. He received a wound which, though not at all dangerous, appeared when I saw him to be very painful. With the exceptions of some threatenings the battle dragged on throughout the day in the Indian like warfare, that, during the pauses of the heavy collisions, raged, apparently without intermission, outside the opposing lines.

On the 12th of May the battlefield lay, before dawn, enveloped in a hazy fog. At four o'clock in the morning of that day the hostile lines burst, as under the sudden bidding of an electric wire, into a fierce cannonade. An explosion in its suddenness, it raged from the first moment of opening, in the full depth of its fury. The metallic peal of the solid shot, the sharp clap and the flat crash of the shell rose from side to side with rapidity. They seemed to shake the very earth with their thunders. That terrific storm, while undiminished in depth, underwent immediately after its first outburst a change in character; for the sharper peals of shot and shell were succeeded by the duller thuds, that, hurling forward grape and canister, told of a struggle deepened into the sternness of close quarters.

The suddenness of the thunders with which the artillery rent the air was not greater than that with which the deafening storm burst from the infantry. The musketry that followed immediately after the first gun was so great in its volume from its opening that it bespoke clearly the presence of large masses of men. Rising in a deep roll, one and unbroken, its blended ringing declared that the hostile thousands from whom it swelled up must have met in conflict, hand to hand. The peals in quick succession of the artillery did not drown its voice; but on it went distinctly, a flowing roar that rose to heaven, like the constant outcry of a rushing river. Divination was not necessary with all those evidences to tell me, as I rose from my blanket in the rear, that, as in the case of our own conflict at Inkerman, an attack prepared with deliberation in close proximity to the Confederate lines had moved suddenly from the cover of the morning fog.

The field works that protected Ewell's right on the morning of the 12th extended through a wood. They occupied the line of a low bridge, and, by what appears to me to be a grave error, lay somewhat down its reverse slope. An enemy approaching them could not be seen from some parts of the works until he had appeared over the rise, in their immediate front. Retreating from them, he received, once behind that swell of ground, protection from the fire of part of those defenses. The course of the breastworks followed that of the bridge, and accordingly formed at one place a salient with an angle so small as to be almost acute. It consisted of two lines which ran one parallel with the other, and containing between them a space sufficiently wide for a line of battle, described by military engineers as a "double sap." Epaulements were placed in support of the whole at several points of the line; and, at the salient, sufficient for so many as twenty guns. A general understanding of the position may be obtained from this description, after it has been stated that the sides of the salient, subject as they were, in the event of an attack, to enfilade from its apex, were protected for some distance down the line with a series of short traverses.

Gen. J. M. Jones's brigade occupied the salient. On the left of Jones's men were formed the Stonewall brigade, under Walker, and next in order in the line of battle were the Louisianians under Hays. The right of Jones, who held the salient, rested on the brigade of Stewart. Such was the distribution on the morning of the 12th, behind the breastworks of Ewell's right wing, of the men constituting the division of Gen. Edward Johnston. On the right of the division was an unoccupied part of the works about two hundred yards in length, and further on that staunch brigade of Wilcox's division—Lane's. Jones's brigade had sent one of its best regiments—the twenty-first Virginia—from the salient, to cover the gap between Stewart and Lane as skirmishers. Two others were also sent out of the works in

Appendix. 457

the same capacity, with the view of protecting the angle of the position from sudden attack. But three regiments of the brigade remained to defend a weak point that had been held previously by six. Of twenty guns that had been placed in the salient, sixteen had, under an expectation entertained during the night of an attack upon the extreme right, been withdrawn. Such was the array and strength of Ewell's right on the morning of the 12th.

Johnston, informed at 3 o'clock, a. m., that the enemy was massing in his front, sent off in hot haste for guns to replace those that had been removed from his works during the night.

In the meantime the signs in front began rapidly to take the definite form of an attack. His skirmishers came in at short notice, and the forest behind them impressed the senses with the feeling that, wrapt as it was in a fog, it was swarming with the masses of human life. Page's battalion of artillery had, in response to the demand of Gen. Johnston, come up to the salient in a trot; but a tremendous column of the enemy having at that moment emerged from the haze, it arrived only to have its horses shot dead in their traces, and its men mowed down in the act of unlimbering. So terrible was the fire of the enemy that but one of the guns was brought into action. Capt. W. Carter had, with great devotion, succeeded, unassisted, in making that ready for work; and, standing at it, heroically alone, continued until his capture to fire it, charged with grape and canister, into the Federal ranks.

Gen. Johnston had no sooner become aware of the exact point of attack than he rushed towards the salient. He was too late. The column that had burst from the fog upon that weak point held it already in possession. Three regiments which had been left in line for its defense had fled before the storming mass without firing a shot. Johnston, caught in the rush of friend and foe, was made prisoner, and was thus left by the bad conduct of some of his own men to waste his brave spirit ingloriously in prison. His bravery is of the antique. His conduct as a general officer was marked by constancy and address. A great favorite with Lieut. Gen. Ewell, he was known amongst the rank and file, in affectionate recognition of his courage and obstinacy, as "Old Blucher."

The salient carried, and one-half of Jones's men killed, wounded or captured, the enemy poured through the Confederate line in immense force. The Stonewall brigade, on the immediate left of the gap thus opened in the Confederate ranks, became exposed on the right flank. Gen. Walker, its chief, attempted immediately to swing that wing around, but while in the act was disabled by a very severe wound in the side. Pressed hotly by the Federal advance, that movement became then, after even the brief delay consequent on that accident, impossible. The pressure upon its flank having commenced, many of the men forced into disorder were killed, wounded or captured; but several of the regiments, wheeling into position behind the short traverses running back from their breastworks, disputed every foot of ground they held with a steadiness worthy of their traditions. Col. Terry, while holding with unflinching firmness one of those short fronts, received a severe wound. The Stonewall brigade, however, overborne by the movement upon its flank, was finally forced back; and what of it was neither captured, wounded nor killed, found protection behind the battle array of the brigade that had been in line on its left—Hays's Louisianians.

Stewart's brigade, on the right of the regiments that had occupied the salient, was taken by the surging masses of the Federalists in flank. Those of them who were neither captured, killed nor wounded found shelter behind the brigade that had been in line upon their right—Lane's, of Wilcox's division. Engaged in front with a heavy column of the enemy, Lane, on learning of the miscarriage at the salient, became alarmed for his left flank; and having immediately swung his line around almost squarely with its original position, he encountered the enemy's triumphant advance. Charging in fine style he drove it back after a contest that must have cost it dearly. His North Carolinians thus won the glory of being the first to stem the tide of Federal victory on the right.

While the Stonewall brigade fought and fell back, that next on its left—Hays's—had time to swing around. Col. Monaghan, its senior colonel, being in command, it confronted the rushing advance to the left. Standing behind a traverse that extended perpendicularly from the original position of the brigade, it presented a front as firm as a ledge of rock. The wave of the enemy's triumph surged up to that barrier; but having broken upon it in mere spray, left the honor of the arrest of its overflow on that side of the field to those houseless, landless warriors of Louisiana.

Between Hays's men on the one side and Lane's on the other, the Federalists had driven all opposition from their path. For a width of a mile they had swept the works of their defenders; but, though complete masters within that limit, they were confronted by an impassable barrier on the one hand and on the other. Pouring through the gap they had made, their masses formed rapidly from the right and from the left, with the view of turning the line of Hays on that side and of Lane on this, by pressure on those officers' exposed flanks.

Apprehension of attack during the night on the front of Hays had led to the transfer to its support of the fine brigade of Pegram. The other brigades of the division under the command of Gordon—two—were, at the time of the assault upon the salient, half a mile to the left. Springing forward without orders, Gordon had moved at double quick in the direction of the fire that had burst upon the dawn in sudden thunders. Rushing into the fog, he could see neither friend nor foe; but, guided by the instincts of a soldier, still sped forward rapidly under the bidding of the battle's hoarsest roar. The thick haze into whose unknown depth he drove on, soon lit its murderous terrors, as he closed into the conflict, with lurid flashes; and, in the next instant, flung out a sheet of lightning that hurled about the ears of his advancing ranks a very tempest of bullets.

Gordon had come up in column. Gen. R. D. Johnston's brigade, first upon the field, he threw rapidly into line, and launching it against the enemy through the fog, checked the advance. Having arrested thus at one point the surging ranks of the foe, he sought to stop him as he swept around his right. The torrent streaming rapidly in that direction, he was about to be borne back by the flank, when, bringing up his own brigade, its firm line presented to the river like rush an additional width of barrier. The living flood of Federal triumph, dashing against it in vain, swept still farther around, again threatening the Confederate right with destruction under a rapid movement upon its flank. Gordon by this time having brought up his third brigade —Pegram's—forms it, under the command of Col. Huffman, somewhat detached from the others, across the new front of the enemy's advance. The whole line then delivered a murderous volley into the dim masses of human life that stood before it shrouded—and very, very many of them winding sheeted—in the morning fog. Instantly seizing the colors of his center regiment of his own brigade, Gordon spurred forward under a storm of bullets ordering a charge. His men rushed upon the misty ranks that they had just cut gashes through with their deadly fire. Their fury bore down all resistance. The charge had become a chase. Huddling the Federalists in headlong flight over the breastworks that had been held during the night by Stewart, that murderous race was continued for half a mile beyond. Opposition had disappeared before the pursuit; still, however, it held its way in unabated fury. Starting out suddenly from the fog upon a hostile force in line, Gordon's demand for surrender having, in the confusion of his sudden appearance, obtained no reply, the Federalists fell where they had but a moment before stood in lusty life, a battle array of dead and dying.

The enemy still held the ground he had won on Stewart's left. Gordon falling back, therefore occupied the works he had carried so gloriously. His charge had cost the Confederates the services for a time of Brig. Gen. R. D. Johnston. That gallant officer was disabled by a wound that is, however, not very severe. Col. Jones, a soldier of high promise, lay on the field wounded mortally. Lieut. Col. McArthur and Col. Garrett, both officers of ability, gave up upon that field their life blood in manly assertion of the liberties that have been handed down to them from our common ancestors of the days of Runneymeade. Terribly, however, were the Confederates' lives, lost in that moment, avenged. For a width of three hundred yards the Federal slain were scattered over a length of three-quarters of a mile; and, in all the open fields included within that space, lay a sickening slaughter. Four guns that had been taken at the enemy's advance were, during the charge, recaptured, and in the absence of horses, sent by hand some distance to the rear.

The Federalists continued to hold their ground in the salient and along the line of the works, to the left of that angle, within a short distance of the position held by Monaghan's (Hays's) Louisianians. Ramseaur's North Carolinians of Rodes's division formed, covering Monaghan's right, and, being ordered to charge, were received by the enemy with stubborn resistance. The desperate character of the struggle along that brigade front was told terribly in hoarseness and rapidity of its musketry. So close was the fighting there for a time that fire of friend and foe rose up rattling in one common roar. Ramseaur's North Carolinians dropped from the ranks thick and fast, but still he continued with glorious constancy to gain ground foot by foot. Pressing under a fierce fire resolutely on, on, on, the struggle was about to become one of hand to hand, when the Federalists shrunk from that bloody trial. Driven back, they were not defeated. The earthworks being at the moment in their immediate rear, they bounded to the opposite side; and, having thus placed them in their front, renewed the conflict. A rush of an instant brought Ramseaur's fellows to this side of the defenses; and though they crouched close to the slopes, under enfilade from the guns of the salient, their musketry rattled in deep and deadly fire on the enemy that stood in overwhelming numbers but a few yards from their front. Those brave North Carolinians had thus, in one of the very hottest conflicts of the day, succeeded in driving the enemy from the works that had been occupied during the night by a brigade which, until the 12th of May, had never yet yielded to a foe—the Stonewall.

The Confederate line had been re-established by Ramseaur to the position held during the night by Gen. J. M. Jones's left. It had been restored by Gordon to the point occupied during the same time by Jones's right. The gap originally made remained, however, still in the possession of the enemy; and with it all the guns—with the exception of the four retaken by Gordon—that had been captured at the time of the rush into the salient. Through that the Federal masses swept out between the flank of Gordon—of Pegram's brigade—on the one hand, and of Ramseur on the other, endeavoring, by movements to the right and to the left in conjunction with heavy attacks in front, to give the unrecovered space greater width. They still protruded from the open interval between the flanks of these officers, and continued to press still forward with the view of preventing their connection by an intervening array of battle. Moving out in tremendous force with the ultimate purpose of driving them still farther apart and of turning their lines, they were encountered by the stern front of Perrin's Alabamians, of Rodes's division.

Perrin met the crushing weight of the advance unaided. He sought to insert his line between Gordon's left—Pegram's men—and the right of the brave fellows under Ramseur. Receiving the shock of the forward movement as a rock hurls back a wave of the sea, he pressed after the recoil, foot by foot. Closing in on it slowly, he succeeded, after a severe struggle, in pressing it back into the breastworks of the salient—for a part, be it recollected, a "double sap"—under a fire of musketry that exceeded anything I ever heard in its rapidity and volume. It roared unceasingly, a very river of death. Forcing his way on with heroic resolution, now straining forward, then standing in obstinate resistance, and next, for a moment, yielding stubbornly, as the mortal struggle swayed from side to side, Perrin kept with indomitable courage laboring onward, inch by inch. Aided by the fire of Ramseur's men on the left flank of the Federalists, he succeeded finally in driving them from part of the works on that officer's right. Perrin fell dead at the head of his brigade, and Col. J. C. Sanders succeeded to command.

The gap in the Confederate array had been reduced to a small extent by Perrin's left. The other part of his line continued to swing heavily backwards and forwards as the tide of battle rolled from side to side. Shattered terribly by the severity of the contest, he was reinforced by Harris's Mississippians, of Anderson's division, and by McGowan's South Carolinians, of Wilcox's division. The heaviness of the fire at the point where these brigades went into action was terrible. Two young oaks, each upwards of twelve inches in diameter, pierced so often across their trunks, were thus actually cut down, to the serious injury of some of McGowan's men, by minnie bullets.

Fresh troops being put in continually, in front of Harris and McGowan, the contest grew in fierceness. Reeling to and fro for the width of a brigade front it surged now to this side, then to that, over a bloody space of two hundred and fifty yards. The guns that had been captured in the salient by the rush of the first attack lay, during the fierce struggle, in their original position, at one time within the onward roll of the Federal lines, and at another enclosed within the surging ranks of the Confederates. Maj. Cutshaw, a gallant officer of the battalion of artillery, whose pieces lay thus between the ebb and flow of battle, hung devotedly in their immediate rear; and watching the moment that saw them included in the advancing array of the Confederate infantry, sprang forward from his lair in the thicket to load them with canister and grape. Bang! bang! bang! he plied them in hot haste; and thus tearing the ranks of the enemy at close quarters into shreds, he continued with rare steadfastness, hurling his thunders until the line of his supports had begun once more to yield. Retiring again and again as the tide of strife rolled back upon him, he continued on each occasion to watch his opportunity in patient resolution; and whenever the battle surged onward, bounded to his guns to work them with the same ardor and with the same havoc.

McGowan behaved gloriously in the struggle for the works at the salient. He fell, in its progress, painfully, but I hope not dangerously, wounded. Several of his best officers yielded up their lives on that field of blood. Gen. Harris set a brilliant example to his brigade in the stern strife; but though he escaped accident in the tempest of bullets which swept on the wings of death around him, he lost heavily. His losses in officers included some men of high promise. Col. Baker and Lieut. Fletus, of the sixteenth Mississippians, and Col. Hardin, of the nineteenth, are not amongst the least of the gallant soldiers who fell dead from the Confederate lines in that murderous salient. South Carolinians and Mississippians continued, however, to rival each other in their persistent striving to recover the captured works, and finally obtained firm possession of them still further in advance of the foothold that had been secured in them previously by Perrin. Consolidating within the defenses thus far recovered on the left of the salient, the strife was renewed in their front—and very often so close to the muzzles of their rifles as the opposite slopes of the breastworks behind which they crouched under enfilade from the apex of the salient.

From four o'clock in the morning until half past one the struggle within the salient had raged in terrible fierceness. At the expiration of that time it sunk into a comparative lull. The roll of the heavy skirmish shooting went on without intermission, however, around that angle of blood, and swelled after a brief break in the main contest into the furious roar of a renewed attack. The restored front on each side of the salient burst into threadlike flashes; and from two o'clock through the evening until nightfall, and from nightfall until midnight, and from midnight until the approach of dawn of the 13th, a close and rapid fusilade rushed up in commingled roar from the contending ranks. At one time bursting through the gap on Gordon's right and endangering his flank; at others raging up to the face of the very works held by that officer, by McGowan, by Harris, by Sanders and by Ramseaur, the conflict raged furiously until, the enemy repelled firmly at all points of his attack, it settled long after midnight into the sharp and venomous whizzings of the sharpshooters' rifles.

The four guns that Gordon had recaptured still remained two hundred yards in his rear. They could not be removed under the terrible fire that swept over the ground they occupied. Fourteen guns remained in the possession of the enemy, and with these four constituted substantially the only object of continuing the murderous struggle for the salient. The conditions of that contest had changed Lee's policy of defense for that of attack, and had thus made a further maintenance of it highly expedient. A material advantage, of some importance to the enemy, lay in the possession of the height on which the salient stood; but even this did not, in the opinion of the commander in chief, justify an avoidable waste of the lives of his men. Before dawn on the morning of the 13th a line of works had been thrown up by the pioneers of the second corps, under Maj. Green, half a mile rear of the point to which the contest of the day had been narrowed; and, connecting the original defenses on the right with those on the left by a route considerably shorter, presented a favorable position for return to the policy of defense. Covered by skirmishing, the gallant fellows who had fought their way so stubbornly over the bloody ground within the salient into the works that had been captured by the enemy in his rush of the morning of the 12th, retired before day on the 13th to that new line.

In the battles of the Ny no officer earned such glory as Gen. Gordon. His admirable flank movement at the Wilderness, his repulse of the enemy's rush through the position of Dole, and his dash and skill in stemming the Federal torrent from the salient on the 12th won the admiration of the army. Gen. Lee acknowledged on the field publicly the great services of that officer, and, informing him at the time that he should ask for his promotion, has had him rewarded with the rank of major general.

The battles, ending with the morning of the 13th, had closed. A more stubborn contest than that of the 12th has not been witnessed during the war. The losses of the Confederates during those struggles include between two and three thousand prisoners, eighteen guns, and from six to seven thousand killed and wounded. Those of the enemy in the conflict of the 10th and of the 12th, including as they do the disaster at the hands of Early's flanking force, the murderous repulses from the front of Field, and from that of Dole, and the terrible havoc of Gordon's charge on the right of the salient, cannot have been less than from fifteen to twenty thousand in killed and wounded. The rotting dead found unburied on the ground the Federalists occupied during this contest presented a spectacle utterly horrible in the immensity of their numbers.

During the campaign the losses in Ewell's corps, according to an official statement of the chief of its medical staff—Dr. Hunter Maguire—does not exceed thirty-five hundred in killed and wounded, after summing the losses of each of its brigades up to the 13th of this month. With this basis of approximate estimate, and the further fact that the number of wounded that had been sent to the rear up to the 19th by those devoted men, the Richmond committee for the relief of the wounded, had not reached ten thousand, including those disabled by sickness, there can be very little doubt of the conclusion that Lee's total losses in killed and wounded, inclusive of the battle of the 12th, have not overrun at most eleven or twelve thousand. About three thousand five hundred prisoners added to that, the depletion of his forces by the battles of the campaign up to this time is fully represented, I should think, by fourteen or fifteen thousand men. Grant's army has shown—in the increasing feebleness of and longer intervals between his attacks, in his change from offense to defense, from fighting to manœuvreing—unmistakable evidence of the crippling unavoidable, under losses that, including about four thousand prisoners, must certainly amount to forty thousand, but that fall, in all probability, not much short of fifty thousand.

CHAPTER XXVI.

LANE'S SHARPSHOOTERS.

Gen. Lane, in the history of his brigade, pays this short tribute to his battalion of sharpshooters, which is both abstract and summary, and dismisses the subject:

"Our corps of sharpshooters was organized in the fall of 1863 at Liberty Mills. It was composed of picked marksmen and brave men. Its officers, too, were cool and brave. This fine body of men were not only instructed in skirmish drill, but were frequently practiced in calculating and stepping off distances, firing at targets and similar exercises, which rendered them very efficient. The first commander was the intrepid Capt. John G. Knox, of the seventh regiment, who was captured in the wilderness. Capt. Wm. T. Nickolson, of the thirty-seventh, another brave young officer, temporarily commanded them until Maj. Thomas J. Wooten, of the eighteenth, was assigned as their permanent commander. Maj. Wooten was exceedingly modest, but a cool, cautious and fearless young officer, who was universally beloved by his men.

"This body, composed of men from the different regiments of the brigade, first distinguished themselves under Knox in the Wilderness, where they dashed into the enemy on the left of the road and captured a large number of prisoners. On the 12th of May, at Spottsylvania court house, under Nickolson, they were kept out a long time in front of the salient to the left of the Fredericksburg road, where they behaved with great gallantry in the presence of Gen. Lee, and were complimented by him on the field. Under Wooten they established a still more glorious reputation, especially in their first dash at the enemy's picket line, which called forth a complimentary communication from superior headquarters; in their double quick deployments and advance, and captures in the battle of Jones's farm; in their sudden rush into the enemy's disordered ranks and large captures at the Pegram house, and in the part they bore in the recapture of the (McIlwaine) hill, taken from us on the day of Gordon's attack on Fort Steadman. They also behaved with great gallantry when Grant broke our lines at Petersburg, and on the retreat to Appomattox court house they were frequently thrown forward to fight the enemy when the brigade was not engaged."—*Vol. X, page 206, "Southern Historical Papers."*

***

The above sketch, though complimentary, is meagre, a mere intimation of the splendid record of this magnificent battalion. There was no better corps in the entire line of Lee's sharpshooters than the battalion commanded by Maj. Thos. J. Wooten. Like its gallant commander it was absolutely fearless, and a complete record of its daring deeds during that terrible campaign from the Wilderness to Appomattox would fill a volume of most thrilling interest, and one that would enrich as well as adorn the history of our great struggle. I know whereof I speak.

EVANS'S (GA.) SHARPSHOOTERS.

The battalion of sharpshooters of Evans's Georgia brigade, under command of Capt. Wm. Kaigler, according to his own statement, led his brigade successfully in the last conflict in which the Army of Northern Virginia was engaged. Gen. Gordon, of whose division Evans's brigade constituted a part, was ordered by the commanding general to make an assault on the Federal lines drawn across the Lynchburg road on the line of his retreat, and, if possible, to cut his way through, that the army might follow. Without hesitation Gen. Gordon formed his corps and proceeded to the desperate task assigned him. He moved to the assault with Evans's division in front. Kaigler's sharpshooters were deployed and thrown forward, and soon became engaged. Then, gathering up his full strength, Kaigler charged and broke the enemy's lines, capturing several pieces of artillery and a number of prisoners. About this time notice of the surrender was received by Gen. Evans, who suspended the movement and retired.

The dash made by the sharpshooters was a brilliant success, and proved to be, according to Kaigler's contention, the last tilt between the two contending armies.

Capt. Kaigler supports his position by the following: Gen. Evans says in a letter to Capt. Kaigler: "There is no question in my mind of the fact that the last shot fired and the last capture made by the army under Gen. Lee were through you and your picked corps of sharpshooters. * * * It is one of the proudest of my thoughts that we were shooting with all our might when the army was surrendered; and I have not the slightest doubt, captain, that you burned the last grain of powder and directed the last Confederate bullet from the great old army of Gen. Lee."

The Philadelphia Times says: "On the morning of the surrender Gen. Evans was ordered by Gen. Gordon to place his division in order of battle across the Lynchburg road. Capt. Kaigler, commanding the division skirmishers, moved in front and the division itself followed soon after. In their advance they encountered a line of dismounted cavalry and drove them back. Once more they were suddenly threatened in flank, when Evans changed the front of one brigade under heavy fire and made an attack, supporting Kaigler, who made a dash and a capture. This occurred after orders were issued for their return to camp, but which had not been received. Receiving the orders, they returned to camp and found that Lee had surrendered."

This incident in the history of Evans's sharpshooters indicates a splendid record behind it, which, so far as I know, has never been published. And whether Captain Kaigler's contention that he fired the last gun at Appomattox court house — which is controverted by some—be true or not, his achievements on that eventful day are worthy of preservation in the annals of that revolutionary period.

McRAE'S (N. C.) SHARPSHOOTERS.

The battalion of sharpshooters of McRae's brigade was commanded by Capt. Lilly, the fame of whose exploits in "the forefront of battle" was known throughout the army, is scarcely mentioned in the history of that terrible campaign.

The writer happens to know that when the sixth Federal corps captured our picket lines west of the Weldon railroad, after Gordon's splendid failure at Fort Steadman, March 25, 1865, Lilly's battalion was the only command on that long picket line that successfully resisted the Federal onslaught, and held his position against all odds until the entire line on both sides of him was swept back, and until he was ordered to retire. But the story of his campaigns has gone into oblivion like those of so many others in that arduous and hazardous service.

The following letter from Sergt. L. D. Davis, a member of that gallant corps, is all that I have been able to gather:

DEAR SIR AND COMRADE: Replying to yours of the 5th inst., requesting that I contribute for insertion in your book, "Lee's Sharpshooters," a short sketch of the part I played in that wonderful campaign, "from the Wilderness to Appomattox," I have to say that it has been so long since, and all my energies, both mental and physical, have been so completely taxed in fighting the battles of life, that I have forgotten nearly all of my operations except the "hairbreadth escapes," of which I will mention a few, and then you can insert, or not, any part of it or none, as you see proper. I only want your book to refresh my memory, and feel that in its perusal the humble part I played will be brought back to my recollection. To begin:

I remember very distinctly that our brigade was engaged in the opening of the battle of the Wilderness on the morning of May 5, 1864, but it is not my recollection that the sharpshooters were thrown out. If so, the line of battle overtook us and the whole line advanced through that scrubby, small growth of (principally) blackjack timber until near 12 m. From then on to Spottsylvania, and from there to Petersburg, my recollection is very indistinct, further than to remember that it was almost one continuous battle.

For some time after reaching Petersburg our regiment occupied the "blow up," and while there the sharpshooters kept up a continuous fire through port holes from breastworks.

Some time along in the latter part of summer or early fall we (the brigade) sallied forth down on the South Side railroad to intercept and prevent the enemy from capturing that important road. Arriving there the command was halted, and in less time than it takes to tell it the sharpshooters were thrown forward and advanced in a jiffy. We soon found the enemy's sharpshooters, completely routed them, advanced up to their line of battle and engaged it until our line came up and relieved us. Acting then as provost guard, I was so engaged personally that I did not discover a full line of battle of the enemy right at us in the rear. I was captured, and it did seem to me that a dozen or more Federals would take charge of us *two* as prisoners, in spite of all their captain could do; anyhow, he sent three of his men to the rear with two of us. They got lost; and we five lay out in the woods all night. Ladd and I were so agreeable with them that we gained their entire confidence. The next morning they were completely lost; and pledging them that we were more than willing to be prisoners of war, they let us guide them out; but to their chagrin we pilotted them into our own command. At this battle all our commissioned and non-commissioned officers were captured, and

I was made orderly, and commanded the company for quite a while.

On evacuating Richmond and Petersburg, April 2, 1865, I was called on by the major commanding the regiment to make a detail to reinforce the picket line; the other orderlies were so tardy in sending forward their quota that Maj. Steadman directed Lieut. Sneed — then commanding the company — to take his company and reinforce the picket line. We moved off at once, with instructions to hold the same at all hazards. I was directed to pick five men and occupy a farm house in the near distance. After gaining the house we did not have to wait but a few minutes before we saw, as appeared to us, the whole Federal army advancing slowly but surely upon us. With my squad I arranged every detail of combat. We loaded and fired into them as men never did before, perhaps, until seeing that we were about to become prisoners, I ordered a retreat, and from the back door sent out one at a time. Seeing the enemy picking up the dirt all around my men as they almost flew back to our breastworks, and knowing that I was to make the run last, the enemy right upon me, my feelings can better be imagined than described. I made the break, and it seems now as then that I did not touch the ground in but two or three places. Ladd and I made the run successfully and soon reached our lines, left there to cover the retreat; and after resting awhile we pushed on and overtook our own command the second day after. We then reorganized the regiment as best we could, but only had about fifty men out of an original number of twelve hundred. From then on to the surrender our rations were shelled corn. During the entire term of service I was in seventeen pitched battles, captured five times, was exchanged once, got away three times, and paroled at Appomattox, and have that parole now.

This statement is abbreviated, disconnected and not satisfactory to myself, but am satisfied that as soon as I shall have seen your book my mind will be refreshed, when I might be able to give many and more interesting details which perhaps you as well as I have overlooked.

I came to this State in the winter of '66-'67 without a dollar on arrival. Have settled five different places. Have now a fine farm, out of debt, fine stock of all kinds from horses to goats, and neither expect nor desire Senator Butler's bill to become a law.

The Army of Northern Virginia was composed of three (3) army corps, nine (9) divisions, and about thirty-six (36) brigades, exclusive of artillery and cavalry.

To each of which (brigades) there was attached a battalion of sharpshooters, composed of from two to four companies, and from one hundred and twenty-five to two hundred picked men to the battalion. Of this array of sharpshooters the author only mentions some six or eight battalions, because of the absolute silence of history as to their existence, operations and achievements. Like the gallant brigades to which they belonged, it remains a question as to which performed the best service or earned the highest honors. In vain has the writer searched the records for data upon which to base a story of their exploits; but, finding nothing, he is constrained to conclude that whatever of distinction they may have won was absorbed in the official reports of each engagement, and accredited to the brigades to which they were severally attached. From what has been said of the few battalions mentioned, it readily appears that if an accurate and detailed account could be given of each of the thirty-six battalions in their distinctive capacity as sharpshooters, many chapters of absorbing interest would be added to the volumes of Southern history already written of that stirring period.

The correspondent of the London Morning Herald, whose articles on the battles of the Wilderness and Spottsylvania court house are herein above inserted, evidently wrote after both battles were fought; for while he adheres somewhat closely to the facts in gross, he is mixed in his details, and attributes to one field incidents which belong to the other. Besides, his letters in style are somewhat florid and exorbitant, and had to be toned down in such degree as to speak the truth.

The story of " Lee's Sharpshooters," however, is based upon the personal experience of the author, as noted in his pocket diary at the time, and upon facts contributed by others who were on the field and knew whereof they wrote.

The style of the book as a whole, though somewhat rambling and desultory, is the best that the author could do under the circumstances, and the little volume is given to the public for what it is worth, trusting that it may fall under the eye of some skilled writer and evoke his interest in this fruitful theme, so that the investigation thus begun shall be pursued until full and exact justice shall have been done to each and every battalion that stood with "Lee's Sharpshooters" in the "Forefront of Battle."

OMEGA.

www.ingramcontent.com/pod-product-compliance
Lightning Source LLC
Chambersburg PA
CBHW021425300426
44114CB00010B/650